God and Truth

Is God a necessary being? Infinite yet simple? Creator of a world that seems equally able to explain itself? In this volume, prizewinning philosopher Lenn Goodman probes key religious questions against the backdrop of sacred texts and philosophical classics. In dialogue with a range of philosophers from Plato and Aristotle to Philo, Maimonides, Spinoza, Hume, and Kant, he examines the relationship between truth and the idea of God. Exploring the nexus between theism and logic, he probes ontological and design arguments, the anthropic principle, the problem of evil, the nature of justice and fairness, and the purpose and meaning of art. Goodman provocatively asks what science would look like if scientists allowed themselves to voice religious responses to their discoveries, as Einstein did. Finally, he probes the insights and examples of the morally virtuous, such as Moses, Albert Schweitzer, and Mahatma Gandhi.

Lenn E. Goodman is Professor of Philosophy and Andrew W. Mellon Professor of the Humanities at Vanderbilt University and recipient of the American Philosophical Association's Baumgardt Prize.

Cambridge Studies in Religion, Philosophy, and Society

Series Editors

Paul K. Moser, *Loyola University, Chicago*
Chad Meister, *Bethel College, Indiana*

This is a series of interdisciplinary texts devoted to major-level courses in religion, philosophy, and related fields. It includes original, current, and wide-spanning contributions by leading scholars from various disciplines that (a) focus on the central academic topics in religion and philosophy, (b) are seminal and up-to-date regarding recent developments in scholarship on the various key topics, and (c) incorporate, with needed precision and depth, the major differing perspectives and backgrounds – the central voices of the major religions and the religious, philosophical, and sociological viewpoints that cover the intellectual landscape today. Cambridge Studies in Religion, Philosophy, and Society is a direct response to this recent and widespread interest and need.

Recent Books in the Series

Allen W. Wood
Kant and Religion

Michael McGhee
Spirituality for the Godless: Buddhism, Humanism, and Religion

William B. Parsons
Freud and Religion

Charles Taliaferro and Jil Evans
Is God Invisible?: An Essay on Religion and Aesthetics

David Wenham
Jesus in Context: Making Sense of the Historical Figure

Paul W. Gooch
Paul and Religion: Unfinished Conversations

Herman Philipse
Reason and Religion: Evaluating and Explaining Belief in Gods

Phillip H. Wiebe
Religious Experience: Implications for What Is Real

Norman Russell
Theosis and Religion: Participation in Divine Life in the Eastern and Western Traditions

Amy E. Black and Douglas L. Koopman
Civil Religion and the Renewal of American Politics

God and Truth

An Essay on Reason and Religious Ideas

LENN E. GOODMAN
Vanderbilt University

Shaftesbury Road, Cambridge CB2 8EA, United Kingdom

One Liberty Plaza, 20th Floor, New York, NY 10006, USA

477 Williamstown Road, Port Melbourne, VIC 3207, Australia

314–321, 3rd Floor, Plot 3, Splendor Forum, Jasola District Centre,
New Delhi – 110025, India

103 Penang Road, #05-06/07, Visioncrest Commercial, Singapore 238467

Cambridge University Press is part of Cambridge University Press & Assessment,
a department of the University of Cambridge.

We share the University's mission to contribute to society through the pursuit of
education, learning and research at the highest international levels of excellence.

www.cambridge.org
Information on this title: www.cambridge.org/9781108472142

DOI: 10.1017/9781108601207

© Lenn E. Goodman 2026

This publication is in copyright. Subject to statutory exception and to the provisions
of relevant collective licensing agreements, no reproduction of any part may take
place without the written permission of Cambridge University Press & Assessment.

When citing this work, please include a reference to the DOI 10.1017/9781108601207

First published 2026

A catalogue record for this publication is available from the British Library

Library of Congress Cataloging-in-Publication Data
NAMES: Goodman, Lenn Evan, 1944- author
TITLE: God and truth : an essay on reason and religious ideas / Lenn E. Goodman, Vanderbilt University, Tennessee.
DESCRIPTION: Cambridge, United Kingdom ; New York, NY, USA : Cambridge University Press, 2025. | Series: Cambridge studies in religion, philosophy, and society | Includes bibliographical references and index.
IDENTIFIERS: LCCN 2025023031 (print) | LCCN 2025023032 (ebook) | ISBN 9781108472142 hardback | ISBN 9781108459044 paperback | ISBN 9781108601207 epub
SUBJECTS: LCSH: God | God (Judaism) | Truth–Religious aspects–Judaism | Faith and reason
CLASSIFICATION: LCC BL473 .G66 2025 (print) | LCC BL473 (ebook) | DDC 211–dc23/eng/
20250516
LC record available at https://lccn.loc.gov/2025023031
LC ebook record available at https://lccn.loc.gov/2025023032

ISBN 978-1-108-47214-2 Hardback
ISBN 978-1-108-45904-4 Paperback

Cambridge University Press & Assessment has no responsibility for the persistence
or accuracy of URLs for external or third-party internet websites referred to in this
publication and does not guarantee that any content on such websites is, or will
remain, accurate or appropriate.

For EU product safety concerns, contact us at Calle de José Abascal,
56, 1°, 28003 Madrid, Spain, or email eugpsr@cambridge.org

Contents

Preface		*page* vii
List of Abbreviations		ix
	Introduction	1
1	Logic and God	12
2	God and Mathematics	64
3	God and Science	97
4	God and Value	144
Bibliography		181
Index		187

Preface

My profound thanks to my friend Ophir Ospovat for his critical help in formatting and finalizing the index.

Abbreviations

B	Babylonian Talmud
DND	Cicero, *De Natura Deorum*
J	Jerusalem Talmud
LCL	Loeb Classical Library
M	The Mishnah
SVF	*Stoicorum Veterum Fragmenta*, ed. H. F. A. von Arnim

References to Spinoza's *Ethics* follow the standard usage, listing part, proposition, and demonstration, corollary, scholium, or appendix. For other Spinoza citations, citations generally include the volume and page number in Gebhardt's critical edition of the Latin original.

The word LORD in small caps, as shown here, stands in for the Tetragrammaton.

References to Maimonides' *Guide to the Perplexed* include part and chapter number followed, as needed, by the page, recto or verso, in Munk's critical edition of the Judaeo-Arabic original. These page numbers are shown marginally in Joel's edition, in the Pines translation, and in the new Goodman-Lieberman translation.

Introduction

Biblically, we Jews identify God with Truth and Truth with Justice. But we also identify Justice in its highest form (*tzedakah*) with generosity or grace (*hesed*) and grace in turn with the beauty that finds its source and highest peak in God.

My purpose in this book is to argue for God's truth as the highest reality. I will argue that God is the unique and ultimate One, the Highest, in whom the infinity of things find their unity, mirroring the unity of His infinite Presence. Those thoughts reflect God's causal ultimacy and fecundity, His goodness and generosity as the Beauty beyond perceptible beauty, the ingenuity of design, of which He is the ultimate Source, and the generosity that models the love we humans owe each other and the regard we owe all creatures.

I'll lace together here the biblical usages that warrant my claims made in the first sentence of this introduction before I summarize the argument of this book's four chapters.

We find the Hebrew word for truth applied to God in its core sense of faithful trustworthiness (see Psalms 115:1, 117:2, 138:2) when Abraham's servant sees in Rebecca the marks of character that he seeks in the wife he has been charged to find for Isaac. Having met her at the city well in Haran, and having received water from her for himself and for his camels and rewarded and honored her with gold jewelry, he asks her about her parentage and about a place to stay the night and keep his camels. Her answer: *"We have ample straw and fodder, and room for you to lodge." The man bowed down and prostrated himself before the* LORD, *saying, "Blessed be the* LORD, *my master's God, who has not forsaken His truth and favor toward my master. The* LORD *has led me to my master's brethren."* (Genesis 24:24–27).

Truth here is paired with grace, as it will be again in the epiphany Moses will experience at Sinai soon after the troubling episode of the golden calf. He hopes to learn from God's ways the character he must cultivate in himself if he is to govern his people. Mercy, grace, and patience are prominent among the attributes of God's governance that Moses hears, along with love and truth. And the mention of truth leads on to thoughts of justice. For God's grace, we learn, as if listening along with Moses, does not hold the guilty guiltless (Exodus 34:6–7). The Psalmist reflects this revelation to Moses of God's goodness and truth, saying, *all the pathways of the* LORD *are truth and grace* (25:10; cf. 86:15). The aspiration inspired by those words is of us too to walk in God's ways of truth (26:3–4; cf. 57:4–11), a truth that the Psalmist calls protective, finding it so regularly paired with love (61:8).

Etymology shows the links of truth with justice. For the Arabic root *s-d-q* means truth. A *sadiq* is a friend, reliable and true; but with a slight shift in vocalization, the same root identifies a saint. A *tzaddik*, in Hebrew, is a saint; and the same root bears the sense of being in the right, vindicated legally. The Arabic word *sadaqa*, like the Hebrew *tzedakah*, means charity. We readily see why. For justice in full measure calls on one to give all persons their due, and indeed all that one would ask for oneself, were the positions of giver and recipient reversed.

Noah, we read, was a *tzaddik*, a just man, by sharp contrast with the others of his generation (Genesis 6:9). And we are commanded to use just weights and measures (Leviticus 19:36, Deuteronomy 25:15), a natural transferred epithet, calling a weight or measure just, as if to reflect the rightness of an act and reflect back on the actor. Underlying this nest of cognate terms is the idea of deserts: A fair measure is what is deserved, whether of grain or flour, fabric or funds in a fair exchange. That, we learn, matters to God: *a false balance is loathesome to the* LORD; *a just weight is His delight!* (Proverbs 11:1).

The Torah is not shy about universalizing such norms and stating them as imperatives: *Justice, justice shalt thou pursue!* (Deuteronomy 16:20), it commands. The emphatic repetition, says Ibn Ezra, the doyen of medieval biblical grammarians, means to stress that one must pursue justice all one's life and vigorously pursue it, win or lose or draw. As Bahya ben Asher added, the same divine imperative commands justice toward everyone. And one of the Hasidic masters pressed the point: The same commandment forbids any use of unjust means even to attain worthy ends.

The Torah commands the institution of a system of justice (Deuteronomy 16:18). And the Rabbis identify that imperative as the one positive commandment among the seven given by God to humanity at large, every descendant of Noah, as they put it. Joseph Hertz (1872–1946), Chief Rabbi of the British Empire, wrote in his commentary on the Pentateuch, "Justice is not the only ethical quality in God or man, nor is it the highest quality; but it is the basis for all the others." Rabbi Hertz goes on to quote F. Adler: "Justice is the awe-inspired respect for the personality of others, and their inalienable rights."[1]

Since justice is of such moment in God's eyes, it is not surprising that as the Mosaic Torah rises to its climax in the Song of Moses, God is called *the Rock whose work is perfect. For all His ways are fair, a faithful God, who does no wrong, just and upright He* (Deuteronomy 32:4; cf. Nehemiah 9:33, Job 4:17). For, as Elihu argues in the Book of Job, only the just rule rightfully; and God, who rules all things, is eminently just (*tzadik kabir*, Job 34:17).

God's truth is His justice, but it is also His grace and favor. So the Psalmist, hoping to escape the threat of death, argues that the dead cannot praise God and testify to His truth (30:10; cf. 31:6). Their testimony will be God's thanks. His truth here is His saving help (cf. 43:3, 69:14, 71:22), as the Midrash explains (Psalms Rabbah 30.6), comparing the reversal celebrated as the psalm ends (30:10–13) to the denouement of the crisis recorded in the Book of Esther (4:3, 9:19).

As for beauty, Isaiah uses the term *hadar* when he pictures the land itself rejoicing at God's coming to set things right on earth, flowers in bloom, the desert turned as lovely as Carmel and Sharon (35:2). The tasteful dress of the good wife in Proverbs 31 is, again, a thing *of dignity and beauty*, as the paean to her puts it (*'oz ve-hadar levushah*, 31:25). Absalom was beautiful, so was Alcibiades in his time. Yet their beauty was tarnished even as it shone. But God, the Psalmist says, is clothed in beauty (104:1). I recall Tom Paine's thought here, grasping that image and glossing it midrashically: The beauty in which God is said to be clothed is but the earthly show and shadow of a higher beauty, veiled in physicality to accommodate to our human awareness. The beauty we see in God's works, the beauty of the sunset, the stars, or the aurora, is only the curtain enrobing the transcendent beauty of the Maker who transcends them (Psalms 111:2–4).

The paradigm of beauty, for the Psalmist, is God Himself: All the gods of the nations are noughts – *The* LORD *made the heavens! Majesty and*

---

[1] Hertz, *The Pentateuch and Haftorahs*, on Deuteronomy 16:18–20. For the passage from Friedrich C. Adler (1771–1828), see 821.

beauty attend Him, glory and splendor in His sanctum (96:5–6). God's sanctum, as the poet pictures it, might be sought high in the heavens, whose sublimity befits His beauty. Yet God's manifestations fall far short of His true beauty, which is His holiness (1 Chronicles 16:29). Lesser beauties aspire to such loveliness, and rightly so – as do the moral and intellectual/spiritual beauty that we humans reach for in our thoughts and practices, pointing toward that Higher Beauty that is their Source and Goal.

In Chapter 1, "Logic and God," I turn to the startling first epiphany of God to Moses at the burning bush. Reduced from the royal palace in which he was raised to the exile of a fugitive, Moses remains a man of spirit, of curiosity, and of principle, loyal to his people, although living as a shepherd in the household of his father-in-law. It is there, in exile, that God reveals His name to Moses and gives him his mission: to confront Pharaoh, free his people Israel, and bring them back that very mountain to receive a new law and the way of life that law prescribes, a gift and a charge from the God of their ancestors.

Drawing on Maimonides' reading of God's message to Moses, I argue that the name God gives Moses to relate to his people back in Egypt, as proof of His absoluteness, cannot have been a mere name. For, as Maimonides argues, had it been familiar to them already, it would prove nothing. And had it been unfamiliar it would have been even less effectual. Rather, that strange name *I am that I am*, encapsulated in the Tetragrammaton, if it were to prove anything at all, must have embodied an argument that the elders among the Israelites could be expected to grasp and find convincing. It was, as Maimonides argues, a compact statement in essence anticipating what we would call the ontological argument, the argument that what is absolute cannot fail to exist.

The chapter has some words to say about the familiar dismissal of such arguments by Hume and Kant, running back to Gaunilon's response to the ontological argument set out by Anselm of Canterbury in the eleventh century. We can see anticipations of Anselm's intuition in the writings of Philo of Alexandria and in kindred thoughts in Avicenna and al-Ghazali. The argument, as I read it, is not wholly a priori, not based on logic alone, nor, on mere analysis, of the idea of divinity. For it presupposes, inter alia, a hierarchy of being. Otherwise, Anselm would have been unable to speak of greater or lesser beings and call God a being "than which none more perfect can be conceived." Spinoza will play a significant role here since he takes seriously the idea of God's absoluteness. But the chapter will also consider a version of the ontological argument framed by Kurt Gödel.

And it ends with a discussion of the linkage seen by Maimonides and Spinoza (and before them by Plato, Aristotle, and the Neoplatonic philosophers) between knowing God and loving God – and being known and loved by God.

Chapter 2, "God and Mathematics," seeks to examine the relationship of two ideas about God that seem, on the face of it, to exclude each other: God's oneness and His infiniteness. From a Jewish standpoint, the tensions between God's unity and God's infinity may seem especially insurmountable. For the Torah's affirmation of God's unity (Deuteronomy 6:4) has been a watchword of Judaism immemorially. Initially, God's oneness, as proclaimed to Israel, might have meant little more than the affirmation that all Israelites, despite tribal differences, bear allegiance to the same one God. But the God of Israel, as heard in the Mosaic Torah, does affirm that there is no other (4:35). And He insists that no rival deity shall be recognized (Exodus 20:3). He firmly forbids the making of any image that might try to bring divinity down to earth and under human control (20:4–6). And His law condemns all forms of necromancy and theurgy (Leviticus 19:31, 20:6, 27; Deuteronomy 18:11). He is the sole deity, creator, ruler, and judge of all the universe. We humans do not control God. That is part of what we mean in declaring God unique.

There will be no pagan pantheon in Judaism and no Trinity or Duality of deities. Jewish martyrs died with the proclamation of God's unity on their lips. And, as if in tribute to their sacrifices, Jewish philosophers carry the idea of God's unity to a peak of simplicity. Maimonides, for one, argues that even conceptually God is indivisible, or He could not be a being of absolute necessity (*Guide* I 51, 58a). The very idea of attributes proper to God, he argues, is a mere projection of human traits and therefore a worse affront conceptually to God and His unity than even pagan worship (*Guide* I 36, 54–56). How, then, does the affirmation of God's absolute simplicity square with thoughts of God's infiniteness – which, like unity and uniqueness, anchor the biblical idea of divinity?

Georg Cantor, the modern mathematician who did the most to make sense of the idea of infinity, was a pious Lutheran and did associate God with his thoughts about infinity. But, as a mathematical Platonist, Cantor is less able than he might have been to help us relate God's unity to intuitions of divine infinity. Philo proves to be of greater help here. For he anticipates Plotinus in overcoming Aristotle's discomfort with thoughts of infinity. Aristotle does affirm the infinite divisibility of a continuum like that of time or space, and he does hold the cosmos to be infinitely old. But he stoutly denies that *any* magnitude, even the universe itself, can be infinite, leaning on an unworthy sophism that denies that any *magnitude* can be infinite, since any size must be bounded and therefore finite. Critically for our purposes, Aristotle finds the idea of infinity inconsistent with his profound conception of God as pure and perfect actuality.

But Philo, like his rabbinical contemporaries, was inspired by biblical images of God's boundlessness. Encouraged by Stoic thoughts of the energy and dynamism of the divine, he did not find God's unity and perfection incompatible with thoughts of His boundless creativity, wisdom, and inspiration. Later monotheists, with Philo's help, were well prepared for Plotinus' bold appropriation of the ideas of infinity and power that Peripatetics had long held in the Aristotelian keep of potentiality and want of definition.

Here again Spinoza is the conceptual virtuoso who, by his courageous rigor, can reveal the harmony of unity and infinity in God. Denying that the world, or even a body, or time or geometric space is composed of separate parts, Spinoza discerns the unity of nature, not just spatially but in his own far more inclusive and dynamic sense. The holism here is indeed organic. It underwrites a monism that had long stood tantalizingly at a remove for radical monotheists, frustrated by the difficulty of fulfilling their hope to see all things in God (and God in all things) without, as a result, swallowing up God in nature, or swallowing up nature in God.

Spinoza's bold expedient of recognizing thought and extension not as substances, as they had been for Descartes, but as attributes of the one *and infinite God*, who expresses Himself in infinite attributes (each one of which is a facet of divinity but none of which collapses his infinity or exhausts His oneness) allows him to pay tribute to God's unity without compromising the boundless diversity in which God's unity and infinite power expresses itself. This chapter owes a special debt to the philosopher Errol Harris, who articulated Spinoza's strategy with brilliant clarity. And it examines some of the monistic pretensions of the Kabbalah, exposed by Louis Jacobs.

Chapter 3, "God and Science," explores, the impact of the idea of divine design, partly by reviewing the Stoic version of the design argument captured like a moth in the ancient amber of Cicero's dialogue *On the Nature of the Gods*, and partly by way of a current approach advanced by Stephen Barr, a Catholic physicist. Following up on ideas that he credits to Brandon Carter, Barr has assembled an array of pretty basic facts known to physics today about the nature of the universe we inhabit. He marshals eleven of these in his book *Modern Physics and Ancient*

Faith, none of them matters of logical necessity or inherent in the most basic demands of physics, but any one of which is a critically necessary to the rise of life or the kind of physics and chemistry that would make life possible, or even a universe any more hospitable than the welter and waste the Torah invites us to imagine (since we can't picture sheer nothingness) in suggesting what things might have been like absent God's act of creation.

Barr labels the facts he calendars "anthropic coincidences." The term 'anthropic,' as speculative cosmologists have been using it in recent decades, is meant to suggest a world made for us – or even *by* us, as ventured by those who have drunk deep of idealist fantasy, a world that answers to our understanding because it is in fact the product of our own thought processes. Barr is far more modest than that. But he does observe, speaking as a cosmologist, that unless certain parameters had been just so, we and our world could never have come to be.

Barr's use of the word 'coincidences' plays with light irony on the thought that whoever hopes to hold onto the idea that the world just happened, as if by chance, would have some pretty tall explaining to do. Scriptural monotheists do not abandon causality when they confront totality. And they do not believe that any finite or determinate being just has to exist, as if its existence were self-explanatory. The idea of creation rests on the recognition that all things known to our experience are contingent. Barr's point is that even with the barest givens at the outset (for the red shift argues that there was an outset), there were some pretty tricky bobbins to thread before anything could arise at all like a habitable world. That makes Barr's "coincidences" well worth contemplating.

Moving on from Barr's elenchus, our chapter warns of some of the pitfalls of anthropocentrism that mar Stoic ideas of design. But it takes seriously the idea that nature is a coherent system. Those thoughts lead us to Maimonides' recognition that the unity of nature makes a powerful case for the unity of God. Religion and science stand together here. For today's exponents of a multiverse, like their Epicurean predecessors with their infinite worlds, are all too ready to abandon the coherence of the natural sciences. Yet the idea of consilience, central to the commitment to the practices of scientific authority on which all cosmology depends, both rests on and sustains recognition of causal coherence. An atheological bias skews the intentions and contentions of the exponents of a multiverse here: Recognition of universal natural laws, they fear, might give color to the thought that nature is built to a plan.

Chapter 4, "God and Value," looks to moral, aesthetic, and political values as God's hallmarks in nature at large and in human life specifically. Moral realism is a key corollary of theism. Some derive the very notion of a moral law from the commands of God. Yet the more extreme versions of divine command theory, we find, breed a variety of theistic subjectivism that saps the very authority of the idea of divinity that it may have been intended to uphold.

Kant is right, I would argue, that piety sees moral duties as divine imperatives. But since we often have a clearer sense of right and wrong than of divine moral sovereignty, it makes more sense, I think, to see God's absoluteness through our (still fallible) recognition of moral truths. Maimonides strikes the right balance here, I believe, by arguing that biblically God and His justice are inseparable (*Guide* III 17, 35a). Clearly, then, the argument can run either way: One might proceed from God to morals (insofar as one has reliable knowledge of God's expectations) or from morals to God (insofar as one's moral compass is in good order and not skewed by appetite and convention, cranked up to overweening heights of passion by the play of imagination). But, given the vulnerability of human moral and theological apprehensions, it may be best prudently to rely on moral and theological traditions to serve as checks on any temptation to slide toward excess in one direction or the other. For misguided amoral or theological hubris all too readily skews human judgment in these domains and predictably results in a moral and theological train wreck.

Turning, more happily, to thoughts of beauty, I think we do see the colors of God's palette where we seek them, in nature, just as reflective scientists can see God's handwriting there as well. So, I think it worthwhile to recognize that the arts use their vehicles of painting, music, sculpture, and the rest when they aim creatively to convey the insights of their makers as to the play of God's grace and wisdom in nature, including human nature. I chose a few examples of artists to exemplify the point in the inevitably brief compass of the chapter, focusing on the two friends Anton Chekhov and the Jewish landscape painter Isaac Levitan to help make the point and drawing a few lines from John Dewey, where his experience of art marked an exception to his committed and too often doctrinaire pragmatism. What drew me to Levitan and Chekhov here was partly their affinity for one another, which allowed Chekhov to put into words the spirit and spirituality that Levitan far more readily expressed in paint. Other artists get briefer mention in what can barely touch on so vast a topic as artistic truth. Not all art, of course, need be celebratory. Some of the greatest artworks of paint or pen are critical; some, despairing. These too have truths to share. But I do bracket kitsch and propaganda for their crude reliance on emotive cliches and invidious or simply vicious stereotypes. I also set aside works like those of Lucien Freud and Francis Bacon, who have seemed keener to evoke shock and disgust than to communicate the grounds of their discontent with life itself and the human condition.

Turning to ethics and politics, I think Gandhi stands out as a moral virtuoso in modern times, much as Tolstoy or Dostoevsky did as literary virtuosi. So, I have a few words to say in this final chapter about Gandhi's project of *satyagraha*, the quest for truth and the imperative it lays down for us. In my book *In Defense of Truth*, I spoke at some length about Gandhi's campaigns in this public and more personal domain, which found a paradigm case in his leadership of the courageous and portentous salt march to the sea. So, it did not seem appropriate to expatiate on the same emblematic topic here. But I do urge interested readers to have a look, and I do think everyone should be interested in the moral, communal, and political lessons to be learned from the example probed there. I did, however, want to close this book with reflections on what I take to be the nexus between truth and morals.

Moral truth, this final chapter argues, bears that name and exerts the imperative it lays before us because moral obligations reflect the claims of beings. Deserts spring from the conatus found in every being, the dynamic claim of all beings to existence, and their striving to persist and perfect their being and express their reality in the best ways accessible to them. Even a rock, a mountain, or a waterfall has its own mode of being and expression. Solidity and the inertial tendency of bodies to remain in motion once they are moving are exemplary of conatus elementally. So is the gravitational attraction of one body for another.

But conatus takes more dynamic forms with the approach toward what Lucretius called the shores of life: Viruses reach for life; bacteria strive to persist, multiplying and experimenting collectively with varied unselfconscious genetic strategies in the rapid turnover of their generations. Teamwork is a key theme among such strategies, evident even among mosses and corals and in many other lifeforms. But as life advances in evolutionary terms and by evolutionary means, individuality grows more prominent – bringing with it the threat of death, reflecting the growing prominence of individuality among living beings.

The rise of sexual reproduction, found in all the higher plants and animals, allows the lineages of living beings to harness the play of chance itself, experimenting genetically but mixing and matching the results so as to retain successful genes but mask or mute the impact of less helpful alleles – and, most notably, by combining the contributions of male and female parents in the discrete, but not inviolable, chromosomes. The effect is to shuffle the genetic deck without shredding the cards. At every evolutionary phase in the rise, proliferation, and evolutionary advance of life, a good is present, locally defined in terms of the claims of the creatures and their lineages. But that local good is itself emergent, as purposes become increasingly autonomous and individuated, reaching a stage ultimately, in the case of persons, who are free in some measure to choose and guide their own purposes and projects.

Just as we have a moral obligation to face facts, we are called morally, as conscious beings, to treat all beings as what they are. The moral charge, accordingly, is twofold: (1) to respect the claims of beings, animate and even inanimate, insofar as they are compatible with one another and with the more stately and ambitious claims of higher beings and (2) to pay deference to the claims to life and self-perfection of persons and of those individuals that stand at the penumbra of personhood because they are becoming persons or have been persons.

The deserts of persons, as moral subjects, mark the boundaries of what we properly call rights and dignities. But all living beings deserve our regard for what they are, that is, for the claims they make, equilibrated according to the relative weight of those claims and the claims of other beings. The effort to define the parameters of such concerns is, I believe, among the chief functions of cultures in modulating the norms of a social order. Some individuals and some cultures address such concerns by vegetarianism or veganism. In Judaism, the laws of kashrut pursue such a goal, aiming to meet human nutritional needs without undue oppression of birds and beasts. We have similar rules aiming to spare the soil, giving it its own sabbaths of years, in keeping with its rhythms (Leviticus 25:2–7), just as self-use is regulated by a more human rhythm of days (Exodus 20:8–11). And we seek to sustain human bodily dignity by banning tattoos, scarification, and mutilation (Leviticus 19:28). Even the corpse of an executed criminal must be buried by nightfall (Deuteronomy 21:23).

Inanimate nature as well as animal and plant life are respected through the blanket prohibition of wanton waste and destruction, the ordinance of *bal tashhit*. The general imperative forbidding wanton destruction is broadened rabbinically from the biblical prohibition of cutting down fruit trees in a siege (Deuteronomy 20:19). As Abraham Chill explained

The wanton destruction of trees in war is a sign of unbridled barbarism. The Rabbis extended the concept of *bal tashhit* to include any act of unprincipled waste or destruction of things that can be of benefit to man. Reckless demolition is an effrontery against God, since everything is His creation.[2]

Rabbi Chill goes on to quote the classic *Sefer ha-Hinukh* by an anonymous fourteenth-century Levite sage of Barcelona:

To the righteous person, no man is so unimportant that one may ignore his loss and not try to save him. In the same light no living thing, not even a mustard seed, is so insignificant that it may be destroyed without reasonable cause.[3]

The affirmative side of our respect for human deserts, is represented by the demands of charity and by making healing a communal obligation, grounded ultimately in the obligation to preserve a human life. But respect for human life goes hand in hand in Judaism within the treatment of human understanding as an end in itself, reflecting the premise that each individual is an autonomous end.

---

[2] Chill, *The* Mitzvot, 444.
[3] Chill, *The* Mitzvot, 444; see also Goodman, "Respect for Nature."

I

Logic and God

What has God to do with logic? There are those who say that God sets the parameters of logic and is hardly bound by our notions of necessity. But others consider the very idea of God the least logical of human notions. Logic, to them, is the bastion of reason, and they voice their view that the idea of God is irrational by their passionate denials. Romantics may welcome thoughts of irrationality. But for others, such thoughts are a barrier: An exclusionary naturalism is not fence enough for the most passionate, keen to exclude God not just from nature but from the realm of possibility. Kant is perhaps subtlest here. Betraying his mixed emotions, he leaves no ontological or cosmological argument unturned but grasps God firmly as a postulate of morals, where he feels surer of his footing.[1]

Kant defeated the ontological argument, so he believed, by finding existence to be no true predicate. Affirming that a thing exists, he argued, adds nothing to its description. Besides, he added, all existential propositions are synthetic. That leaves no room for a being whose essence is its existence. Having routed the ontological argument, Kant dismisses its cosmological cousin. For the strongest type of cosmological argument, as he saw, points to the idea of a necessary being. Lesser appeals may speak of "a greater power." But only the contrast of necessity with contingency yields the absoluteness called for in full-throated acknowledgment of the God of monotheism – short of resort to thoughts of creatio ex nihilo.

Only propositions, we're taught, not beings, have modalities. But surely if a necessary proposition asserts that something is real, there is a

---

[1] I assay the argument in "Kant's Moral Case for God."

necessary being. It's hard to see how that inference can be denied without begging the question at issue. If a necessary truth is one that it is contradictory to deny, that's just what exponents of an ontological argument say of God's existence: Given the right idea of God, it's impossible to deny that God exists. To hold that only the "empty" truths of logic or mathematics can be matters of necessity is, again, to beg the question. The ontological argument affirms that the reality of a Being of absolute perfection is a truth that cannot be denied. For its denial contravenes the very idea of absoluteness.

The rub in Kant's elenchus: Its two premises contradict one another: To call all existential propositions synthetic is to admit that affirming that a thing exists does add something to its notion. The predicate in a synthetic proposition does add to what's given in the idea of the subject. That's what Avicenna was assuming when he called 'existence' a predicate. But Kant contends that existence is not a proper predicate. If that is so, he must give up his Humean claim that all existential propositions are synthetic. Hume's claim serves well Kant's aim of confining scientific assertions to a domain where empirical evidence is relevant and accessible. But its pertinence in theological debates is readily disputed. For what the natural theologian who upholds the soundness of the ontological argument understands by calling God the necessary being is that God is not subject to the general rule that all beings are contingent. Ordinary beings, the kind familiar to our experience are contingent. They come and go. We can watch them enter and exit the world we know. So there's no internal contradiction in denying the existence of any one of them. But God, the theist holds, cannot fail to exist. And those who see no contradiction in denying God's reality are most likely positing some other sort of being to which they apply the name of God. In other words, they have begged the question.

One might try to help Kant out by choosing for him between the two legs that prop up his case: Is existence a proper predicate after all, or is the notion that all existential propositions are synthetic somehow dispensable? For Kant, at least, that choice was out of reach. The denial that existence is a predicate rests on the analysis of the logical structure of judgments that underlies Kant's doctrine of categories. But the affirmation that all existential propositions are synthetic is the battle flag of Kant's commitment to empiricism.

The conflicting premises reflect Kant's neglect of his own warnings about the limits of pure reason. Both premises are symptomatic of the same overreach, sprung from the source of Kant's first antinomy, the effort to determine, by pure reason, whether the world is created or eternal: The denial that existence is a predicate reflects the Aristotelian (and Averroist) metaphysics of necessity, where existence is inseparable from the concept of such realities as the species of things. The notion that all existential propositions are synthetic rests on a Humean commitment to empiricism. But it also reflects the scriptural (and Avicennan) conception of all determinate being as contingent, grounded ultimately in the biblical recognition that no mere natural fact is categorically necessary. The antinomy that snags Kant here, as I wrote years ago, "stems from considering beings now as possible, now as real." It echoes "the same confusion that Kant found at the root of the original antinomy between creation and eternity."[2]

We cannot draw claims about what exists from logic alone. To be a fair arbiter of truth, logic should preserve its metaphysical neutrality. And purely formal truths don't seem to have the purchase on reality needed to reach an existential conclusion. But must an ontological argument rest on logic alone? Such arguments typically appeal to the idea of a perfect being. So, they presume a hierarchy of being/value, with God at the peak and all else descending from Him. When Anselm argued that a most perfect being must exist, a being "than which none greater can be conceived" (*Proslogion* 2.18), he was presuming just such an idea in the notion of greatness he deployed. To deny him such premises is not to find a fallacy in his argument. It's more like asking him to box without raising his hands above his waist.

Philosophy is universal. But idioms vary. So, we may not always notice the affinities of Aristotle's "Man, by nature, is a social animal" (*Politics* I 2, 1253a3) to the biblical *It is not good for the man to be alone* (Genesis 2:18) – or the well-known koan, "Have you heard the sound of one hand clapping?" What Aristotle states in terms of taxonomy, exploiting Plato's method of division (*Phaedrus*, 265DE, *Sophist* 253D, *Statesman* 285A–286D, *Laws* 965C) and his own biological bent, the Torah makes a value judgment of God's, pointing onward to the two sexes at the foundation of society and the human condition. Genesis dramatizes that theme, as though the downside of solitude were an ill just discovered by God and remedied by couplehood: Where Aristotle classifies, biblical explanations are displayed historically, as they are when Genesis presents its analysis of creation by reference to a phased sequence of days. Adam finds the

---

[2] See Goodman, *God of Abraham*, 70; cf. Avicenna, 101–4.

counterpart he was lacking (Genesis 2:20–23), and she proves to be a helpmeet, in Tyndale's brilliant coinage, rendering the Hebrew *'ezer kenegdo*. Woman and man, Adam finds, are not alien to one another. Seeing how the two can enhance one another's lives puts flesh on the bones of God's appraisal. The Zen challenge, like Aristotle's biological inference and God's dismissal of isolation, bespeaks positive norms about comity, community, and collaboration. The normative thrust is implicit. It grows rather more explicit in Spinoza's caution against egoism, couched, for the benefit of an interlocutor of utilitarian outlook: "Nothing is more useful to man than man" (E4p18s).

God's words, then, in His first epiphany to Moses open doors to an argument of the ontological type, as Maimonides suggests in his close reading of the biblical account of the name God revealed to Moses at the burning bush (*Guide* I 63, glossing Exodus 3:13–14; 4:1). Like the allied tradition of Platonic philosophy, the argument Maimonides elicits from the text assumes the identity of reality and perfection. The same vision, of value and reality walking hand-in-hand, is shared by all the philosophers who reach for an ontological type of argument. So, it's hardly surprising that when Spinoza sought to render unproblematic the intuitions about God's necessary being that Descartes and Anselm had made central in their philosophies, he relied on the same premise: "By reality and perfection I understand the same thing" (E2d6). He too frames an argument of the ontological type. Can the intuitions articulated in such lines of argument sustain an affirmation of God's reality? Do such reasonings still bear fruitful insights?

BEING AND NECESSITY

Parmenides, the first Greek to inquire after being as such, inaugurates Greek metaphysics with an epiphany couched as a grammar lesson. The goddess of his vision teaches him the logic of being by laying out for him the ultimate dichotomy, between *is* and *is not*. Not content with that primal either/or, she presses on to *interpret* her disjunction (a barebones version of the law of contradiction), by forcing a choice between the two alternatives. The survivor is *esti*, "it is." The goddess then spells out the impact of that thought in an uncompromising monism: We are not told at the start just *what* is. In a way we can't be. But we do learn, overhearing the philosopher poet's tuition by the goddess, that the subject of *esti* must be unique. For negation of any sort has been excluded: There cannot be *another* since it would *not be* its alternative, and *is not* has been excluded.

Nor can it have parts, since any part would *not be* another. No predicate can be assigned it that distinguishes it from anything else. For that something would *not be* what the other was, and there is no *is not*. Nor can this subject change. For what it became would *not be* what it was. Still less can it be thought to come to be. For that would mean it came from what it *was not*.

Much of the history of philosophy in the West reflects varied efforts to grapple with Parmenides' elenchus. Aristotle shows, in the *Categories*, that the monistic inferences Parmenides pursued rest on a fallacy, confusing the existential with the predicative sense(s) of the verb "to be": The 'is' we use to affirm that a thing is real is not the 'is' we need when saying "this is green" or "it is late." To deny a predicate to a thing is not to deny that the thing exists. Aristotle here vindicates change and multiplicity and convicts the goddess of equivocation. But, impressed by Parmenides' raising the question about being as such, Aristotle does not brand him a sophist. Plato, entranced by Parmenides' monisim, preserved the unity he had sought, finding it in the Form of the Good, an ultimate unity beyond the change and multiplicity we encounter in this world, which Plato called not 'being' but 'becoming.' The world of change, he conceded, was equivocal to the root – lying between reality and unreality.[3]

Aristotle, too, sought unity and found it both in the cosmos and in his highest God. He saw immutability as well, in the heavens and in the essences of things. And he sought and saw other unities: in the body of an organism, in a sentence, story line or plot, and in the fabric of a well-ordered city. Where Plato had made the Form of the Good his first cause and highest God, Aristotle saw divine causation in the aspiration of all things toward actuality. But the fullness of actuality is present only in the divine Intelligence that moves the heavens through their love of its perfection and their quest for a perfection of their own. That dynamic found expression, for him, in nature's rational plan, plainest in the invariant motions of the heavens and undeniable in the anatomy of living beings, where nature, like a consummate craftsman, does nothing in vain. Change itself was immutable in its patterns, as Heraclitus had suggested, when he advised inquirers cowed by the universal flux and flow of things to "look to the common."[4] By such means we can find the unity behind ungovernable diversity. The world itself, for Aristotle, is one and divine. Its eternal and unchanging species preserve stability even in the exchange of forms

---

[3] See Seligman, *Being and Not-Being*.
[4] Heraclitus, frgs. 1–2, ap. Sextus, *Adv. Math.* 7.132–33; in Kirk, Raven, and Schofield, 186–87.

among the elements, by an impersonal oversight, as if to anticipate what Stoics will call providence.

GOD'S I AM

What then of the Torah's counterpart to the ontological argument? The goddess in Parmenides' vision points to the Absolute by way of the verb to be. "It is," she teaches, pressing the point to urge the uniqueness, immutability, and absolute simplicity of her subject. But she broaches no imperative beyond the need to choose Truth over Appearances. In Moses' encounter, God speaks for Himself. *Ehyeh*, He says, I AM, not *estin*, it is. I AM, shall be God's watchword and the name He chooses best to be known by. God affirms His absoluteness when He says, I AM THAT I AM (Exodus 3:14). Yet, even before offering that gnomic expression, He calls Himself the God of Moses' father and forebears (3:6) and voices His concern and love: He has heard Israel's cries. He knows His people's agony as slaves under genocidal taskmasters; He remembers His covenant with their ancestors (2:23–24). Caring is not foreign here. God's absoluteness is moral.

Moses, too, has something to remember. For the bonds that bind him to his people define and circumscribe his mission. Called by name, by God's voice, hearing it call him, *"Moses, Moses!,"* he is responsive, primed to serve, even before the scope of his mission is spoken. A fugitive in Midian, tending his father-in-law's sheep, he answers, like a servant or a child, *hineni*, *"Here I am"* (3:4). He too has seen his people's suffering (2:11). Standing barefoot on ground has heard called holy, he confronts a God who has set aside transcendence and stepped out of the wings of history, morally engaged and existentially committed.

The God that Abraham, Isaac, and Jacob knew had promised their offspring a land and a destiny (Genesis 18:19; 26:3; 28:13–15). Israel, now in crisis, was ready for fulfillment of God's promise: No longer a mere clan, they had become a nation, forged in the crucible of slavery. They now would need to follow their fathers' God and receive the land they had been promised – and, with it, as they little knew, the law inscribing their destiny as a holy, dedicated people (Leviticus 20:26), a nation of priests (Exodus 19:6), living the life of a law where slavery was not absolute and even debt was not lifelong, where God Himself held title to the land,[5] where persons

---

[5] Joseph's dream readings saved Egypt from famine, but his policies shifted Egypt's land to its priests. The visions of Moses saved Israel not only from Egypt but from Egypt's ways (Leviticus 18:3).

and even the soil win respite, not for what they have done but for what they are. In their new life, the generations of Israel will see God's promise kept, that all the families of the earth will bless themselves in Abraham's name (Genesis 12:3). For, as Moses promises in his final address, when Israel lives by God's laws, the nations of the world will say, *"What a great nation, to have the divine so near!" – as the* LORD *our God is to us whenever we call upon Him!* (Deuteronomy 4:7).

God's absoluteness is the heart of the message Moses must deliver, implicit in the name God chooses to be known by. For the God of Abraham is no tribal spirit lured into a fetish or objectified in a monarch's will. He is the God of the universe (Genesis 21:33). So His transcendence does not stand aloof and apart but is all-embracing; His commands are not capricious but replete with generosity and the overflow of wisdom, evident in the act of creation and in the energies which that divine act bestows on nature, emblematic in the sight that drew Moses' gaze, a bush aflame but unconsumed.

Moses now must give up his exile. God is present, but He does not act alone. Israel must rise to the occasion and embrace their liberation. They must join hands and voices, accepting the liberty and commitment to life implicit in God's caring. God imparts His message and mission to Moses. But Moses will not act without Aaron, and the two men cannot lead until Israel is ready to be led.

Unlike Parmenides, Moses rode no chariot to the gates of night and day. He first heard God speak from a bush, having stepped aside from his shepherding to see a fire that would not die down and sputter out. The sight was portentous, but Moses approached more curious than ready to decode such symbols. Parmenides opens his hexameters by saying that the chariot the goddess sent for him, drawn by wise mares and guided by daughters of the sun, its axle blazing in the socket, making the naves sing, carried him as far as his heart desired. But Moses was pursuing no vision quest when, quite unexpectedly, he was called by God. The name he heard God use, as in the vision Parmenides relates, was an affirmation of being – but spoken in the first person, not the third. The God who called Himself *I AM* was at once the subject and the object of this epiphany. There was no goddess to speak for Him, and being did not lie somewhere in the background as an object. The fullness of Being was God Himself.

Self-reference lay at the heart of the Mosaic theophany: God introduced Himself as the Absolute. Yet the thrust of His message was no paradox negating all negation, as if to eclipse the world. For even as

He affirmed His absoluteness, He cited His connection with Moses and his forebears: He was the God whose voice those forefathers had heard and whose signs they had seen. This God did not dismiss as illusory the world of history and change, as Parmenides' goddess would do. Nor did He urge escape from the world, as the summons Plato voiced would do (*Theaetetus* 176b). Rather, He brought a clear charge of responsibility, issuing clear and immediate imperatives about the suffering of the nation He called His own, remembering, He says, His covenant with their ancestors: Moses must return to free his brethren. Their bitter life was no mere "way of seeming"; their bondage and oppression were within God's ken and inimical to His love, not to be denied but to be confronted and overcome.

Moses must make haste to shoulder the risks and tasks of leadership. He must face and face down Pharaoh and lead his understandably skeptical people out of bondage. Beyond that, he must help them restore their connection with their forefathers' God, make clearer to the least of them than it ever was in the flickering epiphanies of those forebears or in Abraham's poignant colloquies with his God, just who that God is and what He expects of the nation He calls His own. Moses is charged to restore, enlarge, and strengthen the covenant of Israel with a God they cannot see, let alone control with words or offerings or sacred names. For, beyond emancipation, he will be called on to promulgate a new and comprehensive law for Israel and institute a way of life that will make them worthy of that law, bound together by love of God and of one another.

The Torah will introduce God's law against the backdrop of its narrative of the creation and the early, faltering steps of humankind. In that narrative's account of the world's creation, Israel will learn that the Creator is the very Absolute who revealed Himself to Moses at the burning bush. For stirring in the account of creation in Genesis is the idea of nature as a totality, *heaven and earth*, Genesis will call it. And looming large behind that wholeness, the unseen God that Moses had encountered.

Mosaic thoughts of God's absoluteness meet images of the creative act when the Author of creation, called simply God, or the Divine (*elohim*), in the Torah's first mention of the world's creation (Genesis 1:1–2:3), will be called *the* LORD *God*, using the Tetragrammaton, when the narrative speaks of His relation to humanity (2:4–22): Mankind's Guide and Judge is the same God Moses met at the burning bush, before a word of Genesis was written. His saving power is an expression of His absoluteness. Later generations will so take to heart that home truth as to take it for granted: God's commitment to creation and compassion for humanity are expressions of His ultimacy. The God of Israel's fathers is the same that Moses was taught to call I AM.

A NECESSARY BEING

To Maimonides, God's *I AM THAT I AM* is more than a name. The words were meant to bear an argument for Moses to pass on to Israel's leaders. They too must see God's absoluteness and learn the true character of their fathers' God. Maimonides reads the name that Moses heard from God at the burning bush as an argument that Moses' hearers were expected to find cogent and that his own readers will recognize as a proof. For part of Maimonides' aim is to bridge the Torah's revelatory idiom to forms familiar to thinkers at home in Aristotelian syllogistics and dialectics.[6]

When Moses says, "They will ask me, 'What is his name?' What shall I tell them?" (Exodus 3:13). Why did Moses need an answer to this question? He says, "They will not believe me. They will not listen to me. They will say, 'The LORD did not appear to you!'" (Exodus 4:1). It is very clear that this is how anyone claiming to be a prophet should be met, until he offers proof. But if, as it seems, it was just a matter of giving a name, either Israel already knew that name, or they had never heard of it. (*Guide* I 63, 81a)

We are rightly suspicious, Maimonides declares, of anyone claiming to speak in God's name. Such claims deserve the critical response they get. That's especially true in times of crisis, among an oppressed people, as Maimonides and his contemporaries had bitter reason to know. Had Moses brought Israel a mere name, Maimonides asks, how would that convince the people of anything?

If it was familiar, Moses proved nothing by relating it. They knew it the same as he. But if they had never heard of it, what showed that it was God's name – assuming that knowing His name would count as proof? (*Guide* I 63, 81ab)

A novel name might seem mere gibberish.

Others before Moses had known epiphanies. But even Abraham, who had proclaimed the universal God (Genesis 21:33) and linked that

---

[6] See *Guide* II 15, 33b. All quotations from Maimonides' *Guide to the Perplexed* are from the translation by Lenn Goodman and Phillip Lieberman, by Part, Chapter, and Page numbers in Salomon Munk's edition of the Arabic original, 1856–66. So, the present reference is to Part II, Chapter 15, Page 33 verso.

thought to the demands of universal justice, in pleading for the Cities of the Plain: *Will not the Judge of all the earth do justice?* (Genesis 18:25) – even he did not encounter God as Moses did, mind to mind, as it were (cf. Numbers 12:8 as cited at *Guide* II 24, 54b 45, 97a). Abraham was not the prophet to bring the people founded by his insights a divinely inspired law, a canon of precepts making God's absoluteness present in no carving or casting but in a law to live by, a law that would convince the nations of the earth that those blessed by its precepts have God in their midst (Deuteronomy 4:6–8; and see *Guide* II 13, 28; 19, 44ab; 35, 77; 39, 84.).

Moses saw God's image in humanity[7] and framed his sense of God's perfection in no smoky vision or halting words trying to lend concreteness to abstractions by invoking images of violence or truculence. What God's *I am* signified for him and will come to mean for anyone ready to learn from what he taught was that the sum and summit of truth, goodness, and beauty lies in God Himself, the Source of all being and of every true value fairly captured by the mind. The God who gave expression to Himself in the act of creation, then, as Abraham had sensed (Genesis 14:22), speaks more explicitly in the precepts of the Torah than He had implicitly in the world He created. For what God and Moses talked about for forty days and nights on Mount Sinai was law (Exodus 34:28–32).

Eliciting the sense he finds in the first Mosaic epiphany, at the burning bush, Maimonides spells out the argument he finds in God's words:

> When God revealed Himself to our Teacher Moses and charged him to bring this message to the people, Moses said: "The first thing they ask me will be to prove to them that there really is a universal God. Then I will say that He sent me." For in those days only a handful had any sense of God's reality . . . .
>
> So God taught Moses what he would need to impart to convince them that God exists: *I am that I am*. This "name" derives from the verb to be (*h-y-h*), to exist. For *hayah* signifies existence. There is no difference in Hebrew between 'is' and 'exists.' The key is the repetition in the predicate of the word for existence. For *asher* (*that*) is a relative pronoun, the same as 'that' in Arabic. It calls for a predicate complement. But here the first term, in the position of the subject, is *I AM*; and the second, which should characterize the *I AM*, is again *I AM* – as if it said right out: This Subject is its own predicate, clearly conveying the idea that He exists but not by way of existence – in a word, the Real that is the Real, the Necessarily Existent. That is what the proof inevitably comes down to: that there is a Necessary Being, one that cannot fail to exist . . . .
>
> Once God has taught Moses the arguments to convince the learned of Israel that He exists – for He then tells Moses, *Go and gather the elders of Israel*

---

[7] See Goodman, *The Holy One of Israel*, chapter 8.

(Exodus 3:16) – and promises that they will understand and accept what He had imparted to him, Moses renews his question: "And once they have accepted God's existence based on these rational proofs, what evidence have I that this God sent me?" It was then that he was given his miracle.

Evidently, in anticipating the question, *What is His name?* Moses just meant "They will say: 'Who is it that you claim sent you?'" But out of reverence and deference he phrased it as, *What is His name?* – as if to say: "No one is so benighted as to be unaware of You and Your Reality. But if I am asked Your name, what manner of being does it signify?" He thought it unseemly to address God in terms of anyone's ignorance of His existence, so he put it in terms of not knowing His name rather than not recognizing the One named.

The name *Yah*, similarly, signifies eternal reality. *Shaddai* is based on *dai*, sufficient, as in *the material sufficed them* (*dayyam*) (Exodus 36:7), the letter *shin* stands for *asher*, that, as in *she-kevar*, (*that are already*) (Ecclesiastes 4:2). The sense of *Shaddai*, then: the Self-sufficient – He who depends on nothing else in giving being or in sustaining His creation but suffices unto Himself in doing so. Every name for God, then, as you see, is either derivative or polysemous like *Rock* and such. No name refers to Him directly but the Tetragrammaton, the explicit name, since it signifies no attribute but His sheer reality alone. Implicit in His absolute existence is His eternity, i.e., necessary existence. You can see how the argument unfolds. (*Guide* I 63.)

What, then, is the argument that Maimonides sees so compactly contained in God's I AM THAT I AM? He might have made a cosmological appeal, as is done in the opening lines of Genesis – and in Avicenna's reasoning, well known to Maimonides – that if anything at all exists something must exist necessarily. But the argument Maimonides finds in God's Self-affirmation and encapsulated in the Tetragrammaton cuts shy of all conditionals and relations. For our knowledge of God does not rest entirely on our knowing other things, as if God Himself depended on us or on His world. The argument Moses was given, captured in the "name" God conveys to Moses and invites him to share with the people, focuses on God's absoluteness: The Absolute cannot fail to exist – in God's words, I AM THAT I AM.

PHILO'S INTUITIONS

Does the argument that Maimonides sees in God's I AM THAT I AM fit the frame fashioned for the ontological argument by Anselm, the sainted Italian Archbishop of Canterbury in Norman times? Anselm himself, when questioned by Lanfranc, his one-time monastic mentor, assigned his proof's paternity to Augustine. But the argument, still widely debated today, is rooted in Platonic metaphysics. Philo pursues the intuitions at its heart. As David Winston writes:

Although Philo sometimes employs the well-known teleological and cosmological arguments for the existence of God which had already been formulated by Plato, Aristotle, and the Stoics, he clearly indicates that the demonstration of the existence of God from his actions is only for those who have not been initiated into the highest mysteries and are thus constrained to advance from down to up by a sort of heavenly ladder and conjecture the Deity's existence through plausible inference. The genuine worshipers and true friends of God, however, are those who apprehend him through himself without the cooperation of reasoned inference, as light is seen by light.[8]

Philo compares the direct approach he favors with the Stoics' reliance on arguments from design.[9] Appealing to the beauty and regularity of the heavenly movements and treating the world on the analogy of a well-planned city or a well-managed estate, or a painting or work of sculpture, Stoic philosophers found marks of providence all through the cosmos. A ship or even a garment, Philo writes, echoing Stoic tropes, can hardly fail to prompt thoughts about its maker.[10]

Schematizing his preferences developmentally, Philo pictures "early thinkers" scanning the world for marks of God's work and citing the evidence "before their eyes." The Stoics, he explains, whose philosophy "was reputed the best," advanced but little beyond those sense-bound primitives: Seeking to know the Artificer from His works, they were blinkered by their materialism. A more perfect mind, cleansed of the dross of the senses, "gains its knowledge of the First Cause not from created things, as one may learn of the substance from the shadow, but by raising the eyes above creation" to "a clear vision of the uncreated." A purified mind aspires to apprehend not just the shadow but God Himself.[11]

Closely tracking Wolfson's reading of Philo's texts, Winston sees an affinity between Philo's expectations and Plato's remarks about *noesis* in his famous discussion of the Divided Line in the *Republic*. Perhaps the first known account of a graph, Plato's treatment matched the phases of knowledge with those of reality and value: Knowledge is of what is; ignorance contends with what is not – leaving opinion or belief afloat between the two – its object, what Plato will call becoming. The sequence points toward a supreme object of thought, the Form of the Good, the

---

[8] Winston, *Logos and Mystical Theology in Philo*, 44. Winston notes Spinoza's echoing thought at *Short Treatise* 1.1.10, Gebhardt 1.18.
[9] See *SVF* 2.1009–20; Cicero, *DND* 2.16–17, 3.26; cf. Aristotle, *On Philosophy*, Fragment 13.
[10] Philo, *De Specialibus Legibus* 1.33–35 LCL 7.118–19.
[11] Philo, *Legum Allegoriae* 3.97–103, LCL 1.366–71.

sum and Source of all reality, the necessary condition of all intelligibility, and ultimate anchor of every sound inference.

Our access to any truth, as Plato sees it, depends ultimately on Truth itself (*Republic* 476, 508A–11D) – just as any relative good or worldly beauty presupposes an ultimate Goodness or Beauty; and the partial unity and relative constancy we may seek presumes an absolute Unity and Constancy. The Necessary Being, in other words, sustains all lesser beings and is presumed in all sound and successful reasoning. Necessity underwrites contingency.

What Plato's reasoning pointed toward, then, is our intuition, spoken, unspoken, or even overtly denied, of a First Principle. It is by such awareness that reason nears and reaches its goal: The groundings of our reasoning are literally hypotheses, that is, underpinnings, footings, springboards to a reality that rests on no lesser assumption but serves us, rather, as the starting point of all inference and understanding. Once at the height where the grappling hooks of reasoning find purchase, and once able to grasp the ideas that spring from the supreme simplicity of Truth itself, one can descend again, Plato promises, rappelling downwards sustained by pure ideas alone (*Republic* 511 BC).

Plato, as Winston notes, explains this trajectory not much further on: "When one starts by the light reason alone, without the aid of sense perception, to find the reality of each thing and does not give up until by reason itself he grasps the Good, he reaches reason's highest object" (532AB).[12] If reason is our epistemic dowsing stick, it points steadily toward the Source, the Form of the Good, the highest reality, on which all else depends.

Plato's treasure map to that highest peak and down again is predictably creased by controversy. But the likeliest reading of the path, as Winston writes, suggests "a sudden intuition of the First Principle" (cf. *Symposium* 210E; *Seventh Letter* 341CD) – in Philo's terms, an immediate awareness of God. Plato's talk of dialectic suggests (despite the unexpectedness of Moses' call) that the intuition need not be sudden. Consummation may come suddenly. But hard reasoning, life experience, and disciplined study may be needed first. And continued reasoning, experience, discipline, and study may be needed to preserve the memory and the meaning of such moments from distortion, distraction, narrowing, or highjacking by the trolls that haunt such mountain pathways.

---

[12] Winston, *Philo of Alexandria* [Selections], editor's introduction, 29.

Philo is keenly aware of God's absoluteness. And, like Anselm, he favors an argument whose immediacy mirrors God's self-sufficiency and the immediacy of His Self-presentation to those who love Him. We do not find Philo framing his intuitive case in syllogistic form, as Anselm does when he proposes that a most perfect being cannot lack existence, lest it be surpassed by a lesser being or even one that is merely notional. But, truth be told, syllogistic reasoning *is* discursive and therefore vulnerable to the kind of slippage that our temporality allows, given our reliance on memory as our reasoning advances. That is the weakness in cosmological arguments like the argument from design: Human reasoning can falter, and images of God as a craftsman are feeble ultimately, not deeply satisfying, too projective to approach God's truth with satisfying intimacy and ultimacy. *Noesis*, pure rational intuition, as Plato urged, readily outstrips *dianoia*, stepwise reasoning. Hence the preference for the sheer immediacy promised by an ontological approach.

But has Philo in fact distilled a strictly ontological argument? Winston's talk of the "imprinting" of the idea of God on the philosopher's mind suggests an appeal to Stoic notions that our idea of God was among God's gifts. If that was Philo's view, his privileging of direct knowledge grows hard to distinguish from appeals to mystical experience or revelation. Assaying Philo's contributions, Wolfson finds, "The only new element introduced by him into these arguments is his substitution of revelation for Plato's recollection of the ideas and the Stoics' innateness of the idea of God."[13]

Plato is the clear source of Philo's discontent with bare cosmological arguments like the appeal to "the wonderful procession of the seasons" that Plato fathered upon Socrates in the *Philebus* (28DE). Philo has still less reason for delight in the "easy" appeal to the fact that belief in gods is found among "all Greeks and all foreigners," a case that Plato put into the mouth of the Athenian stranger in the *Laws* (886A), responding to the atheism of dissolute youths.

The cosmological myth that Plato framed so tellingly in the *Timaeus* is not a false road or a mere byway in Philo's estimation. It parallels the well-traveled road on which the biblical creation narrative is a chief landmark. But Philo does see a higher road that promises serenity and peace because it allays the doubts that dog the steps of any inductive inference.[14] Here, in promises of a more direct encounter for reason with

---

[13] Wolfson, *Philo* 2.92.
[14] Philo, *De Somniis* 1.44, LCL 5.318–19 and see the note on LCL 5.597. Liddell/Scott shows that *deuteros plous* originally meant a second-best route. Thus see *Legum Allegoria* 3.100–102, LCL 1.368–69.

God, Philo sees the route adumbrated when Moses beseeched God to show Himself, *that I may know Thee* (LXX Exodus 33:13) – directly, not by His works alone. He finds Moses hearing God Himself commend that more direct approach in his final song: *"See, see, that I AM"* (LXX Deuteronomy 32:39). 'See' has no physical sense here, Philo urges. Intellectual insight is what God urges. This Moses received when God singled him out: *Moses alone shall approach the* LORD (Exodus 24:2; cf. Numbers 12:6–8, Deuteronomy 5:28).[15]

Others may share such direct awareness. But Philo contrasts it with the inferential knowledge borne by design arguments. To make the point, he compares Moses with Bezalel, chief architect of the desert Tabernacle (Exodus 31:2–11, 35:30–35). For Bezalel, the arch-copyist, worked to the pattern Moses gave him. His very name betrays that he worked not from the light but "from God's shadow" – (*be-zel-el*).[16] Pagan Temples might be ascribed to the handiwork of the pagan gods,[17] but Israel's desert Tabernacle was the work of human hands and minds, integrating the contributions of skilled collaborators, apprentices, the acolytes of Bezalel's genius. The design of the Mosaic Law reflects a still deeper intimacy.

The shadow Philo sees suggested in Bezalel's name is not mere darkness, of course. This shadow is God's, after all, lambent with the aura of the Original. And shadows, Philo admits, do bear hints of the substance that casts them. But God is the Reality[18] – ὁ ὤν the Real, as the Septuagint inscribes it, emulating the Tetragrammaton, which is composed of the Hebrew letters of the verb "to be," but of four consonants rather than the three of a usual Hebrew root. Just as works of art, for Plato, are but imitations (or intimations) of the values and ideas that an artist seeks to express or celebrate, the natural world known to human eyes and minds is, for Philo, a shimmering shadow of God's word and the wisdom it bodies forth. But direct knowledge shines like noontide, banishing mere shadows. The fullness of the Law gives normative expression to all that Moses saw in God's rich Sufficiency.

KINDRED SPIRITS

Plotinus, as Winston notes, uses much the same language as Philo in praise of a direct approach to God: "This is the true end set before the

---

[15] Philo, *De Posteritate Caini* 28, 167, LCL 2.342–45, 426–27.
[16] Philo, *Legum Allegoria* 3.100–103, LCL 1.368–71.
[17] Yakov Dolgopolsky-Geva in the *Koren Tanakh – Exodus*, 172.
[18] Philo, *De Abrahamo* 119–23, LCL 62–65.

soul, to see the Highest *by* the Highest and not by any other light – to see the Highest, which is also its means of seeing. For what illuminates the soul is also what it must see, just as we do not see the sun by any light but its own" (*Enneads* 5.3.17).[19] The core image, of knowing light by light, almost Empedoclean, is invoked by Aristotle when he identifies the power that enlivens reason (*De Anima* III 5). Maimonides echoes the thought: Light makes objects visible but also reveals itself (*Guide* II 4, 14a). Thus, the celebrated line of the Psalmist: *For with Thee is the fount of light; by Thy light do we see light* (Psalms 36:10). Kindred affirmations of a direct avenue for the mind to God are found in Ghazali (1058–1111) and in the Jewish exegete, poet, and philosopher Abraham Ibn Ezra (ca. 1092–1167).

The strong, Ghazali wrote, know God directly and see all things through Him; weaker spirits know God through His works.[20] That latter way of knowing reflects the teaching of Ghazali's mentor, al-Juwayni, that at the first signs of puberty a Muslim boy should learn to prove God's existence. Such a proof would predicate our world on God's reality, since nothing – let alone a world – could conceivably create itself. But stronger souls, Ghazali writes, may know God first and see all things through Him. Ghazali alludes here to the sustained sense of divine presence sought by Sufis, whose intimacy with God he admires, the meed of Sufi practice.[21] As Sufis were fond of saying, one does not need a candle to see the sun.

Ibn Ezra, too, contrasts direct knowledge of God with that derivable from and derivative of study of the cosmos. Anticipating Maimonides, he understands that when Moses beseeched God, *let me know Thy ways* (Exodus 33:13), he was seeking to fathom God's governance of nature. In leading his people, he knew he needed guidance (33:12) and hoped to model his leadership on God's rule. Hence the stress on grace, mercy, and compassion when God proclaims His "attributes" (34:6). But, like Philo – and, like al-Makki (d. 996), a warmly acknowledged source of Ghazali's Sufi pietism – Ibn Ezra favors the more direct route.

Judah Halevi (ca. 1075–141), Ibn Ezra writes (at Exodus 20:2), asked him why he thought the Decalogue begins *I am the* LORD *thy God, who brought thee out of the land of Egypt, out of the house of bondage* (Exodus 20:2) rather than, say, "who created heaven and earth."

---

[19] Tr. after Winston alongside MacKenna/Dillon. At *Enneads* 5.5.10, Plotinus urges one not to seek the Good through anything but itself, lest one behold "only its trace."
[20] Al-Ghazali, *Ihya'* Book 36, Bayan 6, 4 (Cairo, 1968); tr. Ormsby, 71.
[21] Al-Ghazali, *Munqidh*, ed. Jabre, Arabic 35–36, French 95–96; and in Watt, *The Faith and Practice*, 54–55.

Replying to his poet/philosopher friend, Ibn Ezra named three kinds of hearers among the Israelites gathered to receive the Decalogue: The intelligent might well learn God's ways from study of nature, tracing the hallmarks of design and grace in the cosmic order, the fashioning of animals, plants, and minerals, and – not least – the human body. But the broader need among the throngs at Sinai was not for a course in astronomy or physiology. God spoke to their shared experience: They had been slaves in Egypt, and He had saved them from that slave house. The appeal was existential. But the most enlightened, Ibn Ezra proposes, needed no such reminders of their recent history. For them, *I am the LORD* sufficed. Was that an argument, we ask, or just a Self-assertion?

An argument to be parsed as ontological, whether scriptural or Platonic in inspiration, draws its impact from the entailment of God's reality by His absoluteness. If that entailment is intuitive, the case made is rightly called immediate or direct. But is the appeal, then, to mystical experience? How can we distinguish the rational intuition that Philo or Ibn Ezra points to from an appeal, say, to what William James called a sense of "presence"[22] or what William Alston called "perceiving God"?[23]

Intuitions are so like sensations that Ghazali, using a Sufi metaphor, spoke of mystic moments in terms of "taste" (*dhawq*), taking them to be irrefragable, un-analyzable, and ineffable – although still in need of guidance and experience for their impact to be adequately grasped and translated into practice. But if such experience is simply a sensation, where is its cogency? How does its immediacy make it communicable, let alone corroborate the claim it was taken to confirm? How could Moses, as Maimonides would have it, expect its utterance to command credence among the skeptical elders of his people and convince them of God's reality?

Clearly, the rational intuitions at the beating heart of an argument of the ontological type must differ from, say, a mystic's sense of being overwhelmed or Alston's sense of being loved and sustained by God? Drawing a line between a sense of cosmic unity and the rational intuition that powers an ontological argument is little helped by Kant's dismissal of the very idea of rational intuitions – although, to some, such intuitions seem indispensable in mathematics, or, indeed, in recognizing truth of any kind.

Maimonides, for his part, balks at the notion that inferences about God and His reality are anchored solely and sufficiently in our experience

---

[22] James, *Varieties of Religious Experience*, 58–68.   [23] Alston, *Perceiving God*, 1–67.

in the world. For such experience is inevitably rooted in the senses and bound up in imaginative modes of thinking (see *Guide* I 76, 126a). He acknowledges that higher truths about God have their signals and semaphores in temporal experience – as they must if prophets are to perform their poetic task of addressing (and inspiring) humanity in human language (*Guide* I 26, 29ab; 46, 51b). Still, prophets, perforce, use the poetic language of revelation rather than speak academically ("a mode of exposition," he writes, "that only a handful, with reason's help can follow"). The difference of idiom does not render scriptural arguments any less sound than those of accredited philosophers (II 15, 33b). But the differences of idiom make it part of the task of the exegete to mediate and bridge the gap between poetic and philosophical modes of discourse, allowing motivated (and well-prepared) seekers and inquirers to discover the philosophical force of prophetic poesy.

The phenomenal simplicity of any intuition troubles distinctions between argument and experience by exiling intuitions of any sort into the realm of the ineffable. The sound of $C^{\#}$ on the trumpet can be known only by experience. But the idea of God's perfection seems not quite as ineffable as that. For we do have access to value notions that can help orient our quest. Anselm does appeal to Gaunilon's religious experience. And he readily uses written words to convey his argument and to answer the monk's critique. He does appeal to experience, but he does not rest his case on it. And rightly so. For experience demands interpretation. But an argument, unlike the intuition that may spark it, is communicable – as Maimonides has it that God's *I AM* was and remains.

Rational intuitions, quite unlike sensations, lay claim to truth. So, they have implications and are subject to critique. They are, indeed, at risk of crumbling if the propositions that seek to state them prove incoherent. Rational intuitions are not just attitudes like racism or fellow feeling. Mathematical and logical axioms, for example, despite their immediacy and the difficulty of breaking them down into parts or deriving them from other thoughts without circularity, do make distinctive truth claims. They are pregnant with consequences: Theorems derive their truth from axioms – and throngs of ordinary propositions, experiential and inferential as well as theoretical, lean on them and dare not cross them. The Torah's mitzvot have a like dependence on the (sometimes contested) normativity of the first item in the Decalogue: *I am the* LORD *thy God* clearly does more than affirm a fact. Its force is prescriptive in much the way that an axiom's truth demands credence for every proposition that presumes it or follows from it. For if we know what God is and what the word God portends, we must also sense a well of value here; and indeed, of value that is directive.

Granted, the subjective immediacy and seeming simplicity of intuitions does make it hard to see an argument in an intuition. Yet intuitions, like axioms, are often called on in the lives of persons, nations, and cultures to sustain great bodies of moral, aesthetic, spiritual, pragmatic, and emotional content. Like axioms, intuitions are teased from the domain they underwrite (and tested and refined there too). But their power far outstrips the inductive. Are intuitions of any type, then – and those critical to spiritual and religious life specifically – merely subjective? Intuitions, even the perceptual kind that model the rest, are not as indivisible as may appear. Like the atom, a sensory intuition proves to have parts and a history.[24] So do concepts, of course: Background and context assign meaning, impact, and implications even to our most compact thoughts. With that thought in mind, we can look back again to Philo – and forward to Maimonides and Spinoza.

The pure intuition Philo praises, bearing the certitude that seekers long for, is often said to reflect God's presence, hypostatized, perhaps, and even personified as the Shekhina. Is that Presence an intermediary or a state of mind? Does it afford a capstan for an ontological argument? Or is Philo simply citing mystical experience when he speaks of God's Self-revelation? Philo, as Wolfson allows, might have had in mind Stoic notions of an innate God idea.[25] Yet, in Philo's talk of a direct proof, Wolfson does see an ancestral link to the ontological argument. Winston, retracing Wolfson's footsteps, thinks it "evident that Philo had accepted an early form of the ontological argument as it had been formulated by the Stoics and Middle Platonists, an analytical argument that discovered the concept of God imprinted on the human mind."[26] That last phrase preserves the ambiguity we're confronting: Was Philo reaching toward or touching an ontological argument, or was he just acknowledging reflexes written in our minds, as irrepressible as a shudder or a sneeze?

Talk of an innate God-idea echoes Stoic thoughts and wakes the specious appeal of arguments *ex consensu gentium*. Talk of an innate God-idea clearly anticipates Descartes' thesis that he, in his finitude, cannot have spawned the idea of perfection he discovers in his mind.

---

[24] For the neurological history and complexity of our sensations, see Goodman and Caramenico, *Coming to Mind*, chapter 2.
[25] See Cicero, *De Natura Deorum* 1.44, 2.12.
[26] Winston, *Logos and Mystical Theology*, 46.

Such suasions are not robust. For, even if ideas of divinity are indeed universal, it may be, as today's evolutionary psychologists maintain, that such notions, although illusory, persist because they have (or once had) some adaptive utility, by projecting a social consciousness and, when full blown, a readiness to make sacrifices for others' sake.

Descartes' idea of perfection, truth be told, does not need a perfect being as its author or source. It may be the mere reflex of the imperfection Descartes finds in himself, given his experience of doubt – just as a sense of sin and guilt may project ideas of a supreme judge, forgiver, and redeemer. Surely a mathematician as keen as Descartes would hardly be incapable of extrapolating from a sense of his own limitations to the projection of their negation, in thoughts of a being powerful in every way that he was weak and perfect in every faculty that he found lacking in himself. How, then, do we reach the idea of a perfect being?

MAIMONIDES IN HIS OWN VOICE

Maimonides opens his "Second Torah" (the plain meaning of the bold title he gave his code of Jewish law, the *Mishneh Torah*) not with an account of the creation like the opening of first Torah but with a call to recognize God as the ground of all understanding.

> The ultimate anchor and the pillar of all understanding is to know that there exists a Prime Being who gives being to all that is: There would be no heaven, no earth, nor anything in between, were it not true that He is real. Were it conceivable that He did not exist, nothing else would be. But if, conceivably, there were nothing else, He alone would exist: The non-existence of anything else would not negate His being. For all things depend on Him. But He, blessed be He, depends none of them, nor on them all. His being, then, is unique. Thus, our prophet's words, *The LORD God is Truth* (Jeremiah 10:10) – He alone! Nothing else is real in the way that He is. As the Torah says, *There is none but He* (Deuteronomy 4:35) – nothing else has His true reality. (Laws of the Foundations of the Torah 1.1)

The Torah sets out its laws against the backdrop of cosmic history, introducing God as the Creator and swiftly spiraling down to a thumbnail history of life on earth, the early generations of humankind, and the Patriarchs of Israel. But in codifying the full body of the rabbinic laws that flesh out the biblical constitution, Maimonides turns from the Torah's narrative idiom to its metaphysical foundations, anchoring the Law not in the epiphany at Sinai but in God's ultimacy as the necessary being, on whom all else, and so all understanding, depend.

Tellingly, he links his famous opening lines of the *Mishneh Torah* to Moses' first epiphany by heading the work's four first clauses with the four letters of the Tetragrammaton, the name he understands to name God directly and by no mere epithet or metaphor like King or Father (I 61). It is in this name that he sees God's necessary being not only affirmed but proven.

In affirming that all else depends on God, Maimonides affirms that were it conceivable that God did not exist, nothing else would exist. But the relation is not symmetrical: Were all else to fail to exist, God would exist alone. God is not alone in fact. There are other beings, ourselves among them. But Maimonides' idea of God as the uniquely necessary being harks back to Plato. The idea had been taken up by Philo, who calls God *to ontos on*, the Real, the one true reality.[27] Taking a page from Avicenna, just as Avicenna took a page from scripture, Maimonides sees all finite beings as contingent. For there is no internal contradiction in denying the existence of any of them, or all. It is along these lines, Maimonides reasons, that God presented Himself to Moses as Self-sufficing, promising His humble prophet that his fellow Israelites would see the argument implicit in the divine *I AM* and find it convincing.

It was God's Self-sufficiency that Moses intended when he said that God alone is real, a thought that Jeremiah echoed in calling God the Truth: God alone is necessary in Himself. All other beings are dependent on His being. Spinoza, similarly, will say of God, "all other things cannot in any way be or be conceived without or beyond Him." So he, too, will call God the Truth.[28] But, where Maimonides gentled the Torah's saying, *There is none but He* (Deuteronomy 4:35), taking it to mean that nothing else is real in quite the way that God is, as the one being whose existence is not contingent, Spinoza faces into the wind: Taking contingency itself to be an illusion, he calls God the only true substance.

Arguments for God's existence, ultimately, must be either ontological or cosmological. In the cosmological type, salient in Genesis, Maimonides finds an affirmation of the dependence of all the world on God's act. But he finds the ontological counterpart of that idea in the Tetragrammaton. Drawing on scriptural thoughts of creation and on the theology of the Islamic *kalam*, Avicenna had argued for God's necessary being cosmologically, by recognizing the contingency of all finite and determinate things: Since the world's existence has no necessity of its own but only the necessity derived from its dependence on God, Avicenna can argue

---

[27] Philo, *Quod Deus Immutabilis Sit* 11, *De Ebrietate* 83, LCL 3.16, 358.
[28] Spinoza, *Short Treatise*, I, chapters 3 and 5, Gebhardt 1.35, 63.

that no contingent being would exist without the necessary being on which all else, ultimately, depends.

Avicenna's harsh critic al-Ghazali sets necessity ahead of contingency when he urges, as if echoing Philo, that "the strong" in faith know God directly and see all things through Him, whereas weaker natures know God through their experience of nature. The highest way, Ghazali writes, is "by calling God as witness for all creation." But this path "surpasses most people's understanding," so "there is no point in even bringing it up in books." The "lower, easier path" is "not wholly beyond one's grasp." That would be by calling creation to witness in behalf of God. Even here there are pitfalls: Worldly passions may distract one, and "the sheer vastness and fullness of the subject" may set the argument beyond adequate treatment. For "There is not a speck of dust from the highest heavens to the boundaries of both worlds that does not hold prodigies of wondrous significance pointing to God's absolute omnipotence and perfect wisdom."[29] Given the contrasting difficulty and ease of the two paths, it is only natural to turn from the higher if more direct route to the indirect but gentler pathway, reflection on God's acts. Such a turning itself may imprint a virtual image of the ontological argument, reflected, perhaps, in Sufi ecstasies. For as Kant suspected, the cosmological line of reasoning, given its head, will yield implicitly to reasoning of the ontological sort. For creation, to be absolute, must have an absolute Creator.

Once that is seen, an argument of the ontological type proves indispensable, if natural theology is to advance beyond the world God is conceived to have created. A cosmological argument of the familiar sort, invoking images of a craftsman God, cannot reach the pinnacle of God's absoluteness. Appeals to the natural order, the fitting of means to ends, the beauty and bounty of nature, or even the reality and truth of love cannot fly high enough to escape the gravity of the senses. Such thoughts fill the quiver of natural theology, but they cannot point beyond a higher being to reach thoughts of a being of infinite perfection. Only absolute creation, as affirmed in Genesis or proposed in Avicenna's contingency argument, overcomes this weakness of cosmological arguments of the familiar type, with their earthbound imagery. Only if creation is ex nihilo is God's causal role absolute and His grace infinite, since there was no prior desert to address and no prior substrate to serve or resist His will.

---

[29] Al-Ghazali, *Ihya'*.

Maimonides' reading of the Tetragrammaton, then, rightly returns us to the idea dear to Avicenna of a necessary being. That, for Maimonides, was the core idea embedded in God's I AM and unfurled in His favored "name" I AM THAT I AM. These words, as Maimonides reads them, invoke no natural epithet like 'king' or 'father,' but point beyond themselves to the highest reach of God's transcendence, beyond the topmost of Aristotle's categories: For just as absolute creation sets God apart from the world, God's necessary being sets Him apart from all other beings. (*Guide* I 52, 60b–61a; cf. 57, 69b; 63, 82b).

God, Maimonides argues, is not just the world's Cause, the Maker introduced in Genesis. He is also the formal and final cause of all things (*Guide* I 69). For behind each substantial form that gives a thing its nature stands a more general idea; and such ideas, bestowed by the Active Intellect, in its role as Form Giver, depend ultimately on God's universal good – pursued by all things in their distinctive ways. For, as Maimonides argues, God "produces only being, and all being is good" – as the Torah attests: *God saw all that He had made, and lo, it was very good* (Genesis 1:31, cited at *Guide* III 10, 17a).

The plainest difficulty with any version of the ontological argument is the intuitive recognition that existential inferences cannot find solid ground to stand on in mere appeals to logic. Yet we have already noted that every classical version of the ontological argument for God's existence invokes a metaphysical premise in the idea of a perfect being. Does Maimonides himself invoke such a premise? Indeed he does. Even before the first chapter of the *Guide*, he speaks of Jacob's ladder and contrasts it with the description of the married harlot of Proverbs 7. The symbolism in that latter case, he argues, is meant to represent matter's lust for form and "to warn against chasing bodily pleasures and passions. But much of the detail here is circumstantial and merely corroborative, meant only to render more vivid the mental image of the seductress, who will be contrasted (in Proverbs 31) with what Maimonides takes to be the image of disciplined matter, compared implicitly to a good woman, "who is no harlot but is wholeheartedly devoted to her family's welfare and her husband's interests." But the symbolism invoked in the account of Jacob's dream at the place he came to call Beth El (Genesis 28:10–17), Maimonides stresses, is to be read far more closely. Every detail here is portentous. And of the ladder Jacob saw in his dream, Maimonides writes, "Every expression in this image adds another idea to the import of the figure as a whole" (*Guide* Introduction, 71b).

Maimonides takes his time in unwrapping the symbolism of the ladder seen by Jacob in his dream. But he opens the cabinet just a bit when he explains that in biblical parlance rising and descending need not refer to positions but can stand in for shifts in rank, success, or social status – and, most critically, to God's rank in the order of being. For, as he explains, "He is the highest of the high, not spatially but in majesty, reality, and sublimity" (*Guide* I 10, 19b). If we've paid attention to Maimonides' caution that we need to mark the significance of every expression in the Torah's description of what Jacob saw in his dream at Beth El, it won't be lost on us that God, in Jacob's vision, was not situated on the ladder but atop it and that the ladder itself had its base on the earth (Genesis 28:12–13). To Maimonides' philosophically attuned poetic sensibilities, the symbolism cannot fail to evoke two images from ancient philosophy: the ladder of love in Plato's *Symposium* and, perhaps even more tellingly, the rather more abstract image of the Divided Line in Plato's *Republic*.

The Ladder of Love (*Symposium* 210–12) is of critical import here because it maps the course of a human soul's rising aspirations from physical appetites and passions to moral and then spiritual fulfillment in the apprehension of divine Beauty Itself. Jacob's ladder, Maimonides stresses, is anchored on earth, but God Himself is atop it: "All who ascend climb by this ladder and must know Him. For He is there eternally at the summit." The angels, here Maimonides urges, are prophets. "After rising to a certain rung comes descent with what was gained, to govern and teach those on earth." (*Guide* I 15). Maimonides makes a point of God's presence atop the ladder of Jacob's dream. But even its anchoring in the earth, emblematic of the embodiment, from which we are challenged and invited to rise is also the means by which each of us *can* rise. The rungs climbed by the angels seen in Jacob's dream map the phases or stages to be attained in the individual's quest for perfection.

The ladder seen in Jacob's dream orients us to the hierarchy of holiness (*Guide* I 10, 19b) that human reason challenges us to ascend. So here, in Jacob's dream that Maimonides challenges us to read so closely (and in its counterpart in Plato's *Symposium*), we find the ontic premise that any ontological argument, including the one that Maimonides discovers in the name revealed by God to Moses at the burning bush, must include if any such argument is to rise from the plane of logical gamesmanship.

But what vindicates that hierarchy? How can one know that it is real? Here one will need reference to the Divided Line of the *Republic*, to validate, orient, and stabilize that hierarchy of being/perfection, by mapping its ontic and axiological import in epistemic terms. Plato introduces the image of the Divided Line (*Republic* 6.509D–11E) with a somewhat oblique allusion to a play on the Greek words for mind and heaven. The line, as he has Socrates describe it, is divided unequally, and its two segments are divided in turn in the same proportions as the whole. In the lowest portion, he finds images, and above that their originals, that is, animals, plants, artifacts, and such. In the upper section, he finds things intelligible: geometrical figures and mathematical facts and relations, with concepts above them, leading on to the first principle. Socrates grades the four phases of the line by their degree of clarity. But it should come as no surprise that the hierarchy suggested is graded by the approach of each sort of object to truth itself. The hierarchy in clarity will suggest a stepwise approach to Truth itself, which orients the entire scheme, which Plato introduces as a prelude to his celebrated Myth of the Cave, with which Book VII of the *Republic* opens. But what matters to us here is that the line, despite Plato's lack of access to the geometry of Cartesian coordinates, is a chart: The degrees of clarity map the reality and worth in the objects apprehended at each stage of one's ascent: The greater the clarity the greater the reality and worth of each variety of object. Here too, as in the *Symposium*, Maimonides profits. For God is at the summit of the hierarchy, orienting the whole. And the epistemic hierarchy, invoked in terms of clarity, vindicates and validates the ontic and axiological hierarchy. So, its phases are not without argument. We know not just that there are (pace Aristotle) degrees of reality and degrees of value, both describable in the language of perfection, but also that we have the scale right, from the material to the increasingly intellectual, with God, in Maimonides as in Plato, above description but perhaps most adequately conceived, at least in human minds, as a pure and perfect intellect – something of which our own minds, as images of God, give us some intelligible idea.

It is through the essences of things that God gives character to all things and stability to the cycles we see in the play and dance and work of nature. That, Maimonides argues, is why God is called *Life of the Universe* (Daniel 12:7, cited at *Guide* I 72, 103b): He gives all beings the energies that render them alive, literally or metaphorically. So, as the source of the dynamic essences of all that is, God is the source of purpose in all beings. He is, then, not just their Cause or Maker but also their ultimate final cause. For "The goal of all things is to emulate His perfection, so far as in them lies" (*Guide* I 69, 90ab).

For us, Maimonides' deference to Aristotelian, Platonic, and Neoplatonic forms may beseech some indulgence. But the core idea of God as the necessary being whose grace and wisdom give content and direction to all things remains robust regardless of paradigms: The same bowshot traces back to Philo and beyond, to the opening lines of Genesis, and from Moses' first epiphany at the burning bush forward to Spinoza and down to our own days.

KNOWLEDGE OF THE THIRD KIND

Spinoza opens his *Ethics* by treating of God and substance, defining *causa sui* as that whose essence implies its existence (E1d1). Descartes had begun his *Meditations* with hyperbolic doubt.[30] But his psychological version of the cosmological argument, proposing God as the author of his idea of perfection, was what enabled him to draw back into metaphysics from his profession of skepticism: Doubting had taught him that he could not himself have generated the idea of perfection that he found in his mind. It must have come from a perfect being – for, as the scholastics had taught, a cause must have at least as much reality (formally or eminently) as its effect.

God, Descartes reasoned, is no deceiver. For only a perfect being could deceive one undetectably, given one's access to the methods of scientific inquiry that he himself was pioneering. But evil is an imperfection. So a perfect being would not gratuitously deceive.[31] If there is no omnipotent deceiver, reasoning can be trusted, so long as one holds fast to clear and distinct ideas and inferences soundly based on them. Here, as in tracing the divine Source of his idea of perfection, Descartes had relied on the equation of power with perfection (and thus, of wisdom with justice and generosity), metaphysical axioms at the core of monotheism.

Hyperbolic doubt, Spinoza could see, was a piece of Cartesian theater. God had been waiting in the wings all along to rescue the philosopher from solipsism. Logically speaking, just as Maimonides had taught in the

---

[30] Spinoza blames predecessors for failing "to observe the proper order in philosophical inquiry. For the divine nature, which they should have considered before all else – it being prior both in cognition and in Nature – they have taken to be last in the order of cognition" – although "all are agreed that God is the sole cause of all things" and so should be understood as that without which "nothing can be or be conceived." E2p10cs, Gebhardt 2.93 l. 30–94 l. 9.

[31] Spinoza spells out Descartes' reasoning in his *Principles of the Philosophy of Descartes, demonstrated in Geometrical Manner*, Gebhardt 1.147–48.

opening lines of the *Mishneh Torah*, God was the foundation of all knowledge; and God, not doubt, was the sound and forthright starting point. Hence the opening of the *Ethics* with thoughts of God. Only a Self-caused being could be the Ground of all else – things that cannot be conceived by reference to themselves alone but whose existence must be predicated on that of God.

If God is Self-caused and if substance (rigorously conceived) must exist in itself and be conceived through itself, Spinoza reasoned, substance cannot fail to exist. It depends on nothing else and is therefore free (E1a7, p7, 17c2). Thought and Extension, which Descartes had called substances and struggled to relate to one another, become attributes, two of the infinite ways in which God's perfection expresses itself (E1p8, 11). But God's infinite other attributes, each infinite in its own distinctive way, remain unknown to us since we have nothing in common with them.

Spinoza states at the outset of his early work, the *Short Treatise on God, Man, and his Wellbeing*,[32] that God's existence can be proved both a priori and a posteriori. Like Philo, he favors the more direct approach: Once we have an adequate idea of God, we cannot fail to recognize His reality. Spinoza here retraces the reasoning that God told Moses would convince his fellow Israelites of His reality: Given the idea of God's absoluteness, one cannot deny His existence. As Spinoza writes in the *Ethics*, "Were someone to say that he has a clear and distinct – i.e. true – idea of substance yet doubts whether such a thing exists, that would be the same as saying he had a true idea yet doubts if it were false" (1p8s2).

Since God is a necessary being, affirmations of His existence may sound rather like tautologies: They are undeniable, so long as a sound idea of God is firmly held in mind. But, unlike common, garden-variety tautologies, such affirmations are not empty. Their burden is existential. Errol Harris may help today's readers adjust to Spinoza's assumption that a necessary truth may bear existential content: "Reason," Harris explains, "may be viewed, used and treated merely as an analytic instrument ... as it was by Hume when he declared that reason was 'the slave of the passions.' But reason, in a higher form is constructive and

---

[32] Spinoza's *Short Treatise* survived in manuscript in the hands of his friend and publisher Jan Rieuwertsz. Rediscovered in 1704 by Gottlieb Stolle, a professor from Jena, in the hands of Rieuwertsz's son, it was not published until 1862. The present reference is to Part I, Chapter 1 of the surviving text, *Gebhardt* 1.15–18.

prescriptive, the source of order and systematic completeness which establishes the ultimate standards of truth and perfection."[33]

Harris welcomes Spinoza's warmer, richer alternative to Humean instrumentalist, functionalist accounts of reason as the mere servant of our appetites and passions. As Jon Miller notes, Spinoza does not exclude reason from such bath-drawing roles. But, as Miller also stresses, reason has nobler work to do: Like Aristotle and Plato before him, Spinoza sees reason coming into its own when it moves beyond the often-banal task of finding means to our ends and begins to find and choose ends of its own. Reason, Miller adds, is "endowed with a substantial range" of content – including the general ideas that Spinoza calls common notions and the ideas we base on these.[34]

Spinoza, like Descartes, found critical to the sciences concepts cleansed of their sensory accretions. But, like Maimonides, he also found in perfected reason the motive, the means, and the goal of human blessedness, making it reason's role to guide and moderate our desires, setting at their head its own desire to know God (E4App4). "Spinoza," Miller writes, "thought that our most important desires are precisely those that reason generates." More than an instrument or tool, reason is "responsible for why we know what we know, and how we ought to live."[35]

Not surprisingly, given the roles Spinoza assigns to reason, what he means by a priori differs strikingly from the sense familiar to most recent logicians and drummed or drilled into the heads of their students. The meanings of the terms a priori and a posteriori, as Miller shows,[36] have changed substantially since William of Ockham (ca. 1287–1347) gave them "canonical definitions" in his work on demonstration. Ockham's examples are telling: If one knows that certain positions of the heavenly bodies cause a lunar eclipse, then knowing that those bodies are in those positions allows the inference a priori that an eclipse is underway. On the other hand, if one observes a lunar eclipse and knows what positions of the earth and the moon would cause such an eclipse, one can infer a posteriori, the positions of the moon and earth. To Ockham both inferences are demonstrative. But in what he calls the a priori case, one reasons from causes to effects; in the a posteriori case, from effects to causes. It is

---

[33] Harris, *Salvation from Despair*; cf. Carraud, *Causa sive Ratio*.
[34] Miller, "Spinoza and the 'A Priori,'" 577–78.
[35] Miller, "Spinoza and the 'A Priori,'" 556–58, 660–61, citing Ockham's *Summa Logicae* III 2.17; and see Moody, *The Logic of William of Ockham*.
[36] Miller, "Spinoza and the 'A Priori,'" 557–58, 560–61.

not that experience is prior or posterior to the inference. What matters is whether the demonstration starts from causes and infers their effect or starts from the effect and reasons to its cause. Along these lines, the Italian logician Jacopo Zabarella (d. 1589) would write that an ideal demonstration works "from what is prior and better known by nature." Eustachio a Sancto Paulo, a key source for Descartes, wrote that an a priori demonstration proves the conclusion by the cause; an a posteriori demonstration reasons from the effect. Descartes himself, as Miller notes, generally used the term a priori in Ockham's, causal sense.

But Descartes himself, as Miller shows, further modified the sense of "a priori." He had identified as "synthetic" (and therefore a posteriori) the geometrical mode of exposition that Mersenne asked him for at the end of his Second Objections to the *Meditations* (a method that Spinoza ultimately applied, both in reframing Descartes' philosophy and in setting forth his own).[37] The "long series of definitions, postulates, axioms, theorems and problems" characteristic of geometrical reasoning left plenty of room for the slippage possible in discursive reasoning, leaving just the chinks for error that Descartes, a consummate geometer, had been keen to avoid. Moving away from Ockham's focus on causal primacy, Descartes turned his analytic gaze to the epistemic yield of that primacy, understanding the a priori in terms of *immediate* intelligibility: Synthetic reasoning might be sound enough, but ultimately it was not satisfying since "it does not show how the thing in question was discovered." Analysis, by contrast, allows one to make a basic truth his own, "as if he had discovered it for himself."[38]

The method Descartes commended gave a new *epistemic* sense to the term a priori. So, as Miller explains, when Descartes suggests that his own method is Archimedian, his reference is not to causal primacy, as in Ockham, but to the *conceptual* primacy that analysis licenses: With the acid bath of methodical doubt, he could demonstrate the irreducibility of thought to extension. And, relying on the givenness of God's perfection, he could expose the ultimate weakness of hyperbolic doubt and set it aside to let the sciences do their work.[39]

Against this background, we readily understand Spinoza's preference for what he calls an a priori argument. For, as Richard Mason shows,

---

[37] Descartes, ed. Cottingham, Stoothoff, and Murdoch, 2.111 = Adam-Tannery 7.156, quoted in Miller, "Spinoza and the 'A Priori,'" 562–63.
[38] Descartes, Cottingham, Stoothoff, and Murdoch, 2.110–11 = Adam-Tannery 7.155–56, quoted in Miller, "Spinoza and the 'A Priori,'" 562–63.
[39] Miller, "Spinoza and the 'A Priori,'" 564.

Spinoza typically thinks of necessity in terms of causation.⁴⁰ If we wish to understand Spinoza's reasoning, we're better off interpreting what we might incline to read as logical relations in causal terms than try to force Spinoza's judgments about necessity into the straitjacket of formal logic. We do, by a kind of metaphor, or courtesy, call gravitational, chemical, or electrical relations part of the logic of their domains. But the real reference in such cases is causal, not logical in the formal, typically empty, sense favored today.⁴¹

Spinoza relied on Descartes' conception of epistemic primacy when he set out Descartes' system in his *Principles of Descartes' Philosophy*, as the friend noted who introduced the work: We must start where we are certain. Still, as Miller notes, Spinoza did not accept Descartes' claim that the geometrical method was not ultimately analytic.⁴² Spinoza's own practice in philosophy, like Euclid's in geometry, shows that for him analysis and synthesis went hand in hand. For Euclid had analyzed the body of geometrical knowledge so as to find the definitions, axioms, and postulates together necessary and sufficient to derive the body of familiar geometrical truths – just as Maimonides distilled the theses and arguments of the practitioners of kalam, and the rival theses and arguments of the philosophers of Islam so as to find the fundamental premises on which their claims were grounded. *Exposition* of the system itself was synthetic, the fanning out of the peacock's tail. But the work of discovery in each case was analytic. Immediacy, whether in philosophy or in geometry, remained the key to epistemic primacy, just as heuristic fruitfulness remained the test of success. The ideal starting point, whether in geometry or in philosophy, clearly was an intuition. So, in Spinoza's ontological argument, we begin from an intuition.

The a priori argument for God's existence in the *Short Treatise* is itself short and sweet – and notably Philonic: "God, the ultimate Cause of all things and Cause of Himself, makes Himself known through Himself."⁴³

---

⁴⁰ Mason, *The God of* Spinoza, esp. 55–62.
⁴¹ Today's philosophers perhaps can learn from Spinoza here. For understanding the relevance of context and background assumptions, as I argued years ago, can help us dissolve some of the false paradoxes that still bedevil philosophers – not least the questions about analyticity addressed in Quine's "Two Dogmas of Empiricism." See Goodman, *In Defense of Truth*, chapter 4.
⁴² Spinoza, *Principles of the Philosophy of Descartes, demonstrated in Geometrical Manner*, Preface, Gebhardt 1.128, cited in Miller, "Spinoza and the 'A Priori,'" 565–66.
⁴³ *Short Treatise* I, chapter 1, Gebhardt, 18; see note 8.

A posteriori arguments are needed for things that cannot make themselves known but are best known from their external causes. To finite knowers like us, the world's furniture is known in partial, relative, perspectival ways – often, backhandedly, from the effects of things. But just as God exists of Himself, He is best known through Himself. If we know the idea of God clearly, we know that He exists (Gebhardt, 1.15).

It's in the *Short Treatise* that Spinoza (Part I, Chapter 5) identifies Providence with the *conatus*. In the same work, he takes the trouble, perhaps in kindness toward his friends, to prove that the devil, an absolute adversary of God, does not exist. Were any thinking being so malevolent, he urges, it would be our duty to pray for him. But there is no such being, "for whatever duration a thing has results entirely from its perfection." There can be no devil: A being wholly opposed to God and having "absolutely nothing from God" would be nothing.[44] At work here is the equation of reality with perfection that anchors the ontological argument.

At its appearance in the *Ethics*, Spinoza's ontological argument is yet shorter and sweeter. Here it has become a reductio: It is inconceivable that God not exist. For failure to exist would contradict the implication of God's existence by His essence (1p11). Substance must be *Causa Sui* (1p7). For, if we try to conceive of God's nonexistence, we collide with Axiom 7: If anything can be conceived as nonexistent, its essence does not involve existence. But substance is defined (fusing the definitions of Aristotle and Descartes) as what exists in itself and is conceived through itself. It must be *Causa Sui* – in Maimonides' terms, Self-sufficient, necessarily existent.

All things, Spinoza holds, must have a cause, and for anything that does not exist, there must also be a cause, internal or external, of its nonexistence. But in God's case, since God is substance and substance is all there is, there can be no external cause to allow or prevent His being. And, for that matter, nothing can share an attribute with God that might sustain or impede His being. But no internal cause can bar God's existence since God is perfect.

There are those, to be sure, who call the very idea of a necessary being incoherent. But if they invoke the premise needed to power their claim,

---

[44] *Short Treatise* I, chapter 25, G 1.107–108; cf. Maimonides, "All evils are privations" *Guide* III 10, 17a – and the reasoning behind Descartes' recognition that there can be no undetectable deceiver.

that all being is contingent, they beg the question at issue. That is the fatal flaw in any case made against an ontological argument.

Our knowledge of God, for Spinoza, is immediate, just as Philo had hoped. It cannot be drawn from some other thought (hence the weakness of the typical cosmological argument). So, our knowledge of God is not subject to the doubts Descartes feared might dog our certitude about the yield of a course of discursive reasoning. Indeed (echoing Plato as well as Maimonides), for Spinoza, God is the cause or ultimate source of all knowledge: "We are so united with Him by nature that without Him we can neither be nor be known."[45] So much for the epistemic primacy Descartes assigned to self-knowledge! Spinoza here returns to the classical epistemic order: All knowledge, like all things, depends on God.

"Strictly speaking," Harris writes, "if God is defined and conceived as Spinoza requires, no proof of his existence is needed, because the existence of God is then the inescapable presupposition of the existence of any and every thing, and the indispensable presumption of all thinking and all truth."[46] That formulation edges onto cosmological turf. But Spinoza's preference remains ontological: If God failed to exist, He would not be perfect. Hence Spinoza's argument in the *Ethics*: "Conceive, if you can, that God does not exist. Then (by Axiom 7) His essence does not involve existence. But that is absurd. So God exists necessarily" (1p11d).

Those who reject the ontological argument, Harris notes, maintain that no matter how we conceive of God, His existence does not follow.[47] But it's hard to see how that claim can be sustained without begging the question, by denying that existence is a perfection (1p11s) – or, as Spinoza also puts it, a power (cf. Plato, *Sophist* 247e), the very power by which God is *Causa Sui*.

It may help us retrace the workings of Spinoza's argument if we review his account of what he calls knowledge of the third kind, delineated with exceptional clarity by Miller. In knowledge of the first kind, which Spinoza calls opinion or imagination (terms still rife with the stigma of Plato's and Maimonides' disparagement), we rely on our senses, or on words and other signs. But the yield of the senses, for Spinoza as for Descartes, is fragmentary (*mutilata*) and confused. And if we rely on words and other signs, including recollections of past experiences, or

---

[45] *Short Treatise* I chapter 22 § 3, Gebhardt, 1.101 *ll.* 9–11.
[46] Harris, *Salvation from Despair*, 39.
[47] Harris, *Salvation from Despair*, 41. Jonathan Bennett dismisses the ontological argument in Kantian terms as "that notorious paralogism." "Spinoza's Metaphysics," 64.

perhaps on what we have read or been taught, we get no assurance but are left with only subjectivity in hand.

In knowledge of the second kind, we rely on reason. Here, as Spinoza puts it, we use "common notions," general principles accessible to anyone who thinks clearly, to frame a rule under which cases can be marshaled and inferences drawn from the general to the more specific, or to the particular case or cases singled out as instances of a general rule. Sound inferences yield sound conclusions.

But knowledge of the third kind is intuitive, that is, direct and immediate, reliant not on finding and using a general rule abstracted from studying the classes of things but based on immediate grasp a particular essence. One might think here of one's firsthand acquaintance with a good friend or a lover, although in such a case one must always be ready to admit that individuals change and that what we took to be an intuitive awareness might prove to have been anything but. Passions can always distort what we take to be intuitive. Yet intuitive knowledge is real, Spinoza holds, since all reality and all genuine knowledge depend ultimately on God: Our direct apprehension of individual essences springs from our apprehension of some essence as an expression of an aspect of God. In the *demonstratio Dei* that Spinoza privileges as a priori, we rely on our intuition of the reality of God Himself as a perfect and therefore necessary being.

Spinoza uses the problem of naming the fourth proportional to illustrate his distinction among the three ways of knowing: Given three numbers, we are asked to find a fourth that is to the third as the second is to the first (E2p40s). One could, Miller writes, "peek at a neighbor's test," or mechanically multiply the second number by the third and divide the product by the first, with no earthly idea why or how that method works, so long as the calculations are done correctly.[48] In both cases, our answer rests on imagination or opinion: It relies on received opinions, from the test paper viewed across the aisle, or the method taught and perhaps made habitual in the rote performance of "cross-multiplying."

"A more scrupulous or brighter person," Miller writes, might see a general rule applicable to the case at hand. Knowledge reached in this way Spinoza calls rational. It relies on general rules for its soundness. But knowledge of the third kind is more direct and not reliant on reference to a rule: If the numbers are simple enough one can see at a glance, say, that

---

[48] Miller, "Spinoza and the 'A Priori,'" 44–45.

Knowledge of the Third Kind 45

the second is twice the first, so the fourth must be twice the third. Talent, training, and insight matter here. Many of us can "see" with the kind of immediacy Spinoza prized what the fourth proportional would be with three easy numbers. But compare the story told of Karl Gauss, at age six, as legend would have it, swiftly seeing how to sum the numbers from one to one hundred: Seeing that 2+3 would be the same as 3+2, he pictured an array of the numbers to be added; and, recognizing that adding the first to the last, the second to the next to last, yields an array of equal sums, he saw that the sum of the entire sequence would be that sum times the number of pairs, but divided by two to avoid double counting. Gauss relied on no received formula here. Rather, he devised one. That is how creative work in mathematics can be done: not by fishing up a prescribed formula but by framing afresh a pattern perceived – or perhaps by seeing the relevance of an existing rule where its use might not have been customary or familiar. Poets do something similar, as do insightful exegetes like Maimonides. And scientists, for like reasons, often do their most creative work by the application of analogies.

The pitch or range of intuitive insight that Gauss had in mathematics is rare, but it may be possible to enhance such capabilities, not so much by "training," which smacks of rote and regimentation, but by freeing up the mind a bit, as the Gestalt psychologist Max Wertheimer did when he visited a schoolroom where the children had just learned how to calculate the area of a rectangle. He challenged them to find the area of a parallelogram: The rectangle rule does not govern here, but students ready to stop hunting for a prescribed formula found several ways to solve the problem on their own.[49]

In the case of God, searching for set formulae and general rules won't help much more than deference to catechisms and dogmas. For if God is unique, He belongs to no class and (as Maimonides stressed) does not have properties. What's needed, if one hopes to pursue the highest kind of knowledge here, is a direct grasp of what an absolutely infinite being must be. If Spinoza is right that God is the universal cause, such that "whatever is, is in God, and nothing can be or be conceived without him" (E1p15) – an idea to which all theistic traditions at least pay lip service – God's reality cannot be denied without denying the existence of anything at all, an end game that Harris tactfully dubs "self-stultification."[50] To know

---

[49] See Goodman and Caramenico, *Coming to Mind*, 226–27; see Wertheimer, *Productive Thinking*.
[50] Harris, *Salvation from Despair*, 44–45.

God directly, one must confront and contemplate the very idea of ultimate, infinite reality, that perfection whose idea, Descartes reasoned, God must have implanted in his mind.

Does Spinoza lean too heavily on God's identity with all that is? How can he warrant his muscular claim that "Every substance must be infinite" (E1p8) or that the all is not contingent but necessary in its being? He rests his case that the universe exists necessarily on the premise that all things must be caused and thus necessitated: What is not caused externally must be self-caused, and there is nothing beyond the All to give it being: It must be its own cause. As for its infinity, nothing can limit it for the same reason that nothing could have produced it, since nothing has an attribute in common with it. It is for the same reason that Spinoza can affirm that God is infinite absolutely – of infinite attributes, each in its own way expressing infinite reality (E1p9).[51] Only God is infinite in this full, rich sense. And there is, indeed, nothing else.

Spinoza's God does lack some of the key attributes cherished in traditional theologies. But his God is one in a stronger, purer sense than many a theist has proved able to sustain. And his brief does reach a necessary, free being, infinite in infinite ways (E1p16) and uncurtailed in any attribute that expresses perfection. Here he finds a being he thinks worthy of the name of God since it is the cause and ground of all things, itself included. He does attribute knowledge to his God, on the Stoic-sounding grounds of the irreducible presence of intellect in Nature. He adds here his own idea, that the human mind itself is a part of God's infinite intellect.[52]

Granted, Spinoza's God does not perform miracles in any traditional sense[53] or choose favorites. Indeed, as if rising to Maimonides' challenge to press the biblical project inviting us to maximize thoughts of God's transcendence (*Guide* I 59–60), Spinoza invites his reader to conclude that God has no will or purpose, passions or desires, nor even an intellect in the usual sense (E1p17s, Gebhardt 2.62). Such notions, he holds, have

---

[51] See Letter 83, to Tschirnhaus, Gebhardt 4.335 *ll*. 4–7. In Letter 9 to "the Learned Young Man Simon de Vries," ~February, 1663, Spinoza addresses the worry that he has not shown how substance can have multiple attributes. He reminds his "worthy friend" and those whose concerns de Vries voices that he had, in fact, offered two arguments on that score: first, his thesis that the more reality a being has the more attributes must be attributed to it; and second, which he calls decisive: "that the more attributes I attribute to any entity the more existence I am bound to attribute to it; that is, the more I conceive it as truly existent – that is, the more I conceive it as true." Gebhardt 4.45.

[52] Letter 32, to Oldenburg, November 20, 1665; cf. Maimonides' naming human reason as the object of the imagery when Genesis 1:26 calls human reason the image of God within us, *Guide* I 1.

[53] See *TTP* chapter 6, Gebhardt, 3.83–84.

only vexed and confounded traditional theologies, opening their accounts to infusions of myth and magic, since they spring not from any pure idea of divinity but from hopes and fears as unworthy of the subject who projects them as they are of the God on whom they are projected (see *TTP* Preface, Chapter 7).

Wolfson is at pains to note that the immediate knowledge of God that Philo (and Spinoza) upheld is not based on revelation. That is quite true – unless, of course, one agrees with Spinoza that every finite mode is an expression of God's absoluteness and that what the intellect apprehends is the reality of a thing. Revelation, in such a case, would span a broader domain than is often assumed. And Spinoza's thought that one does have an adequate idea of God – if only one allows oneself to entertain it – is, in its way, a brilliant, if bold, resolution of the Torah's affirmation that Moses knew God directly and spoke with Him face to face (Numbers 12:8). But to this we must add that such communion is possible only when one welcomes the conversation, as Abraham welcomed the three strangers who visited him at the Oaks of Mamre (Genesis 18:1).

Spinoza, as Harris explains, does deny "supernatural knowledge" if that is supposed to mean "knowledge involving contravention of the laws of nature."[54] Yet it does not follow "that no legitimate meaning can be given to the idea of divine inspiration. In fact, Spinoza regards all natural (philosophical) knowledge as divine, so far, at the very least, as it is knowledge of the third kind ... knowledge of individual things derived from adequate ideas of God's attributes." For, as Spinoza argues,

> What we know by the natural light is known solely by our knowledge of God and His eternal decrees. But since this natural knowledge is common to all men and rests on foundations that all share, it is not so highly prized by the masses, who are ever eager for what is rare and foreign to their nature. They spurn their natural gifts and typically take prophetic knowledge to exclude natural knowledge – although it has as much right as any knowledge at all to be called divine, being dictated to us, as it were, by God's nature, so far as we share in it, and by God's decrees. (*TTP* 1, Gebhardt 3.15)[55]

---

[54] Harris, *The Substance of Spinoza*, 135, citing *TTP* chapter 1. "A sincere believer in the possibility of supra-rational knowledge," Leo Strauss argued in *Persecution and the Art of Writing*, "would not have declared, as Spinoza does, that man has no access whatever to truth except through sense-perception and reasoning, that reason alone, as distinct from revelation and theology, justly claims to possess the truth" (133). But Strauss slighted Spinoza's most distinctive epistemic idea, celebrating knowledge of the third kind.

[55] Harris quotes the passage in *The Substance of Spinoza*, 135–36.

Even confused and erroneous ideas, as Harris points out, are, for Spinoza, "nothing but true and adequate ideas mutilated and fragmented." We correct them when we know them "as they are in God, in the light of the whole."[56]

Spinoza's God makes no arbitrary choice of a person or a people. Yet the idea of election, like its cousin revelation, is not inconsistent with God's absoluteness, provided that those who are called have themselves chosen God. That last thought resonates with Spinoza's general account of knowledge. For revelation, it seems, is always a two-way street: Minds must be open for insight to take root.

In his analysis of Spinoza's ontological argument,[57] Don Garrett rightly observes that Spinoza appeals to the Principle of Sufficient Reason when he assumes that all things have a cause. Moreover, as we've seen, Spinoza relies on the classic equation of being with perfection, not least in his talk of ability to exist as a strength and inability to exist as a weakness. So, there are metaphysical (rather than merely formal) assumptions at work here. If an ontological argument is expected to demonstrate God's existence by way of logic alone, Spinoza's version fails. Hence the scare quotes on the word "ontological" in the title Garrett gave his article.

But bootstrapping was not Spinoza's metier, if that means trying to extract strong conclusions from weaker premises. Spinoza is quite open about his assumptions, insisting prominently on causality as an axiom: "If a triangle exists, for example, there must be a reason or cause of its existence. If it does not, there must be a reason or cause that prevents it or excludes its existence" – as a square circle, for example, is excluded by its nature, since the notion involves a contradiction (E1a3). Spinoza here anticipates Leibniz's concern that an ontological argument can work only if one knows that God's existence is not impossible, that is, that the idea of a perfect being hides no inner contradiction. But Spinoza does argue that no cause can preclude God's existence: no external cause (since no other substance, if there were such, could have an attribute in common with the Perfect Being so as to limit it) and no internal cause, since there can be no contradiction in the essence of a perfect being.[58]

If God did not exist, Spinoza argues, some lesser being like us would be more potent than the Infinite. Here Spinoza does argue a posteriori, as he admits, since this argument argues from the effect to the cause, when it posits the existence some finite being and so relies on a concept other than

---

[56] Harris, *Salvation from Despair*, 105, citing E2p38 ff.
[57] Garrett, "Spinoza's 'Ontological' Argument," 198–223.
[58] Spinoza's reasoning here is treated in Harris, *Salvation*, 43.

that of God. But what is critical here is that Spinoza's a priori does not exclude premises like the equation of being with perfection or the causal principle best known to us as the Principle of Sufficient Reason. Causality and the identity of being with perfection are metaphysical premises, core truths about reality, the proper domain of metaphysics. There's a nice parallel in Kant himself, although he makes his case not with reference to reality but with deference to experience. For he, too, calls causality a priori (since it is presupposed in experience and not deducible from it) although he hardly sees the causal principle as analytic.

What we see on contemplating Moses' epiphany at the burning bush and its philosophical exegesis by Maimonides, which has its counterparts in the work of philosophers from Philo to Spinoza and beyond, is that the varied formulations of the ontological argument, regardless of their equipage, all center on the same intuition, the idea of a perfect being. Where Plato devoted his life as a philosopher to his sense that goodness must be real, the Mosaic tradition probes the same vein from the opposite mountain face, affirming that what is most real must be good. The philosophically acute have long been hearing each other's voices, confident that light will break through when the seekers on both sides make contact and see that they have been tracking traces of the same intuition.

Two questions face us here: (1) Is there any soundness in the intuition behind these quests for an ontological argument, or is there something fishy in all such arguments that sours the intuition that prompts them? And (2) Does the effort to articulate such arguments drain off the spirit that energizes them, leaving only a sterile shell? To meet the challenge of those two questions, we should first consider the version of the ontological argument left behind, almost shamefacedly, by Kurt Gödel. We may then be more ready to appraise the deeper question by revisiting the thoughts of Maimonides and Spinoza who, like Philo and Ghazali, favored an argument of this type and saw profound connections between the absoluteness it points to and the love of God by and for humanity.

GÖDEL'S ONTOLOGICAL ARGUMENT

Kurt Gödel, perhaps the greatest logician of the twentieth century, was impressive in his ability to frame philosophical questions in terms that made them "amenable to *mathematical* methods."[59] He's best known

---

[59] Mar, "Gödel's Ontological Dreams," 461. Mar credits P. Odifreddi for reversing the familiar rubric "philosophy of mathematics" in favor of the more perspicuous phrase of his essay's title: "Gödel's Mathematics of Philosophy."

today for his Incompleteness Theorem, marking the limits of logical systems by showing that any formal system rich enough to permit constructing a system of arithmetic allows for true propositions that cannot be proved by its premises. Gödel was motivated here, as Gary Mar explains, by his commitment to realism about truth, unsettling the subjectivism that lay, not too well hidden, in the verificationism of the logical positivists.[60]

One of the two first recipients (in 1951) of the Einstein Prize, Gödel saw deep metaphysical consequences in the General Theory of Relativity, allowing him to link the new physics with Parmenidean monism, the time-relativism of Kant, McTaggart's denial of the objective reality of time,[61] and (we might add) Stoic and Augustinian ideas of a higher plane of eternal truth, against which time is projected and within which every moment of history is eternally present. Gödel was cautious in voicing his religious commitments, but the atheism of the Vienna Circle to him seemed a mere "prejudice of the times." In his (unsent) response to the Grandjean questionnaire, he wrote: "My belief is theistic; not pantheistic, following Leibniz rather than Spinoza. Spinoza's God is less than a person. Mine is more than a person."

In notebooks that he wrote around 1941, Gödel set out a version of the ontological proof grounded in modal logic. He did not publish these thoughts, as he told Oscar Morgenstern, lest he be supposed to believe in God. The jottings, Morgenstern inferred, were just a logical exercise. But in February 1970, sensing the approach of death, Gödel entrusted to Dana Scott his *Ontologischer Beweis*.[62] Mar spells out the argument. Its "modal core" was an Anselmian (also Cartesian and even Maimonidean) axiom:

1. It is a necessary truth that if God exists His existence is necessary.

This premise matched Anselm's (and Spinoza's) assumption that a being that might not exist could not be the greatest conceivable, since a necessary being is plainly greater than a contingent one.[63] Then comes the Leibnizian premise, patching the gap that Descartes seemed to have neglected:

2. God's existence is possible.

---

[60] Mar, "Gödel's Ontological Dreams," 470.
[61] Mar, "Gödel's Ontological Dreams," 467.
[62] Gödel, *Collected Works* 4.441; Wang, *Reflections on Kurt Gödel*, 16, 19, 21.
[63] See Adams, "The Logical Structure of Anselm's Arguments," 41–42.

Using Brouwer's Axiom, Mar proposes:

3. If God exists, it is necessary that God's existence is possible.

So

4. In the actual world α it is necessary that if God exists, God's existence is necessary.

But

5. If it is possible that God exists in world α, there is a world β, possible relative to α, in which God does exist – and that, necessarily (by 1).
6. The same necessity would hold in all worlds possible relative to α.

Indeed, Brouwer's Axiom makes the relative possibility relation symmetrical.

So

7. God exists necessarily.

In short, if it is possible that God exists, given that any existence of God is necessary existence, God does exist.

Gödel's argument rests on understanding modalities in terms of possible worlds. That fact highlights the centrality of Leibniz's insistence on the premise that God's existence is possible. For what is possible must be true in some possible world. So if it is true that for God to exist at all He must exist necessarily, the possibility of God's existence anywhere entails the necessity of His existence everywhere – that is, in all possible worlds.

The riposte would come in the assertion that God is *not* a possible being, that there cannot be a necessary or even a greatest conceivable being – perhaps because modalities properly apply only to propositions, not beings, or because the notion of 'greatness' is too amorphous to apply out of the blue to any putative being, actual or virtual, as if such a notion somehow had a clear sense applicable to just anything.

But it seems tendentious to confine modalities to propositions, when true propositions clearly reflect the realities they affirm. There may be some wisdom for us in the broader, classical use of modal concepts, as we've suggested. The more open usage is clearly in play in Spinoza's talk of the strength or weakness of things to exist.

As for greatness, I agree that we need more concrete and richer notions of perfection than are suggested by the familiar omnis (omnipotent, omniscient, etc.), which too often make God sound like a comic book superhero or a strongman at the fair, and breed sophistical questions about whether God can create a rock too heavy for Him to lift – the sort of conundrum that medieval theists routinely dismissed alongside comparable specious notions about, say, whether God could create His like. What we need is more reflection on the dimensionalities of greatness that might apply to the divine. That sort of inquiry would enrich our thinking about God and might turn our thoughts to the unity of knowledge of God with love of God and God's answering knowledge and love for creation.

INTUITION AND ARGUMENT

We can try our wits in disentangling argument from experience in God's *I AM*. But before we exhaust our wits, we should recall, as our Thomistic friends remind us, that the words God gave Moses, as the name to answer Israel's doubts, came in an epiphany. Only language could make that epiphany intelligible and actionable and thus allow its articulation as an argument. Beatitude and contemplation, as the Catholic theologian A. N. Williams argues, are united, for Aquinas, in *theoria*, which, at bottom, he glosses, is contemplation.[64]

The goal, for Thomas, as for Maimonides, is a knowledge of God that fulfills our quest for understanding and a grasp of ultimates and so imparts blessedness. Such knowledge, Williams argues, stems from "a kind of active participation in God's self-knowledge" – a thought that Spinoza would share. And, to Thomas, as to Maimonides, God's knowledge is no mere attribute, separate and distinct; it is "no less than God's own self." So the epiphany of Moses at the burning bush counts as "a divine self-giving."[65] No wonder it is at the same mount that all Israel will hear God's *I AM* (Exodus 3:12, 20:2).

True felicity, for Maimonides arises in a virtuous circle, knowledge guiding love and guided by it. And the flowering of their union is in the contemplative form of prayer that Maimonides deems the highest (III 51,

---

[64] Williams, "Mystical Theology Redux," 57.
[65] Williams, "Mystical Theology Redux," 58–59. As a corollary, Williams argues that, for Thomas, God's unity dissolves the distinction "between pure and applied knowledge," and implies, as regards God, "that in knowing himself he also knows all that he has made." He argues further, that "even in its most practical moments" the Summa "is to be read as an act of contemplation whereby we are united to the mind of God." Maimonides puts that shoe on the other foot, as we've seen, when he argues that even when making a living (or doing battle) Moses and Abraham were never out of touch spiritually with God.

126a), a knowing that puts one in ever closer touch with God and bears fruit in lives of kindness, justice, and generosity (*Guide* III 54, 134b–35a). For Maimonides, unlike many a successor, sees no fatal dichotomy between an active and a contemplative life: Moses and Abraham both had wives and children, earned a living, and engaged in the world. Indeed, Abraham's destiny was to be realized not just personally but in his offspring and successors, as God promised in His covenant for them all: *For I know him, that he will charge his children and his house after him to keep to the way of the* LORD *by doing what is right and just, so that the* LORD *may fulfill for Abraham all that He promised him* (Genesis 18:19).

Abraham's destiny reflects his righteousness. So it is to be pursued and realized morally, spiritually, and intellectually by the nation constituted by his descendants and successors. The key to its shared fulfillment is moral. But that key unlocks an intimacy with God, confirmed at Sinai and manifest when Israel lives by the law God gave Moses (See Deuteronomy 4:6; Numbers 23:23, cited by Maimonides at *Guide* I 4, 15b; II 11, 24a.). It is the Torah, then, that keeps the covenant of Abraham alive.

Head and heart, mind and spirit, are at one as conceived here. For *heart*, as we've noted, is the Torah's name for the mind. Williams captures the zest of such thoughts when he writes of Thomas' citing Gregory's view in fleshing out "his own notion of contemplation," as grounded in a love of God "inflaming us to gaze on God's beauty."[66] Thomas, Williams writes, "envisions no spiritual experience which is not a fully human experience." The same is true of Maimonides, not surprisingly since Thomas was schooled in Maimonides' epistemology: "If we are led to God by our senses as well as by our minds and our hearts, it is because we are embodied …. We are drawn into participation in God's life through the body, mind, and soul …. Our senses and our minds lead us to God, the finite to the Infinite, the created contemplating the Uncreated, that the two may be joined in love."[67]

LOVING GOD

For Spinoza, as Garrett explains, human minds "are parts of the 'infinite intellect of God' (2p1c)." But "human thought has not only a representational but also an affective aspect; and this is possible only if God's thought itself … *also* has an affective aspect." So,

---

[66] Williams, "Mystical Theology Redux," 63.
[67] Williams, "Mystical Theology Redux," 64.

To the extent that one achieves knowledge of the third (and highest) kind – which involves understanding the essences of singular things through the attributes of God, effects through their causes (E2p40s2) – one possesses knowledge in something like the way that God himself does .... In a similar way, knowledge of the third kind involves having affects in something like the way that those affects are in God, and so enables one to participate more completely in what might be called the affective life of God.[68]

We cannot, of course, sustain the world as God does. We are finite *and interested* parties. But a basis can be seen here for emulation of God's love through what Albert Schweitzer called reverence for life and what I have summed up in my general theory of deserts as recognition of deserts in all things.[69]

Those who find Spinoza's God abstract or cold may not have reckoned with his thoughts about God's love – or those affirmative and beneficial affects that the Stoics, and Philo in their wake, called *eupatheiai*, good passions, and that Spinoza called active emotions (3p58), among which he numbered joy, and chief among which he counted love. For Spinoza, as Harris writes, "the power of the intellect, which in the last resort is the true essence of man, is such that it can, through the third kind of knowledge (*scientia intuitiva*), bring him to the knowledge and love of God."[70] As Spinoza writes, in the passage that Harris goes on to quote, "love directed toward the Eternal and Infinite nourishes the mind only with a joy free of all sorrow, something truly worth desiring and seeking with one's every strength." (*TdIE* 1.10 = Gebhardt 2.7 *ll*. 24–26; cf. E4p28). Spinoza prefaced those lines by contrasting the mixed worldly goods that he has found fraught with danger and risk of loss. So here he echoes Maimonides: One must make knowledge of God his highest good, the cynosure of all one's powers and pursuits. For Maimonides, too, saw knowledge of God and love of God as advancing hand in hand. And for both philosophers, the two attainments are not only complementary but reciprocated. For providence, Maimonides argues, reflects our knowledge of God (*Guide* III 51, 125b–27b). And, for Spinoza,

The mind's intellectual love of God is the same as the love by which God loves Himself, not insofar as He is infinite but insofar as He can be parsed in terms of the essence of the human mind considered under the aspect of eternity. That is, the mind's intellectual love of God is part of the infinite love by which God loves Himself.

---

[68] Garrett, "Spinoza's Ethical Theory," 283.
[69] See Goodman, *On Justice; God of Abraham*; Chapter 4.
[70] Harris, *Salvation from Despair*, 165.

It follows that insofar as God loves Himself He loves mankind. So God's love of humanity and the mind's intellectual love of God are one and the same. (E5p36&c)

In the *Short Treatise*, Spinoza argues that we can reach the felicity we seek not by way of belief (as some Christians hope) but only by the direct, intuitive kind of knowledge, whose highest object is God, the best and most glorious of beings, with whom one is drawn to unite. Ultimate felicity is found in the blessedness of such union.[71]

Given our finitude and the infiniteness of the One we seek, such knowledge cannot be comprehensive: "I do not say that we must know Him as He is. It is enough for us to know Him somewhat to unite with Him. For even in our knowledge of the body we do not know it perfectly, as it really is. Yet what a union, and what a love!"[72]

Today we know the body, with all its complexities of form and function, far better than the physiology of Spinoza's day allowed. But one recalls here Galen's point, that we learn to speak using our tongues (and the elephant to use its trunk) despite our knowing little of the detailed anatomy of the muscles that move the tongue (and the elephant's knowing nothing at all of the anatomy of the 40,000 muscles that move its trunk). For, as Spinoza has it, one's mind is the idea of his body and is, in that sense, united with it, although too intricately for our awareness to anatomize, and too intimately for reason to sunder their union by analysis of their concerted action as they act.[73]

We know God directly and immediately, Spinoza argues, since His reality grounds all that we know. So, even if our knowledge starts from as narrow a base as our own bodily sensations, it "finds no rest" there but reaches and roams further, toward knowledge of that without which neither body nor mind can be or be conceived. And, as soon as it knows that being, "it will be united with it in love" – and born again: "At our first birth we were united with the body .... But our second will occur when we become aware in ourselves of the completely different effects of love produced by knowledge of this incorporeal object" – as Spinoza here calls God (*Short Treatise*, Gebhardt 1.101–2). "For since all Nature is one

---

[71] Spinoza, *Short Treatise*, II chapter 22.2, Gebhardt, 1.100.
[72] *Short Treatise* II chapter 22, Gebhardt 1.100 *l*. 23–101 *l*. 1.
[73] Immediate consciousness of the physiological workings of our bodies, were it possible, would, of course, be an unmanageable distraction and would have proved an evolutionary disaster. We see one reason here for the emergence of the mind as a subjecthood that knows and expresses itself in terms irreducible to those of the body and thankfully unaware, largely, of the detailed functioning of our bodily organs.

unique substance whose essence is infinite, all things are united in Nature in one being, which is God" (Gebhardt, 1.101).

For Descartes, Margaret Wilson observes, knowledge, even of God, was "primarily instrumental," a bulwark against skepticism, making way for "a 'firm and permanent' science of nature." But, for Spinoza, "The mind's highest good is knowledge of God, and the mind's highest virtue is to know God" (E4p28).[74] Again Spinoza echoes Maimonides as to the highest goal of human life and aspiration ("Eight Chapters," 4). Spinoza's God, to be sure, is all-inclusive. But he too sees knowledge of God as the critical understanding "that can lead us by the hand, as it were, to knowledge of the human mind and its highest blessedness" (E2, Introduction = Gebhardt 2.84 *ll*. 11–12).

Knowledge of God, Spinoza argues, "incontestably evokes love." That love, as it is for Maimonides, is drawn by God's perfection. Maimonides speaks of a turning toward God (*Guide* III 51, 123a). To Spinoza that might mean looking toward the beauty of the All. In his unfinished, posthumously published early *Treatise on the Improvement of the Mind* (*De Intellectu Emendatione*), Spinoza calls it one's highest good to pursue a perfected nature that will, along with others if possible, enjoy an intellectual union with the whole of Nature – that is, with God (*TdIE* 13, Gebhardt 2.8 *ll*. 25–27). The key to that union: to purify the mind and so improve it as to understand things without error, aiming in all the sciences toward the single goal of personal and, if possible, shared intellectual perfection (*TdIE* 16). So here, as in Maimonides, moral purity supports and enriches intellectual perfection. And here, although Spinoza does not separate God from nature, as Maimonides does, he too sees in the sciences a true route toward knowledge of God. For nature remains, as it was for Maimonides, the expression of God's perfection.

Spinoza never abandoned the goal he set himself in the *TdIE*. For in the *Ethics*, he argues that reason demands that everyone love himself and seek what will truly lead him toward greater perfection, not at others' cost or to their harm but with due regard for them and in collaboration with them (E4p18s). And he holds fast to his Maimonidean thought that human perfection is to be found through the pursuit of knowledge, consummated in knowledge of God.

That point is critical if we are to hear the harmony among the voices in the diachronic chorus gathered before us. For the God who reveals

---

[74] Wilson, "Spinoza's Theory of Knowledge," 90.

Himself to Moses at the burning bush is no abstraction. He presents Himself as the God of Moses' father and forbears, affirming an existential connection to Israel even before revealing His absoluteness, voicing compassion for Israel, as His people, a people He wills to liberate – and before summoning Moses to his role in that liberation.

Maimonides does uphold an act of creation, as Spinoza did not, favoring instead God's eternal Self-expression. So, Maimonides' God exercises choices, as Spinoza's God does not. The Mosaic Absolute that prompts Maimonidean loyalty is ultimate not just ontically but morally and historically. Without engagement with His creatures, God's perfection, as Maimonides sees it, would be incomplete. For God's exaltation is complemented by His omnipresence: His glory would be dulled to nullity were it present only elsewhere. What Isaiah heard the seraphim declare is that all that is proclaims God's glory, His exaltation confirmed by His immediacy; His transcendence, by His immanence.

That thought, that God's immanence is the expression of His transcendence is critical if we are to grasp how we can know and love God: We reach God in the same way that God reaches us, by a knowledge pregnant with love. So when Moses calls on each of his hearers to love God *with all thy heart, and with all thy soul, and with all thy might* (Deuteronomy 6:5), Maimonides reminds us that biblically *heart* means thought, outlook, will, mind, and intent (*Guide* I 39). We are called to know God, and the love invoked by God Himself is not shrouded in a cloud of unknowing but open and alive, enspirited and energized by discovery, rooted in an understanding of nature, viewed and studied, loved and admired as God's work (III 28, 61a).

LOGIC AND LOVE

Love, for an Aristotelian and not less for the Neoplatonic Aristotelians of Maimonides' day, is literally what makes the world go 'round. For the revolutions of the heavens are inspired by an awareness of transcendence, as the heavenly bodies and the minds that drive them in their vast choric dance seek to emulate divine perfection and express their love of the Highest, passing on all that lesser beings can handle of the good shed on them from above.

This cosmic choreography maps the coalescence of love and knowing invited biblically. It should not be slighted when we move beyond the ancient cosmologies. We have ample reason to retire the astral influences and astrological superstitions that hark back to pagan piety. But we still observe a striving toward perfection in all things, each according to its general and specific nature and its individual project and conatus, even without the mediation of the heavenly bodies and their once deified or angelic minds. It is the striving of all beings that anchors their deserts, moral and aesthetic. Even without the ancient cosmology, such love and the knowledge it prompts and feeds remains emulative, aspiring, and expressive, pointing toward the Source of all perfections.

The nisus we observe everywhere in nature is rarely self-aware. For, as ancient and medieval thinkers and poets in the Hebraic tradition fully understood, our bones and organs, and the animals, plants, and minerals we study, use, or admire are hardly conscious. The consciousness is ours when we take in the elegance of nature's design and the energies of the strivings we witness around us as well as in ourselves and one another. Yet the beauty and utility of the design we see everywhere in nature still praises their Creator, and the conatus manifest in all beings still points to Him.

Love of God is natural if God is recognized as the source and summation of all perfection. Yet there is always the risk of projection, capping God's infinitude with the imagined but constraining and delimiting "perfections" of anthropomorphic "attributes," distorting the idea of divinity and setting them in service to selfish appetites or chauvinistic passions. Hence the need for an open spiritual space to accommodate the idea of holiness: Whatever features we might imagine to capture (and exhaust!) God's perfection, we must always recall (as the angels do, in the praises Isaiah overheard) that God Himself is higher. Yet we must not let our thoughts of God vanish into abstractions like wisps of vapor. We can moor our thoughts of God's sanctity in marking the concrete expressions of God's perfection in the recognition of beauty, ingenuity, and grace in nature, and again in the exemplars of virtue, moral principle, and creativity in human lives, as it is in the energy, stability, and even solidity in earthly things. And this we can do even as we recognize the absoluteness of God's perfection, reached for by the ontological style of argument and by God's I AM.

Love of God, as Maimonides reminds us, is the root of genuine worship. But such love depends on knowledge, lest it be derailed, misdirected, or left to lie fallow (*Guide* I 39, III 28; 51, 124b–25a). And love must be enacted – morally, aesthetically, intellectually, creatively. Symbolic (that is, ritual) acts of worship confirm us in the love of God (III 35, 76a) – individually – and, as Spinoza dared to hope, even communally. But such acts are empty without knowing. Hence Maimonides' advice about attaining habits of focus, centered on the meanings of the prayers, poems, and texts of scripture and the liturgy, and his finding the highest worship in quiet contemplation as one lies awake in bed (III 51, 125–26a). These are spiritual counterparts of the practical habits that cultivate the moral virtues, just as communal observances cement our social bonds – and just as the symbols and celebrations that articulate our values and beliefs make those beliefs and the ideas they articulate lasting institutions worthy of the Subject they celebrate (*Guide* II 31).

The care of God for Israel in love and knowledge is attested biblically, Maimonides explains (*Guide* II 43, 91ab), when he glosses the symbols seen in a vision of Zechariah's (11:7): "The people at the start were in the LORD's grace. He guided and led them. They were pleased and delighted to follow, and God was pleased with them and loved them, as it says, *This day hast thou affirmed the* LORD... *and this day hath the* LORD *affirmed thee* ... (Deuteronomy 26:17–18)." It was Israel's trusting in God's care that made the affirmation that Zechariah speaks for. And that ancient bond remains unbroken. As Jeremiah hears God Himself affirm, *I remember in your favor, thy young love as a bride, how you followed Me into the desert, a land unsown* (Jeremiah 2:2) – verses repeatedly chanted on the Day of Atonement, by which we remind ourselves of God's promises and of the actions and choices of Israel's ancestors that gave those promises their strength.

It was active and public, personal and communal expression of allegiance to the one God that cemented the bond Zechariah spoke of. Ceremony is critical here. But the service of God far outstrips its liturgical expression. For love is more than courtship; and courtship means more than love notes, chocolates, and flowers. Actions as well as thoughts and words must be put to work in God's service. "That is why," Maimonides writes, "you find David so urging Solomon to devote himself to these two things: striving to know Him and to serve Him once known: *And thou, Solomon, my son, know thy father's God and serve Him ... if thou seekest Him He will be found of thee* (1 Chronicles 28:9). Once you know Him, devote yourself to Him unreservedly, turn your mind to constant passionate love of Him." (*Guide* III 51, 125a).

God is there to be discovered. But masses and holy water, as Pascal put it, do not add up to faith. They do, however, prepare a ground for it. The same can be said, with all the greater force, of the life of the mitzvot – those that are moral and interpersonal and those inviting and commanding one to study and explore, discover and invent. It's in the moral partnership and intellectual friendship one builds with God that spiritual knowing bears fruit.

The yearning to know God, drawn to God's perfection (*Guide* II 36, 79a), is more than curiosity – although curiosity is where Moses began his rise from a powerful moral sense to his mature eagerness to see God's face, or if not that, to know God's ways (Exodus 3:3; 33:12–13, 18–20; *Guide* I 21, 25b–26a). The sense of God's absoluteness is transfigured, in worship, as what began in love and awe becomes symbolic action and poetically freighted words. So, not surprisingly, worship, in Hebrew, is called work, 'avodah, as it is in the kindred ideas of cult, culture, and cultivation. But talk of *knowing*, in the Torah's Hebrew, points toward more intimate bonds. It alludes to consummation, spiritual and intellectual, and reflects the intimate mutuality presumed when the Torah calls love-making knowing. The same mutuality and intimacy are signaled in our most frequent ritual act, that of blessing God, a practice that would amount to effrontery were it not for God's intimacy with us, communally in His covenant and personally, privately, in contemplation.[75]

The love of God, as Maimonides sees it, like the love of wisdom, with which it is intertwined, is, in its true form, a constant passion – devoted, not merely devout. It builds and strengthens the intellectual bond that links us to God. This existential bond, our human birthright (Genesis 1:26–27, as glossed at *Guide* I:1), given with the first glimmer of human intelligence, Maimonides cautions, is weakened and wasted by distractions (III 51, 125a). Its work is conceptual, not fanciful, trapped on the plane of the imagination. It is best sought in solitude. But its living nerve does not preclude practical engagement, as the lives of Abraham and Moses prove (III 51, 127a) – so long as one does not let passions of pride and precedence reverse the polarity of means and ends and short circuit its productive and creative current. For one is always in God's presence when one acts (without self-deception) in God's behalf.

The motto of such a life, the biblical ideal, at once active and contemplative, is eloquently voiced in the words Maimonides takes up from David, so often blazoned on the interior front wall of a synagogue but rarely grasped in the full rich sense that Maimonides finds in them: *Shiviti ha-Shem le-negdi tamid, I have set the* LORD *ever against me* (Psalms 16:8) – and the paired hemistich not typically posted: *With Him at my right I'll not list*. Maimonides glosses the words of the warrior poet: "He says, 'I never let the thought of Him escape my mind. He is my right hand,

---

[75] See Goodman, *The Holy One of Israel*, 51–57, 62–74.

as it were, its strokes too swift to slight for an instant, lest I list' – lest I fall." (*Guide* III 51, 125b).

A no less poignant image of the union of passion with engagement is elicited by Maimonides from a no less lyrical text:

So rapt may one become in higher things and so joyous in their contemplation that he can converse with people and see to his every need of body and mind without quitting his ecstasy. His heart remains before Him, while outwardly he is with others. The Torah puts it poetically: *I sleep, but my heart waketh – Hark, my beloved knocking!* (Song of Songs 5:2). (*Guide* III 51, 126b–27a)

Concluding his treatment of *teshuvah*, one's moral and spiritual turning toward God, he writes:

It is clearly known that love of the Holy One, blessed be He, is not knit up in one's heart until it possesses one constantly and completely, as it should, and one gives up all else in the world for it, as God commanded us, *with all thy heart, and with all thy soul* (Deuteronomy 6:5). But one can love God only so far as one knows Him: The love reflects the knowledge, much if it be great, less if it be small. So one must devote oneself to understanding and mastery of the sciences and disciplines that will enlighten one about his Maker, so far as one's human powers permit. (*MT* Laws of Repentance 10.6)

SUMMING UP

Like its Hebrew counterpart, Greek metaphysics begins with an epiphany, distilled to a single word, the verb to be – hardly surprising, since metaphysics, as Aristotle conceived it when first setting out its agenda, is an inquiry into "being *qua* being," that is, being as such. Nor is it surprising that both the Greek and Hebraic metaphysical quests should raise their eyes to the heights. For the idea of being *qua* being readily sustains at least two rival readings. Taking 'being' in its widest sense, metaphysics, first philosophy, as Aristotle called it, asks, "What does it mean for a thing – anything – to be?" On that reading, metaphysics becomes the broadest of inquiries: We may study animals, plants, or minerals, but metaphysics asks what *all* realities have in common: What can we say and know about anything just in virtue of the fact that it is? But, in a second sense, that inquiry opens onto the question whether such things as animals, plants, and minerals are all that exists. So metaphysics points toward theology, another of Aristotle's names for first philosophy.

That higher quest is already suggested by the thought that looking for what it means for a thing to be is already to wonder about pure being and what it is that makes things real. Thus, even when we interpret metaphysics as seeking an account, be it ever so thin, of what all things have in common, the inquiry beckons one on to a bolder search, a search for being in a richer, higher sense, for being at its purest. When metaphysics becomes a quest for being par excellence, it becomes theology, the mind's movement spurred by thoughts that first philosophy rightly regards "first things" (*archai*), that is ultimates – ultimate realities, yes, but also ultimate causes and ultimate values – ultimate beauty, truth, goodness, and the wisdom that knows them and knows how to relate them to each other and how to relate oneself and one's life to them.

The implicit message, spurred by our human appetite for ultimacy, prompts a sense, not always tacit, that ultimate reality, ultimate causation, and ultimate value prove, when best known, to be the same. It is here that we discover monotheism, where God is recognized as the Ground of all reality, as the ancient Rabbis intimated when they called God *ha-Maqom*, the Place – the Standpoint. The Mosaic contribution here is to link the thought of absoluteness to the acknowledgment of goodness and its demands for caring and creativity, in the recognition that the transcendence of the Absolute means that bounty and beauty are ever present in the immanence that complements and completes God's transcendence.

The narrative of Genesis employs the narrative idiom but disjoins the fanciful fabric of Babylonian myth to weave a finer, fairer tapestry. Maimonides, for his part, builds on the insights and techniques of Aristotle but curries away much of the pagan piety still clinging to ancient notions of a divine cosmos. Spinoza builds a Euclidean framework and climbs to its summit. Philo adopts and adapts the allegorical methods and tropes of the Stoics. Surface differences may mask the affinities of these varied discourses; but, from the first Mosaic epiphany, an Abrahamic tree grows (Genesis 18:1) where a bush once burned. It's all too easy to miss the deep unity underlying a single, simple intuition.

Pascal famously contrasted the God of the philosophers with the God of Abraham, Isaac, and Jacob – marking a turning point in his personal road to Damascus. And Heidegger, more archly than contritely, remarks of Spinoza's God: "Man can neither fall to his knees in awe nor can he play music and dance before this God."[76] But we don't take our spiritual cues from this unrepentant Nazi. Nor do we learn the logic of Divine unity from a profound trinitarian like Pascal. It was David who danced

---

[76] Heidegger, *Identity and Difference*, 72.

before God, and it is we who fall to our knees, but only before God. To Maimonides, Abraham was the paradigmatic philosophical theologian. For Abraham had no role model to follow and no religious tradition that he could faithfully and wholeheartedly embrace. In Maimonides' eyes, the God of the philosopher and the God of Abraham were one and the same.

2

God and Mathematics

Twice daily observant Jews recite the Shema, opening with the line, *Hear, O Israel, the* LORD *is our God, the* LORD *is One* (Deuteronomy 6:4). We then read the admonition to love God with all our hearts, with all our souls, and with all our might. We are commanded to teach our children God's words – the obligations they prescribe and the values and ideas they inspire. We are to think of them and speak of them at home and in public, on rising and when settling down for the night, and even when traveling: We are to make God's precepts the watchwords of our doings and guides of our thoughts.[1]

The Shema, as Jonathan Sacks wrote, "is the oldest and greatest of our prayers, part of the liturgy since Temple times. Its opening line is among the first words taught to a Jewish child, and among the last words spoken by those who went to their deaths because they were Jews." How did these words become our "supreme declaration of faith"? The Shema "contains no human requests, no praise or plea. It is less a prayer than a prelude to prayer. In prayer, we speak to God. In the Shema, God, through the Torah, speaks to us."[2] Indeed, as Rabbi Sacks stressed, the opening word, from which its name is drawn, means *Listen!* How do words framed as a public declaration, drawn from Moses' final exhortations, become a private meditation recited (often softly) morning and evening, a bedtime prayer – and the last words a dying Jew is charged to say?[3]

---

[1] See Goodman, *The Holy One of Israel*, 55–60.   [2] Sacks, *The Koren Siddur*, 98–99.
[3] Sacks, *Koren Siddur*, 294–95; Birnbaum, *Daily Prayer Book*, 778–80, 787–88. See B. Berakhot 4b, 60b.

Although not framed as a confession of faith, the Shema is a declaration of loyalty. By echoing this charge one turns toward God, affirming His oneness and uniting in spirit with the entire caravan of Israel. Israel's ancient tribes may once have declared their unity by proclaiming their shared allegiance to the same one God. But now Jews unite in this covenant of allegiance: We are not polytheists, dualists, or trinitarians. We unite as a people in affirming God's oneness and uniqueness.

"It does not seem too rash," Richard Mason writes, "to speculate that one legacy of Spinoza's Jewish upbringing that never left him was a repudiation of any thought of many gods or of some kind of multiple God."[4] Spinoza's radical monotheism bespeaks his Jewish heritage, alongside his commitment to the ancient philosophical project, seeking to reconcile the monism of Parmenides with the particolored kaleidoscope of our experience.

Plato and Aristotle, the founders of that project, did hammer together thoughts of a single highest deity beyond multiplicity and change, even though they never banished lesser gods, the ranked legions of deities that return to prominence as intermediaries in the philosophies and pious practice of their Neoplatonic heirs. Faced with centuries of persecution by pagan powers and their Christian successors, Jews rallied their spirits with the Shema, affirming God's oneness, not as a battle cry like *Allahu Akbar* (which means not "God is great!" but "God is greatest!") but as a pledge of solidarity with God and of unity with one another, even in the face of torture, persecution, and death.

For Spinoza, as for Maimonides, God's oneness excludes not just multiple gods but any multiplicity in God. It also entails God's infiniteness. Simplicity underscores the complex idea of God's oneness. For anything divisible, even conceptually, as Maimonides argues, cannot be a necessary being (*Guide* I 51, 58a; 53, 62b). How do the facets of God's oneness – uniqueness, simplicity, and infinity – relate to one another? And how do these pillars of radical monotheism impact images of God as a person, approachable, and responsive, a judge, strict but forgiving, and a creator, even out of His eternity?

INFINITY

Georg Cantor (1845–1918), the founder of mathematical set theory, was perhaps the greatest modern theorist of infinity. An Augustinian Lutheran, Cantor is best known for his proof that there are higher order

---

[4] Mason, *The God of Spinoza*, 39.

infinities beyond that of the rational numbers. For if we order every possible fraction in a grid and map them all for counting, we exhaust the natural numbers. What, then, of the irrationals? For there are infinite irrational numbers just between zero and one. As Cantor saw, there must be uncountable infinities beyond the "countable" infinity of the rational numbers. That thought, for him, resonated with Augustine's discovery of the inadequacy of his thinking in his Manichaean phase, of God as a sort of boundless sea (*Confessions* 7.5, 7.14) – and his realization that he must think otherwise of God's infinity (*vidi te inifinitum aliter*). Cantor orchestrates Augustine's thought here: Just as God transcends time and space, He must transcend any ordinary infinite.[5]

God was the high goal of Augustine's quest; whatever knowledge he acquired, including the knowledge of mathematics that tellingly sets human minds apart from animals, would be used (much as Plato had projected) to pave a path toward God. It is not from the senses that we know numbers and their laws, Augustine argued. Such knowledge cannot be culled from mutable things. Only the light of reason shows us numbers and teaches us their laws. But, although all numbers are composed of ones, the senses show us just the manyness, not the underlying unity.

Cantor was a mathematical Platonist, holding mathematical truths to imply the reality of mathematical entities. For only what exists can be known. Numbers, to be real, Cantor reasoned, must exist in God's mind: The numbers we know reflect the eternal numbers God knows. That thought, for Cantor, proved both God's existence and the infinite vastness of His mind, that we glimpse in the vastness of the *mathematical* universe.

Do thoughts of God's knowledge as the complement of human ignorance topple one into a God-of-the-gaps mode of thinking, as if God and humanity were competitors in a zero-sum game and any advance in human knowledge – say in the natural sciences – pressed God ever deeper into the shadows? A more wholesome and more venturesome spirit, following in Einstein's and Maimonides' footsteps, would trust that the more we know of nature the better we see into some corner of God's mind. Thus, Einstein framed an idea of God in "humble admiration of the infinitely superior spirit that reveals itself in the little that we can comprehend of the knowable world."[6]

---

[5] Drozdek, "Beyond Infinity," 127–40.
[6] Einstein's words here are taken from remarks he made to a banker in Colorado in August 1927. They were repeated in Dukas and Hoffman, eds., *Albert Einstein: The Human Side*, 66, and in Einstein's *New York Times* obituary, April 19, 1955. See *The*

As for Cantor's mathematical Platonism, however, to me the premise seems to come dearer than the outcome it buys. Would we not be better off, before hypostatizing numbers and other mathematicals, just admitting that mathematical truths hold even if they don't *refer* to entities that exist beyond those that we must posit? That seems a stance that Ockham would recommend: Mathematical truths hold true with no need for mathematicals for them to be about, just as moral truths hold true without there being any 'ethicals' for them to be about.[7]

Salient for us in Cantor's thinking about God was his thesis that all human knowledge is grounded in an idea of the Infinite. That idea, as Cantor sees it, is not the product of some process. Rather, it is the grounding needed for any such process to begin: The infinite precedes the finite in the cognitive order, just as it does in the order of being.[8] We need space before we can draw a line or even mark a point. And in the same way nature needs God's infinite power before being can erupt from nothingness. If mathematics, as Plato suspected, is the royal road to knowledge of God, the idea of infinity is the signpost that points the way.

Cantor's privileging of mathematics framed his thinking about nature, where others may feel more at home. So, it might help us put flesh on the bones of Cantor's metaphysics if we think of his scheme cosmologically. The Torah makes such gestures when it speaks not of the universe (and still less of numbers!) but of heaven and earth and not of the nothingness that might have been had there been no act of creation but of the welter and waste (*tohu va-vohu*) it invites us to imagine. We are not asked to picture sheer nothingness, and still less, to fancy an absolute and infinite being.

Quotable Einstein, 204. Einstein told a friend around 1920, "I want to know how God created the world. I am not interested in this or that phenomenon, in the spectrum of this or that element. I want to know his thoughts." In conversation. Einstein said, "In every true searcher of Nature there is a kind of religious reverence, for he finds it impossible to imagine that he is the first to have thought out the exceedingly delicate threads that connect his perceptions" (*Quotable*, 202–4); "a conviction in the reasonableness and comprehensibility of the world, in kinship with religious feelings, is the basis of all the most elegant scientific work" (203).

[7] The realities addressed by moral truths, as I have argued, are not some magical ingredient – natural or "non-natural" property that renders neutral propositions prescriptive. The referents of moral truths and source of their prescriptivity are the bearers of deserts, persons foremost among them, the subjects by whom and about whom moral judgments are properly made. See *In Defense of Truth*, 132–34, 405–6, 409–10; *On Justice*, passim; and Chapter 4.

[8] Drozdek, "Beyond Infinity," 131.

Cantor's metaphysics, like Augustine's, was of a piece with his theology. Thus, his poetic description of the nexus between metaphysics and the sciences, including mathematics:

> The foundation of the principles of mathematics and the natural sciences is the responsibility of metaphysics, which must regard them both as her children, servants, and helpers, which she cannot afford to lose sight of but must always safeguard and control, and which must produce from the wide range of the material and mental realm the building blocks of which her palace can be completed – just as the queen bee residing in her apiary sends out thousands of bees into the garden to suck nectar from the flowers and then, together under her supervision, transform it into honey.[9]

It seems hard to rely on Cantor's mathematical Platonism to sustain one's theism since his Platonism itself is driven and steered, at least in part, by his theological commitments. But Cantor's religious faith does attest to the deep bond between ideas of the infinite and the idea of God, just as his idea of a kind of unity among all the sets he would countenance (an idea grounded in what Kai Hauser calls Cantor's "intuitive style of mathematical reasoning") bespeaks the affinity of his mathematical ideal to God's oneness, a deep intuition of rational mysticism.[10]

Cantor, much taken by Plato's rather Pythagorean treatment of the forms, interprets a set, like a Platonic idea, as "a One over Many."[11] Like Plato's forms, Cantorian sets may aid one in making sense of nature, since they "furnish an 'organic explanation of nature' that is superior to a mechanical one."[12] What Cantor found most arresting in Plato's *Philebus* was the proposal that "the many are one, and the one many" (14c). How are man and ox one, and how is the beautiful one, or the good? Are there truly such unities, as Plato proposes (15ab)?

Plato's method of division provides half an answer to such questions as to the unity to be found in difference. For the members of any natural kind are in some sense one. But to fill in the picture, Plato invokes the contrast between the infinitely, continuously variable and the constancy

---

[9] Cantor, letter to Esser, 1896 in Tapp, "Kardinalität und Kardinäle," here translated after Joanna Van der Veen and Leon Horsten, in "Cantorian Infinity and Philosophical Concepts of God," 133.
[10] Hauser, "Cantor's Absolute in Metaphysics and Mathematics," 172; cf. Hauser, "Cantor's Concept of Set in the Light of Plato's Philebus," 783–805. And for the manifestation of God's infinite grace in the act of creation, Saadiah, On Job, *The Book of Theodicy*, tr. Goodman, 124.
[11] Hauser, "Cantor's Concept," 785–86.
[12] See Cantor's 1883 letter to Wundt, quoted in Hauser, "Cantor's Concept," 787.

in what has come to rest (24A–D). Here we confront the Pythagorean duality of the *apeiron* and *peras* – and the stability emergent between them that we glimpse in nature, in the mixed (*mikton*) that allows us the semblance of knowledge accessible to us in our changeable world: "All things that are ever said to be consist (so the men of old say) of a one and a many, and have in their nature a conjunction of limit and unlimitedness" (16c; cf. 23c). Limit here might be the Form of things in embryo; the unlimited would solidify and precipitate as Matter.

It was in such reflections of Plato's, Hauser argues, that Cantor may have seen the role of mathematical understanding in the natural sciences, at the interface between the ideal and the sensory.[13] Here, it seems, Cantor could see the import and the impact of the definiteness he expected in the elements of a set, undergirding the power of mathematical ideas to stabilize sensory particulars and allow the intelligibility of natural happenings, by construing their phases and components as a unity. The indefiniteness of the ancient *apeiron* may have prompted Cantor, at an early stage, to brand it "an inauthentic infinite." But the more positive understanding of the infinite that he relates to God owes more to Plotinus than to Pythagoras. It is with reference to that richer and more positive idea that Cantor crowns his God with the diadem of absolute infinity.

"To be sure," Hauser writes, "strong axioms of infinity and the orders of transcendence charting the higher infinite were unknown to Cantor. Nevertheless, the basic intuition underlying their formation is implicit in Cantor's doctrine of the Absolute maintaining the uncharacterizability of the totality of all sets in its open-endedness. Some inkling of this is provided by the absolutely unlimited growth of the sequence of transfinite numbers which Cantor saw as an 'appropriate symbol of the Absolute.'"[14]

THE INFINITE AND THE ONE

God's simplicity looms large in the thinking of Maimonides and other radical monotheists. But how, we may ask in the wake of Cantor's learned intuitions, do ideas of God's absolute oneness jibe with thoughts of His infinity, the boundlessness at the core of biblical ideas of God? As we read in the psalms, twice in our morning worship and once again in

---

[13] Hauser, "Cantor's Concept," 790–91.   [14] Hauser, "Cantor's Concept," 796.

the afternoon: *Great is the* LORD *and much to be praised. His greatness, unfathomed* (145:3).[15]

Saadiah sees allusions to God's boundless grace when Isaiah reports God's words, *High as the heavens are above the earth, so high are My ways above your ways and My thoughts above your thoughts* (55:9). For the Psalms apply the same comparison to God's grace. But they also proclaim that God sets our sins at as far a remove from us *as the East from the West* (103:11). Midrashically, Saadiah reasons, "the distance of the eastern horizon from the western is twice that of the heavens from the surface of the earth." So, God's goodness must be infinite: "Since Scripture employs this comparison of His bounty and beneficence once with double the quantity and once singly, we learn that ... in neither case is there a limit or boundary but only a symbolic reckoning." That reading is confirmed by the psalmist's calling God's grace *higher* and *loftier* than the heavens (108:5) – beyond all measure. Less midrashically and more philosophically, Saadiah argues: "His bringing creation into being from nothing is the ultimate act of grace." For there was no prior desert of such bounty.[16]

Is there a tension between affirming God's unity and recognizing the infinite depth and generosity that the psalmist celebrates and Isaiah affirms? Philosophers like Saadiah and Maimonides saw no conflict. Nor did Philo. But it took Spinoza's genius to explain how God might be both infinite and indivisible.

To the founders of Greek philosophy, the idea of the infinite often seemed a borderline concept. To Anaximander (d. ca. 546 BCE) the *apeiron*, was the "indefinite," from which the multifarious world had emerged, diversifying from a pregnant, amorphous mass.[17] But Aristotle, with a pronounced distaste for indeterminacy, took Anaximander's term to signify an unbounded cosmos. With some distaste he wrote, "The infinite turns out to be the contrary of what is said to be. It is not what

---

[15] Psalm 145 is the only psalm called *tehilla*, a paean, as Joseph Hertz notes; yet it is the psalm "from which the whole Book of Psalms received its name *Tehillim*, lit. 'Book of Praises.'" Hertz *Siddur*, 85. The Talmud underscores the centrality of this psalm's celebration of God's grace by promising life in the World to Come to all who recite it, as prescribed, three times each day. Why, the Sages ask, is this particular psalm singled out for such special regard? The answer given: not only does it acknowledge the universality of God's grace, *"on all His works,"* but it underscores the comprehensiveness of God's grace, by its form as an alphabetical acrostic (B. Berakhot 4b).

[16] Saadiah, on Job, *The Book of Theodicy*, tr. Goodman, 124.

[17] See Kirk, Raven, and Schofield, *The Presocratic Philosophers*, 105–20.

has nothing beyond it but what always has something beyond it."[18] For Aristotle, as Leo Sweeney explains, the infinite is inevitably inchoate: "There is always something absent or lacking from it. Thus it is not complete or perfect. In the fourfold scheme of causes, it is plain that the infinite is a cause in the sense of matter, and that its essence is privation."[19]

Linking the infinite with the indefinite, Aristotle bridles at thoughts of an amorphousness ungovernable by the mind. Yet he accepts the infinite divisibility of a continuum. And something of Anaximander's spirit still whispers in his words when he affirms the polyvalent potentials of matter. But even here he seeks a measure of definiteness. For he situates the intelligible specificity of things in their forms but locates (and limits!) their generic potentialities in their matter.

Determinacy, clearly, was the hallmark of being for Aristotle. And to him that meant definition. Hence his discontent with the accidental.[20] Defending the world's eternity against the notion of Pythagoras and Speusippus, "that supreme beauty and goodness are not present in the beginning, he argues that any seed must have come from individuals already present and complete" (*Metaphysics* Λ 7, 1072b32–73a13). And yet, in positing the infinite revolutions of the heavens, Aristotle did suggest (at least by Maimonides' lights) that his God, consummately good and beautiful, and the ultimate cause of all movement over infinite time, must be infinite in power. For no finite body could have an infinite effect, and no infinite body is possible. God, then, must be incorporeal, impassive, and unchanging, but also infinite, at least in the energies that God inspires.[21]

Even so, A. H. Armstrong wrote:
The idea that the First Principle of things, the supreme divinity, is itself in some sense infinite, does not seem to appear clearly and unmistakably in the Greek-speaking world before Philo of Alexandria. It is indeed an idea opposed to the

---

[18] Aristotle, *Physics* II 6, 206b32 with II 7, 207b35–8a4.
[19] Sweeney, *Divine Infinity in Greek and Medieval Thought*, 6.
[20] Aristotle knows that accidental relationships occur – a carpenter might happen to be musical. But such connections hold no interest for him since they are subject to no science. He slights the play of chance in nature and misses the tale told by statistical correlations, beyond the vague notion of "for the most part." See *Metaphysics* I 2, 1026b27–33; *Physics* II 5, 196b15–17. See Owens, *The Doctrine of Being in Aristotelian Metaphysics*, 307–11.
[21] See *Guide* II 1, 6b–7a. Maimonides defended the theism of eternalists by arguing dialectically that only an incorporeal God could keep the spheres in motion over infinite time; see *Guide* I 71, 97a; II 2, 10b–11a.

normal Greek, and especially to the Platonic-Pythagorean way of thinking, for which the good and the divine is essentially form and definition, light and clarity, opposed to vague formless darkness.[22]

Despite the loaded language, contrasting light with darkness, Armstrong does qualify his generalization: not "clearly and unmistakably." For he knows the lines just cited from Λ 7 of the *Metaphysics* and sees clearly that Aristotle's highest deity must have existed long enough to obviate the very idea of a cosmic beginning. For Armstrong, what Aristotle regarded as infinite was God's power, not God Himself. But in that sense, Maimonides reads Aristotle soundly. Yet if Aristotle is big enough to curb his preference for determinacy in behalf of divine (and cosmic) eternity, one should not so cavalierly sacrifice his capacious Peripatetic reasoning just to contrast Greek light with Judaic darkness. Joseph Owens read the contrast of Hellenic with scriptural reasoning much as Armstrong did, if less invidiously, when the alternative was Christian: "Perfect Being for Greeks meant limitation and finitude; for Christians, the perfect Being is infinite. Limitation for the Christians denotes imperfection; while for the Greeks imperfection was implied by infinity."[23]

Posting himself at the boundary between the Hellenic and the Hebraic, as if to preserve the purity of Greek philosophy, Armstrong (in the early article we've quoted) assayed Philo's originality more in the spirit of Hegelian ethno-essentialism than in that of cosmopolitan Alexandria (or imperial Rome!). He cites no text for the idea of divine infinity in Philo but goes on to credit Plotinus, himself a man of Egypt, as "the first Greek philosopher to try to work out with any sort of precision the senses in which infinity can be predicated of the Godhead, and to distinguish them from the evil infinity of formlessness and indefinite multiplicity."[24] Was Philo, then, imprecise?

Plato had called God incorporeal, imperceptible, immovable, and unchanging.[25] He had also called God simplex (*haplou*). Philo, in like spirit, called God inapprehensible (*akataleptou*), unnamable (*akatonomastou*), ineffable (*arrhetou*), uncharacterizable (*apoios*).[26] Where do

---

[22] Armstrong, "Plotinus' Doctrine of the Infinite and Christian Thought," 47. Armstrong cites Guyot, *L'Infinité Divine depuis Philon le Juif jusqu'a Plotin*; and see Sweeney, "Infinity in Plotinus."

[23] Owens, *The Doctrine of Being*, 5 n. 19.   [24] Armstrong, "Plotinus' Doctrine," 47.

[25] Plato, *Sophist* 246B; *Timaeus* 52A and 38 A; *Phaedo* 78D; *Republic* II 382E.

[26] Philo, *De Posteritate Caini*, 169, LCL 2.428–29; *De Somniis* 1.67, LCL 5.330–31; *Quod Deus Immutabilis sit* 62, LCL 3.40–43; *Legum Allegoria* 1.51; 3.36, LCL 1.178–79, 1.324–25, etc. Much in tune with Philo, Maimonides too rejects divine attributes on the ground that they would in some way limit God.

The Infinite and the One

we see infiniteness? We get a taste of Philo's approach in his response to questions about God's abode: "God Himself is called a place. For He contains all things but is ... contained by Himself alone."[27] For Philo, God is His own place – as in early rabbinic usage, where *ha-Maqom*, the Place, becomes a standard epithet of God,[28] having the force sometimes found in phrases like "the Ground of being." More literally, *ha-Maqom* means "the Standpoint." Glossing Exodus 33:21, *Lo there is a place by Me*, Rabbi Jose ben Halafta of Sepphoris (second century), a disciple of Rabbi Akiva's, spelled things out: "The Holy One is the place of the world; the world is not His place" (Genesis Rabbah 68.9).[29]

As if answering Plato, Philo calls God "better than good, elder than the monad, purer than unity, discerned by no one else – for He alone comprehends Himself."[30]

Philo rests his metaphor for God's boundlessness on the Sages' identification of the Torah as the Tree of Life limned in Proverbs (3:18), taking that vivid image to symbolize the dynamism of God's wisdom and the unpent generosity of its Source:

The wealth of God's wisdom is unbounded. It puts forth new shoots after old, never to cease flourishing and renewing its youth. So all who fancy they have reached the limit of any science are simple minded: What seemed to near an end remains far from it.[31]

Armstrong was keen perhaps to credit Plotinus with giving clarity to the idea of God's infiniteness. But Philo, at work long before Plotinus was born, sees no murk or muddiness in the idea. He finds it presaged vividly in the Torah's narrative, as if to anticipate Plotinus' thesis regarding emanation, that when the gift is intellectual the giver bears no loss. That thought, along with the word later adopted as the Hebrew term for emanation, is taken up by Jewish mystics from the Torah's text itself.

---

[27] See Philo, *De Somniis* 1.63, LCL 5.328–29; cf. Plotinus, *Enneads* 5.5.9.
[28] See Urbach, *The Sages* 1.66–69. Translating *Ha-Maqom* as "the Omnipresent," Urbach finds the epithet widespread in early rabbinic discourse and used quite naturally, attesting to its acceptance, although it became rare in time.
[29] Winston, *Selections*, 349 n. 212, sees a possible influence of Philo on Jose b. Halafta's gloss; see Midrash Tehillim on Psalm 90:1, ed. Buber 195b. Winston notes parallels in Origen, *Contra Celsum* 6.71 and Porphyry's *Letter to Anebo*, inter alia.
[30] Philo, *De Praemiis et Poenis* 40, LCL 8.334–35. Philo returns to his earlier words when he calls God "the primal good, the excellent, the happy, the blessed" and argues, in Platonic tones, that God is – being most perfect in every way. *Legatio* 5, LCL 10.4–5. For Philo's new audience in Rome, see Niehoff, *Philo*.
[31] Philo, *De Posteritate Caini*, 151–52, LCL 2.2.417–19.

When Israelites, soon after receiving the gift (and trial) of manna, complain that they want meat, Moses, feeling overwhelmed, makes a complaint of his own. Will he get no help in bearing the burden of this restive generation of former slaves? God's response is couched in a denouement filled with the dramatic irony that so often caps the Torah's narratives, and it frames an outcome leading Moses all the more deeply to appreciate the blessing enfolded in the burden of his leadership.

Moses heard the people weeping with their kin, each at the entrance to his tent. The LORD *was furious; Moses was distraught. "Why did You bring this ill upon Your servant?" he asked the* LORD. *How have I displeased You, to have the burden of this entire nation laid upon me? Did I father all this people? Did I give them birth, that You would have me bear them in my bosom to the land You promised their ancestors, as a nurse carries a nursling? Where can I get meat for this entire nation when they weep at me for meat: "Give us meat to eat!" I cannot carry all this nation by myself. The burden is too great for me. If that is how You mean to treat me, just kill me, if I have found grace in Your eyes. Do not let me witness my own failure."* (Numbers 11:10–15)

God moves to offer Moses help:

"Gather Me seventy elders of Israel, men that you know are senior leaders of the people, and bring them to the Tent of Meeting to assemble with you there. I will come down and speak with you there and share out (atzalti) with them some of the spirit that is on you and set it on them, so that they can bear the burden of the people with you and you need not carry it alone." (11:16–17)

God, miraculously, provides meat for the people, who have already begun to wish they were back in Egypt and to speak wistfully of the slave rations they enjoyed there. But with those cravings met, the idea that others might share Moses' burden takes a surprising turn:

Moses went out and told the people what the LORD *had said. He gathered seventy elders of the nation and stationed them about the Tent. And the* LORD *did come down in a cloud and shared (va-ya'tzel) some of the spirit that was on him and set it on the seventy elders. And, lo, while that spirit rested on them they did prophesy. But it did not last. Two men had stayed in the camp, Eldad and Medad by name, and the spirit rested upon them. The two had been listed but had not gone out to the Tent. A youth ran up and told Moses, "Eldad and Medad are prophesying in the camp!" Joshua the son of Nun, Moses' aide since his youth, spoke up and said, "My lord Moses, make them stop!" But Moses answered, "Are you jealous for me? Would that all the* LORD'*s people were prophets and the* LORD *set His spirit on them all!"* (11:24–29)

As Philo explains, what the elders received meant no loss to Moses:

Do not assume that this kind of taking involves any loss or partition. When fire is lit from fire, it can light a thousand torches but remain undiminished and undisturbed. Just so with knowledge: It makes all its devotees and disciples knowing, without any loss. Often, indeed, the knowledge improves, as they say springs do when water is drawn from them – for they say it grows sweeter. Just so, on-going conversation with others gives them training and practice, improving everyone. If the spirit to be shared with so many were to belong to Moses alone or to some other mortal, it might have crumbled and wasted away. But the spirit that was upon him was the wise, divine, indivisible, unseverable, supreme spirit that spreads everywhere without loss or deficit, conferring its benefits with its wisdom undiminished.[32]

Moses did, in fact, grow in stature, as the episode reveals: Just as he had risen from a fugitive shepherd to a prophet through his epiphany at the burning bush, he now rises from an overburdened soul, all but echoing his people's complaints, to a leader generous in spirit and glad to share his gift with others – although none would prove capable, as he was, of transforming moments of inspiration into concrete guidance. For he, unlike any other inspired person, will fashion his epiphanies into a law and way of life for his nation. But, as Philo sees, anticipating Plotinus, an intellectual gift is undiminished by the giving – and God's gift points beyond the moment of inspiration to the infinite, ever fecund Giver.

Philo knows that God's ultimate reality is hidden. Even Moses had to be told, *No living man can see My face* (Exodus 33:20). Yet God's reality does manifest itself. As Philo sees it, it does so in two ways: in the Logos that is God's wisdom[33] and in the sensible world that reflects that wisdom.[34] The Logos, for Philo, reveals God's goodness or creative power; the natural world reveals His sovereign, royal power. Readers of rabbinic literature will not miss the resonance in Philo's thoughts of timeless perfection and spatiotemporal expression with the classic rabbinic ideas of God's aspects of mercy and justice (*middat ha-rahamim* and *middat ha-din*). But Winston sees something more:

It is not difficult to recognize in these two powers the *apeiron* and *peras*, or the Unlimited and Limit of Plato's *Philebus* (23c–31a), which reappear in Plotinus' two moments in the emergence of *Nous*, where we find undefined or unlimited Intelligible Matter proceeding from the One and then turning back to its source for definition (cf. Proclus, *Elements* 89–92, 159). However, since God's essence as it is in itself is beyond any possibility of human experience or cognition, including the experience of mystic vision, the only attributes that may be applied to God in his supreme state of concealment are those of the *via negativa*... or of the *via eminentiae*.[35]

---

[32] Philo, *De Gigantibus* 24–28, LCL 2.456–59.
[33] Philo, *De Somniis* 1.239, LCL 5. 422–23; *De Confusione Linguarum* 147–48, LCL 4.90–91.
[34] Philo, *De Opificio Mundi* 25, LCL 1.20–21.   [35] Winston, *Selections*, 23.

What Philo bequeathed for his successors, the precipitate of his philosophic reading of the Torah's poetic tribute to God's transcendence, was this question: How are we to reconcile God's unity with His infinite transcendence? Plotinus took up such questions just where Aristotle had set them down. He too found God's infinity in His power, and, echoing Aristotle, wrote, as Armstrong renders his words:

> He who is capable of making all things, what greatness would He have? He is infinite and, if so, would have no physical magnitude. The Principle would be great in this sense that nothing is more powerful than He or even equally so. (*Enneads* 6.7.32)

And again:

> The One is the greatest of all things not in physical magnitude but in power, for that which is without extension is great through power. We must also insist that It is not infinite as though intraversable either in extension or in number but by the unboundedness of its power. (*Enneads* 6.9.6; cf. 2.4.5)

The argument does hark back to Aristotle's appeal to God as the ultimate source of motion and thought but enriched now with thoughts of (timeless) creativity. The notion of power is now enlarged from the sense Aristotle had given it, pointing to matter's limiting impact on the parameters of change, to something active, energetic, and, in what would become its new sense, dynamic. Sweeney paraphrases Plotinus' new departure: "The divine power is so great as to be the source of infinite effects – material existents that are infinitely numerous because they ceaselessly deploy in endlessly recurring world cycles. Unlike Aristotle," Sweeney notes, "Plotinus developed a theory of infinity that is synonymous with perfection and that is applicable to God Himself." For in Plotinus matter is below form and thus indeterminate and imperfect, but God (as Plato had urged) rises above form, and "By this transcendence He is infinite."[36]

TO QUANTITY AND BEYOND

Human thinking, Alfred North Whitehead remarked, reached an early plateau when we humans first saw something in common between five fish and five stones. Abstraction advanced as thinking became more topic-neutral and the mapping of quantities of one sort onto another applied numbers to spatial magnitudes, giving birth to geometry. Egyptian

---

[36] Sweeney, *Divine Infinity*, 7, citing *Enneads* 5.7.1, 3, and 6.2.22 and 6.8.9.

geometry, as schoolchildren were long taught, began as a practical art, used, as its Greek name implies, in surveying the land each year to reset property lines after the Nile flood – or to plot the footprint of a house or temple. Egyptian geometers used rules based on familiar shapes, not unlike the rules of thumb that longshoremen once used to gauge the volume, weight, and value of a cargo.

Tracing the techniques that Greek thinkers devised to put a bridle and a bit on the seeming indeterminacy of space, Husserl pictures Greek geometers refining the Egyptian techniques by notionally dividing complex shapes into smaller, less irregular parts. Estimates of sizes grew more precise as the number of pieces needed to fill a shape with patches increased, and the pieces shrank in size – until, in the ideal case, the steps became infinite and the patches infinitesimal, leaving a shape constituted, paradoxically, by infinite elements of no size.[37] A like drama was played out not just in geometry. For the Pythagoreans found counterparts of the mathematical ordering of space in music, another step toward the universal. Drawn by the beauty of abstraction and the surety of demonstration, Greek mathematicians pressed beyond empiric measures. For their gaze often turned toward the heavens, where direct measurement was impossible.

Removing figures to the realm of thought made them manipulable by the mind: Projected in abstract sketches, they could be compared, doubled or trisected, superimposed, constructed mentally and subjected to logical deductions yielding certainty, or reduction to absurdity. Hence the slave boy's reasoning about the doubling of the square in Plato's *Meno* (82–85), reasoning paramount in triumphs like the proof of Theaetetus (ca. 417–369), that there are just five regular convex polyhedra, the five Platonic solids, as we now call them. Euclid (ca. 325–ca. 270), with an appetite for rigor, demonstrated the intellectual fruitfulness of geometry beyond its practical uses. He modeled the mathematician's ethos in the deductive derivation of his theorems, but also in the analytical work that came first, isolating the axioms, definitions, and postulates and the handful of undefined terms that proved sufficient to yield a full geometric repertoire – and allow for its expansion. Euclid highlighted his analytic triumph by titling his work *The Elements*, giving pride of place to the conceptual building blocks from which the new system was built and might be built again by any mathematically inclined student or inquirer.

---

[37] See Husserl, *The Crisis of European Sciences*.

Geometrical figures were now clearly ideals. Indeed, Proclus identifies Euclid, on the authority of Eratosthenes, as a Platonist, well at home in philosophy.[38] Rigor and precision bore a suitably Platonic price: The figures of which Euclid's theorems are true are not to be found anywhere in the sensory world: A Euclidean circle had no bumps or dents. Its infinite radii were all exactly equal. And any Euclidean figure was built of lines that had no thickness. Assigning such lines more than their one dimension would falsify any theorem about the figures they compose.

We can see why Euclid left the line, point, and plane formally undefined. He can appeal to common notions intuitively by saying that a point is the limit of a line and has no parts. Similarly, he describes a line as a length with no breath. A line can be conceived as the limit of a plane figure and a plane as the limit of a solid. Even 'magnitude' is left undefined formally. For Euclid is rightly chary of introducing circularity into his demonstrations if he defines terms by reference to the concepts they make possible.[39]

Limit was the intuitive key concept here, the very limit (*peras*) that was the first item in the ten pairs that Pythagoras thought primary – his *yin* and *yang*. The opposite of limit was the *apeiron*, the indefinite.[40] It was by using this pair that Cornford thought Pythagoreans derived the remaining pairs in their full set of ten. And we get an inkling here as to why Proclus saw divine unity in the simplicity of the point: "Among non-physical things that exist as ideas apart from matter and as forms grounded in themselves alone, the substance of the simpler is always more primary than the more composite." So, "both in Nous and in the intermediate orders of souls[41] – those natures that directly breathe life into bodies – the limiting factors – have an essential priority over the things they limit, being less divisible, more uniform, and more sovereign." As Proclus explains:

Among non-physical forms unity is more perfect than plurality, the partless than what in any way proceeds from it, and what bounds than what gets its limit from something else. But those forms which, requiring matter, have their basis in what is outside themselves and have departed their own nature to be dispersed among their diverse substrates and have only a borrowed unity, have been allotted more complex rather than simpler ideas. So in the objects that appear in imagination

---

[38] Proclus, *A Commentary on the First Book of Euclid's* Elements, 68.10, 57.
[39] See Euclid, *Elements*, tr. Thomas Heath, 153; and Heath's Commentary, 143–51.
[40] See Arisotle, *Metaphysics* A 5.
[41] For the intermediate status of souls, see Proclus, *Elements of Theology*, props. 188–19.

and in the matter of imagined shapes, as well as in the perceptible things generated by nature, the ideas of bounded objects have priority. Lest an object in three dimensions stretch to infinite size in our thought or perception, it is limited on all sides by planes; and lest a plane slip into boundlessness, the line arrives to contain and define it. The point does the same for a line. In forms separable from matter, the ideas of the boundaries exist in themselves, not in the things bounded. It is because they remain just what they are that they act to bring to be the things dependent on them. But in forms inseparable from matter the limits surrender to what they limit. They settle there and become parts of them, as it were, filled with those lesser traits. So, here the partless partakes of divisibility and the breadthless of breadth. The limiting elements can no longer preserve their simplicity and purity. Matter muddies their precision.[42]

The point, in "the higher regions," Proclus reasons, is entirely without parts. Yet

it secretly contains the potentiality of the Unlimited, by virtue of which it generates all intervals; and the procession of all the intervals does not exhaust its infinite capacity The point, being a limit, preserves its character when things participate in it. But since it also secretly possesses the nature of the Unlimited it strives to be everywhere in the things it bounds. It is present in them infinite times. For among the higher realities – the intelligibles – the Unlimited is the first creative cause and generative power of all things. But in enmattered forms it is imperfect and only potentially everything.[43]

Yes, the point is the ultimate limit of the line – but points are the notional components of all lines, planes, and solids. Here, then, is the ultimate tiny figure that early geometers pursued, the infinitesimal presence never reached in the unending divisions by which geometrical precision was sought – and rigor attained.

Euclidean points and lines, plane and solid figures might seem mere abstractions, artifacts of geometrical theory, not real in the world they notionally help us measure or manipulate. But to a Platonist, the further we abstract from the sensory realm, the closer we draw to reality. The solid objects we handle are but crystallizations in three-space of ideal geometrical figures, just as the music we hear is an audible expression of the numbers that give birth to the sensory world. Euclid, indeed, wrote an *Elements of Music*, extant today in fragments, his counterpart to the *Elements of Geometry*. Leaping upward by what is conventionally called abstraction, and reaching the realm of the real, what the mind discovers at the summit of analysis is the perfect reality of the One, which "does the

---

[42] Proclus, *Commentary on the First Book of Euclid's* Elements, tr. after Morrow, 70–z71.
[43] Proclus, *Commentary on the First Book of Euclid's* Elements, tr. after Morrow, 72–73.

same work in Plato," as Gary Zabel put it, "that the Limit does in Pythagoreanism." And the "indefinite dyad of the Great and Small," Plato's surrogate for matter at its most elemental, "plays the part of the Pythagorean Unlimited."[44]

The Euclidean point, for Proclus, becomes the emblem of divine creativity – and more than an emblem, in a way, since its ebullient quest for omnipresence is its heritage from the perfect Simplicity out of which its compromised simplicity is sprung. It still reflects the absolute unity of the infinite Source, the pure and divine Form of the Good, which Platonists recognize as the true One. Geometry, seen through the eyes of Proclus, poetically mirrors the great arch of Neoplatonic eschatology, as if emulating the creative power of God, bringing the many from the One and allowing their return to Unity.

The dance of unity with infinity that Proclus celebrated was the choreographic work of Plotinus, first plotted by Plato. If infinity, as Aristotle saw, is not a number or a quantity, then as Zabel put it, "The actual infinite" that Aristotle had so studiously shunned, "turns out to be, not a mathematical concept at all, but a purely ontological one." Here shone the purity that Plato had glimpsed in the Form of the Good, transcending all that flows from it, namely, Plotinus' Divine Mind, World Soul, and natural Cosmos. In the wake of Plotinus, 'infinite' will no longer mean indefinite. What is infinite now is the Absolute.

Tellingly (and similarly), just as Plotinus gave new life and a new meaning to the idea of the infinite, he rescued the idea of power from its Aristotelian apprenticeship. For power (*dynamis*), as Aristotle understood it, mapped the (generic) limitations that matter sets to the parameters of change, mediating the transition between what a thing is and what it can become, and obviating the Megarian notion that it is impossible for a thing to become what it is not. Plato had suggested this alternative to the Eleatic elenchus, by proposing in the *Sophist* (247DE) that we regard as real whatever has the power (*dunamis*) to act or be acted upon. Seeing that, in the timeless world of the ideal, creativity need not betoken change, Plotinus boldly rescues the idea of power, giving the term its now familiar, energetic sense: The highest God wields the highest power, producing every lesser being.[45] For, as Plato had urged (*Timaeus* 29d), Goodness is never jealous.

---

[44] Zabel, "Excursus."   [45] See Leigh, "Being and Power in Plato's *Sophist*," 63–85.

SPINOZA WEDS ONENESS TO INFINITY

In a letter to his good friend Lodewijk Meyer, written in the spring of 1663, Spinoza seeks to explain how substance, God, or nature, the sum of all that is, proves to be both one and infinite. "The question of the infinite," he writes, "is always of the greatest difficulty for everyone – insoluble in fact,

> As long as 1) people fail to distinguish what is infinite by its own nature or by definition from what is boundless not by its own essence but by that of its cause. And beyond that, 2) as long as they do not distinguish what is called infinite because it is boundless from that to whose parts we can assign no definite number, although we know their upper and lower limits. And finally, 3) as long as they fail to distinguish what we can know by reason alone and not by imagination from what we can also know by way of the imagination. Had they paid attention to these distinctions, I say, they would never have found themselves overwhelmed by such a throng of difficulties but would have understood clearly what kind of infinity is indivisible and without parts and what kind can, without contradiction be divided into parts. They would also have understood what kind of infinite can, without contradiction, be conceived as greater than another.[46]

The notion that nature, God, or substance cannot be both one and infinite, Spinoza explains, reflects our habit thinking typically of modes, the particulars that we take for the basic furniture of reality: We tend to assume that anything corporeal must have parts – just as some "have convinced themselves that a line is composed of points" imagined as tiny bodies – and so try to prove that a line is not continuous but must consist of indivisible segments.[47] In truth, even a line is both one and (potentially) infinite.

To expose the error of thinking that a figure is composed of discrete parts, Spinoza diagrams two non-concentric circles, one inside the other. If space had parts, he argues, there would be more parts in the larger circle than the smaller. But in truth the "parts" in either would exceed any number, regardless how small the parts or how great the difference in size between the two circles. So, are the unequal numbers equal? The source of the absurdity, Spinoza urges, and the notion to discard, is the assumption that space has parts.[48] As Spinoza insists, "No attribute of a substance

---

[46] Spinoza, Letter 12, April 20, 1663, Gebhardt 4.53 *ll.* 19–28.
[47] Spinoza, Letter 12, Gebhardt 4.56 *ll.* 1–5.
[48] Spinoza, Letter 12, Gebhardt 4.59–60; cf. E2p8s. Spinoza returns to the point years later in writing to Tschirnhaus, Letter 81, May 5, 1676, Gebhardt 4.332. As Shirley explains, Spinoza (like Aristotle) reserves the term number for finite magnitudes: "he will speak of infinity but not of an 'infinite number.' The false assumption that multiplying an infinite

can be conceived from which it follows that the substance can be divided" (E1p13).

Spinoza might readily have dismissed the notion that extension is composed of discrete parts by recognizing the incommensurability of the diagonal of a square with its side, so scandalous to ancient Pythagoreans. For if extension is a continuum, as that incommensurability proves it to be, parts can be separated out and isolated only by abstraction. Extension, for Spinoza then, is not a collection of parts. It forms a continuum, every component dependent on the rest.

Holism here is clearly feeling its oats, and monism is its mission. So, Spinoza does not stop at the geometry of extension but urges that time, too, does not have parts. Bergson would later make a similar point about time: Moments can be isolated only by some conceptual surgery, which, like the more familiar kind, always comes at some cost. The idea has an ancient lineage. For, as Guthrie explains, when Anaximander sought the basis of all things in the *apeiron*, the boundlessness he spoke of was temporal as well as spatial – without beginning or end but an everlasting continuum. It was the "imposition" of number, by the Pythagoreans, as Guthrie puts it, that made time an ordering principle of the cosmos.[49]

The unwary, Spinoza argues, picture time as divisible into separate moments. We can see why Aritstotle calls time "the number of motion" – rather than just the measure of motion – and then adds, "with respect to before and after," stressing time's relativity to a standpoint. But if thought of in such relative terms, Harris explains, unpacking Spinoza's tightly furled thoughts, time is but a projection, an artifact of the imaginative way of thinking that Spinoza contrasts so sharply with conceptual thinking, and with that higher, intuitive thinking that the *Ethics* will call thinking of the third kind.[50]

The partitioning of time, or of extension, Spinoza argues, comes readily to the imagination. But such thinking only feeds a perverse appetite for paradoxes. For imagination is powered (but also constrained) by the senses – not least, we might add, by the sight brain, on which human imagination so largely depends. It is here that Spinoza cards the tangles in which many have entrapped themselves. To the intellect, he reasons, so long as it does not abstract and isolate time, extension, and quantity in

---

number by a finite number (here, two) produces an infinity with 'twice the number of parts' was common to seventeenth-century thinkers and appears also in Newton." Shirley, in Spinoza's *Complete Works*, 956 n. 298.

[49] Guthrie, *A History of Greek Philosophy*, 1.337. [50] See Harris, *Substance*, 67.

general from substance (that is, from God), without which none of these would be real, we can see them all – time, extension, and the physical world itself as infinite, indivisible, and unique – although it is admittedly hard to avoid (sensuous) abstraction: Imagination quite naturally pictures these dimensionalities in isolation from one another and each region or expanse of any of them as though it were discrete. But, in reality (as Einstein's work helped show), they are inseparable from one another and from the larger whole to whose unity they contribute and belong.[51]

Burnt by the paradoxes implicit in attempts to treat time, number, and measure as real, many, Spinoza notes, have denied the reality of the infinite – as though the limitations of human imagination must constrain and contain nature itself. Yet mathematicians know well that there are all sorts of things to which number does not apply and that there are things "that exceed any possible number." To cut clear of such confusions, he argues, one must conclude that some things are infinite by nature and cannot be conceived otherwise, while others are infinite in virtue of their cause.

Driving home his point about the unity of time, Spinoza mounts his own version of Zeno's paradox of the *stadion*:[52] If time had parts, he argues, an hour, say, would never pass. For infinite moments would have to elapse before the least of them could end. The conclusion Spinoza draws, however, is not Zeno's denial that motion is real. For motion, to him, is safely ensconced in the infinite mode of motion and rest. Unity is what's at stake here: Time, like space, is not really divisible.

By making the same claim about time as he does about space, that neither is composed of parts, Spinoza reveals that his target is not time or space alone but nature at large. For him, sound thinking about time, as unitary (as the Stoics held), makes unitary thinking a model for sound thinking about nature itself: The world, then, is best glimpsed from a God's-eye point of view. God, being eternal, is timeless; and timelessness sustains divine omniscience. God surveys history, including human choices, without descending (or falling) into the fray. Rabbi Akiva, we observe, put it well and with inspired concision: "All is overseen, but agency is delegated."[53]

To Spinoza, God's agency is everywhere: All events are expressions of it. But Spinoza's thoughts about God's expression, in and as nature, dovetail with what Maimonides sees as the delegation that Rabbi Akiva

---

[51] Spinoza, Letter 12, Gebhardt 4.56–59. [52] Cf. Aristotle, *Physics* VI 2, 233a22–28.
[53] M. Avot 3:15; cf. Maimonides ad loc. and in *Eight Chapters* 8 and *Guide* II 48.

cited: When I eat dinner, we don't say that God eats; when I learn something new, we don't say that God learned what He did not know timelessly. To Spinoza such facts are best given voice by saying that God, as expressed in the finite modes of my body and mind, is modified or qualified in this or that way.

If the true (or radical) monotheist comes so close to monism as to see God in all things, and if God's knowledge is so comprehensive as to see the world and history timelessly, then we must treat time as a facet of our lifeworld or (in Kant's terms) as the pure form of sensibility in the human mind. That thought is presaged in the Maimonidean thesis that God's knowledge is radically unlike ours: God's timeless knowledge, Maimonides argues, is more like the knowledge an inventor has of a device like a water clock than like our own when we seek to study the clock and reverse-engineer its workings.[54] The same thought is more directly expressed in Ghazali's treatment of time as relative – to natural events, perhaps, as Aristotle had it – but, more tellingly, to our human modes of awareness.

Ghazali, as I wrote years ago, as sharply distinguished from the freethinking physician and philosopher Muhammad ibn Zakariyya' al-Razi, "will make no absolute, eternal, or objective thing of time." Rather, he treats time as nominal and relative to the facts of creation. In his Jerusalem Letter, incorporated into the text of his *Reviving the Religious Sciences*, Ghazali makes it an article of faith that God transcends directionalities. For Him there is no up or down, left or right, forward or back. For all such terms have meaning only relative to our human anatomy, posture, and position. If we were spherical (as the world is), directionality would be different for us: all is relative to our mode of being. Geometry, we could say, might be spherical, as it is for pilots and navigators, rather than grounded in the plane figures familiar from the days when first used in measuring plots of land that were presumed to be planes. Time, in the same way for Ghazali, is relative to the motions of bodies and to the perceptions of beings like us that mark such motions. Accordingly, in the *Incoherence of the Philosophers*, he argues that the same event is called past or future, depending on one's standpoint. Not so for God, who lives beyond time.[55]

---

[54] See *Guide* III 20, 43ab, citing Isaiah 55:8–9: *My thoughts are not your thoughts, and your ways are not My ways, saith the* LORD. *High as the heavens are above the earth, so are My ways above your ways and My thoughts above your thoughts*. For the water clock, see *Guide* III 21, 43b.

[55] Ghazali, Jerusalem Letter 1.7; cf. Plato, *Timaeus* 62d–63a; Aristotle, *Physics* IV 8, 208a4–28, *De Caelo* IV 1, 308a15–20; Heraclitus, SVF 2.133, 166.4. For Ghazali's rejection of the absoluteness of time, see *Tahafut al-Falasifa* Discussion 1, Proof 2, ed.

Recognition of the relativity of time is critical for anyone who hopes to reconcile unity with infinity in the Godhead. Hence Spinoza's pointing beyond temporality in his talk of God. My late friend Roger Scruton captures the point brilliantly, although in an argument meant to show that Spinoza treats all causal relations as logical implications and so to reduce Spinoza's world to a block universe, in which change is impossible. As Scruton put it, "there is a real sense in which nothing in Spinoza's world really 'happens.'"[56] It may help here to remember that the Spinozistic equivalence of causality to implication holds in *both* directions: It's not just that causation amounts to implication; it's also true, as Mason showed, that logical necessities in Spinoza's sights are causal. With causation, as with time, much depends on whether one regards nature from a divine or from a human standpoint. But seeing causal relations as logical implications, as Scruton believes Spinoza does, may help one understand Spinoza's suspension of time on the plane of God's thought and agency. Here's how Scruton phrases Spinoza's view:

> God is, indeed, the cause of everything, but he is the 'eternal' cause. He does not, rightly conceived, participate in change. He is not "in" time, and the conception of time plays no part in the true knowledge of God. While we understand the world in terms of 'change' and 'process,' these descriptions attach only to the modes of God, and not to the divine essence. They express only the partial and confused perception of those who have no complete or adequate idea of the world ... to explain things ultimately we must not relate them to what precedes them in time – since that is merely to relate one mode to another; rather, we must show their timeless relation to the eternal essence of God. An ideal science, therefore, like a true religion, would aim to see the world not in its temporal dimension, but "under the aspect of eternity" (*sub specie aeternitatis*), in the manner of a mathematical proof.[57]

Translating rather more literally, that last famous phrase of Spinoza's becomes "under the gaze of eternity." Spinoza's holism is in full cry here: We understand things adequately not merely as we relate them to one another (as is our wont) but insofar as we can relate them to their ultimate cause and overarching context in the whole that Spinoza calls God or nature. My friend Jeffrey Tlumak sums up the moral Spinoza draws as to the preciousness of the God's-eye view: "So long as we see things

---

and tr. Marmura 30–36; Discussion 11, Marmura 133; cf. the corresponding passages in Ibn Rushd's *Tahafut al-Tahafut*, tr. Van Den Bergh 2.11 and 31 (nn. 13.1 and 41.2). "The very language, 'after' and 'before', already confesses the unreality of time," Plutarch apud Eusebius, *Praeparatio Evangelica* 11. See Goodman, "Time in Islam," 3–19.

[56] Scruton, *Spinoza*, 49.   [57] Scruton, *Spinoza*, 49.

temporally and partially, we are pulled in contrary directions, between natural sensuous concerns and the rational aspiration for eternal totality."[58]

In God's comprehensive knowledge and all-embracing causality, for Spinoza, time collapses, and all is one. God does not preempt natural agency in general or human agency specifically, of course, as some are tempted to presume, as if Spinoza's were some common, garden-variety monism, linked to a common, garden-variety determinism that incoherently regards all causation as external to the agent. For Spinoza sees that persons, like all other beings, do act and interact. But, as he explains, individuals are rightly said to act only insofar as their own conatus determines an outcome. We human beings do act (and act freely), insofar as our actions are our own – and thus, insofar as they reflect our adequate ideas rather than mere passions, the inadequate ideas that make us passive, the butt of circumstance, as we fondly call the external agencies that make us undergoers rather than undertakers.

In his idea of God/nature, Spinoza integrates unity with infinity by the same holistic insight that gives him the continuity of time and extension. Spinoza's infinite substance, as Harris explains, is not an aggregate of "separately independent and separately intelligible parts, which, in consequence, would be prior in conception to the whole ... the whole is prior to, and determines the conception, the nature, and the behavior, of its parts."[59] We understand *anything* adequately, only insofar as we relate it to the whole – that is, to God. Spinoza spells this out for Oldenburg:

> When you ask for my views on how we know "how each part of Nature fits with the rest and accords with the whole," I take it you are asking what makes me think that each part of Nature joins with the rest to form a whole. For how each part in fact fits into a coherent whole, as I said in my last letter, I do not know. One would have to know all of nature and all its parts to know that. But I'll try to show you the reasoning that compels me to hold that it does, only cautioning you first that I do not ascribe to Nature beauty or ugliness, order or confusion. It is only in relation to our imagination that things can be said to be beautiful or ugly, well-ordered or confused.[60]

Spinoza's choice of the word "confused" drives home his point, that the appraisal of order or confusion, like that of beauty or deformity, is in the eye of the beholder, not in nature itself: When one has trouble following the workings of nature, one might ascribe its operations to a

---

[58] Tlumak, *Classical Modern Philosophy*, 98.   [59] Harris, *Substance*, 33.
[60] Spinoza, Letter 32, to Oldenburgh, November 20, 1665, Gebhardt 4.169 *l* 20–170 *l*. 11.

scheme ill-framed, just as one might call an array lovely because one finds it pleasing.⁶¹ Spinoza's letter carefully avoids using passive participles to characterize any aspect of nature, lest he suggest anything in nature externally imposed to meet our needs or please our tastes or fancies. Indeed, as my friend Emanuele Costa stresses, Spinoza's avoidance of passive participles when referring to nature here bespeaks his emphasis on *Natura naturans*.⁶² For nature's integration shows its active, dynamic, and creative face rather than the passive, partitioned aspect known to analysis: Design, as Spinoza sees it holistically, is emergent from the conatus of all things, every mode of every attribute expressing God's agency. Hence, the fit of modes with one another. So, addressing Oldenberg's question, Spinoza writes:

By the coherence of parts I mean just this: that the laws of nature and the nature of each part of it, adjusts itself to minimize any disparity among them. As to parts and wholes, I see things as parts of a whole insofar as their natures fit together as closely as possible. Insofar as parts are disparate, each forms a separate idea in our mind, and we think of it not as a part but as a whole.⁶³

That latter type of thinking, of course, is apt to miss the wholeness of the larger whole. We can think of blood, Spinoza explains, as a single fluid, or we can focus on its components. A tiny worm in the bloodstream, if able to discern those components, might take each particle for a whole, unable to grasp how they all work in concert. Similarly, we humans regularly miss the integration of the cosmos and mistake its parts for wholes, missing the interactions and interconnections that make nature itself, in all its infinite variety and extent, the one real whole.

It is with nature's dynamism in mind that Spinoza, as Harris explains, "rejects the notion of whole and part," a notion that treats any whole "as a mere aggregate subsequent and posterior to its parts conceived as having independent reality."⁶⁴ It's hard to think of a better case against the kind of reductionism that grows like a mold on analytically biased notions and assumes that we understand a thing when we know its parts! The picture projected by the imagination, taking things to be made up of

---

⁶¹ Maimonides notes a like bias: We ascribe what makes sense to us in nature to God's wisdom; what we have trouble understanding, to God's will. But in God's perfect unity will and wisdom are the same.

⁶² As Yitzhak Melamed explains, "The whole-part relation plays an important role in Spinoza's metaphysics, but this role is restricted to the realm that Spinoza calls *natura naturata* (E1p29s), i.e., the realm of modes." "Cohen, Spinoza and the Nature of Pantheism," 4.

⁶³ Letter 32, Gebhardt 4.107a *l* 12–71a *l* 1.   ⁶⁴ Harris, *Substance*, 208.

discrete parts, Spinoza argues, dogs our thinking. And the related error, in thinking of infinity as a number or quantity, underlies the presumption that infinity precludes oneness. We do not understand nature adequately until we recognize that its infinite variety and diversity form an underlying unity.

Parmenides' goddess stood with both feet planted firmly, if roughly, as if unshod, in the logical law of the excluded middle. But we have not received her account, if indeed she had one, of how to relate the way of truth to the way of seeming. And we get no hint of how her admonition to favor the way of truth over the way of seeming might allow us to skirt reliance on negation, which her elenchus was supposed to exclude.

Plato does offer such an account, brilliantly relating truth to seeming, when he links Being with becoming, through the notion of "participation" and the metaphor of imitation. But Plato's reach for unity does still divide the world: Things in the realm of the senses, participate, we are told, in the reality of those higher realities, the universals, that are intelligible but unseen. Particulars "belong to" classes, exemplary of the more perfect, immutable Forms that nest in one another, the more specific in the more general, all, ultimately, in their measure, sharing in the reality and unity of the divine Form of the Good. But the relative unity, goodness, and beauty seen in the world we inhabit, below that highest Form, mounts up as a scaled duality. And Aristotle, content to leave perfect oneness in the pure actuality of the divine Mind, unsullied by change, finds only a qualified unity when he calls on science to celebrate constancy and intelligibility in the species of things.

The idea that cosmic unity is organic is well precedented in Plato, in Aristotle, and in the Stoics. But Spinoza's version of that idea has grown rather stronger than it was in those ancient Greek tributes to nature's unity or than the biblical and rabbinic images of heaven and earth created together and functioning together – as Rabbi Simeon said, in dismissing the dispute of the schools of Hillel and Shammai over which came first, the heavens or the earth: "I am amazed that the fathers of the world," as he honored those pioneering halakhists, "debated this. They were created together, surely, pot and lid, as it is written, *I call them, and they rise together* (Isaiah 48:13)."[65] Spinoza brings thoughts of unity to full fruition when he makes his case that nature/God, although infinite, is not composed of parts.

---

[65] Genesis Rabbah 1.15.

It was finding organic unity at the heart of Spinoza's metaphysics that moved Harry Wolfson to surprise and delight: The macrocosm idea, honored in ancient and medieval cosmologies, was alive and well in Spinoza's infinite cosmos.[66] Philo had argued that the world is one, just as its Creator is.[67] He drew upon Plato's (*Timaeus* 31b–32c) and on Aristotle's commitment to the unity of the cosmos, sustained, as Aristotelians held, by the equipoise and harmony of its parts (*On the Universe* 5). The harmony that Plato ascribed to the work of *philia*, even in geometry (if plane figures were ever to become solids), had been intensified for Philo by an infusion of Stoic vitalism. For Spinoza, such harmony or fit permeates nature all the way down. Vibrant in what we now know as cells and molecules, it would be expressed, as Spinoza sees it, everywhere: all of nature dynamically interactive, each mode dependent on the Whole. It was such thoughts that led Spinoza to resist talk of parts: Nothing exists or can be conceived apart from the Whole. The intellectual love of God that Maimonides had seen as mankind's highest goal returns here as a more primal love, the love in which Aristotle and the ancient and medieval Neoplatonists had found the theme and thesis of the entirety of Nature.

Spinoza's appropriation of the ancient macrocosm idea prompts fresh thoughts as to God's oneness: Spinoza's world, like Maimonides' God, is indivisible even conceptually, so long as our thinking remains conceptual and is not trapped in distortions projected by the imagination. Writing to Tschirnhaus toward the end of his short life, Spinoza underscores the organicity of the cosmos by contrasting his lively vision of nature with Descartes' more static view:

> From extension as Descartes conceives it, as a static mass, it is not just difficult, as you say (Letter 80), but completely impossible, to show that bodies exist. For matter, at rest, while it is so, will remain at rest and will not be roused to motion without some more powerful external cause. That is why I have not hesitated in the past to state that Descartes' principles of things natural are useless, not to say absurd.[68]

Descartes' project of treating material nature wholly in terms of extension (and thus, geometrically) left no room for natural forces (or even solidity, as Leibniz later complained). That, as Shirley explains,[69] left God

---

[66] See Wolfson, *Spinoza* 2.7–8 citing E2p1–13.
[67] Philo, *De Opificio Mundi* 171, LCL 1.136–37.
[68] Spinoza, Letter 81, May 5, 1676, Gebhardt 4.332 *ll*. 16–22.
[69] Shirley, in Spinoza, *Complete Works* 956 n. 299.

to set things in motion. Spinoza, by contrast, will set physical forces inboard, as expressions of each thing's conatus, the inertia evident not just when bodies are at rest but also in their persistence in motion once they move. But inertia, in the newly discovered sense, is just one phase of the dynamism of nature as an organic system. The conatus, manifest in the drive of each mode to sustain itself, free itself from external constraints, grow more self-sufficient, and (if intelligent) more capable of perceiving more things more clearly, is a striving to augment a power of action that belongs, in the first instance, to that mode.[70]

Spinoza does not think the world was created. Nor does his world exist apart from God – although his immanent God, with infinite attributes, remains transcendent and infinitely beyond our totalizing comprehension. For, as Aquinas argued, no finite being can engulf the Infinite. Spinoza's God is no watchmaker, and his world is no mere mechanism. It is the dynamism of nature that fuses unity and infiniteness here. As Spinoza argues, "a substance absolutely infinite must be indivisible" (E1p15s). Spinoza's God is infinite (E1d7), but He is not static or passive – nor are His attributes. As Harris writes,

A blank and featureless unity is the diametrical opposite of an infinite reality (that is, of concrete and complete wholeness); so to try to conceive God as undifferentiated unity is to strive to entertain a flat contradiction.[71]

If God is infinite in reality/perfection, God will be infinitely diversified, in infinite attributes, each, in its own way "infinitely diversified in its own kind." So, the world is not swallowed up in God, as monism so often has seemed to threaten or demand: Diversity of expression is not division. "Within an indivisible whole there may (nay, must) be numerous ... aspects, interdependent elements, and mutually indispensable factors, so related that no division or separation is possible ... although among themselves they may be infinitely changeable and diverse. This is the case, for example, with any living organism." Spinoza's God/universe "is a veritable whole, understood in the only proper and legitimate sense of that word: as a unity which, though diversified, is indivisible."[72]

Epicurean worlds, by contrast, have diverse natural laws, lest reason be forced to acknowledge one mode of explanation adequate to all, and thereby unwittingly pay deference to a single overarching scheme of nature, standing in for God, as the Stoic logos does when it legislates and projects its universal governance, judgment, and plan. In a modern

---

[70] See Harris, *Substance*, 165.   [71] Harris, *Substance*, 24.   [72] Harris, *Substance*, 24.

multiverse, similarly, the avatars of a skeptical "no more" find no epistemic plinth to stand on. They see no cosmological pathway as more rational than another – just as their soulmates in ethical domains acknowledge no moral path that outshines and eclipses and so qualifies to guide, critique, or supersede the another.

Where Maimonides sees Moses looking to nature for knowledge of God, Plato looks to mathematics – and Neoplatonists find their God in Unity itself. But Maimonides, seeing unity in the world, saw in Aristotle's thesis that there is but one world a highroad to monotheism.[73] Today's exponents of a multiverse, by contrast, see no cosmic story more likely than another – although that stance belies the faith of the sciences, on which rest their claims to intellectual authority. But reason, as the tool of science, tracks the likely course of nature when it seeks the best explanation of every phenomenon that we must acknowledge, making consilience the touchstone of veracity. There's more power here than might at first appear, in Plato's calling efforts toward a coherent account of nature "a likely story."

A PRICE TO PAY

The charm of monism is large, as witness the monistic appeal of *wahdat al-wujud* in Sufism and the gentle, if all-encompassing, embrace of ultimate unity that enwraps and bids fair to smother Kabbalah. All through Western intellectual history, monistic leanings ring the changes on (often Neoplatonizing) visions of a higher unity behind the kaleidoscope of experience, the "blooming, buzzing confusion," that William James thought the mind must address. But not every thinker or theorist has the rigor and discipline of a Spinoza adequately to conceive the unity sustaining nature's diversity or to appreciate the cosmic manifold as the expression of an ultimate oneness. Without critical syntheses like those Spinoza devised, unity might seem to swallow up nature's vastness, or multiple worlds disperse and dissolve into infinite atomistic arrays, as they did in the ungoverned worlds of the Epicureans and still do in cosmologies of a multiverse.

Experienced philosophers know that any move one makes comes at a cost. So before one spurns Spinoza's God – too impersonal, etc. – one should consider other efforts, younger than ancient Neoplatonism, to fuse

---

[73] Maimonides, *Guide* I, 72, 100b; Aristotle, *De Caelo* I 5–9; *Metaphysics* Ë 8, 1074a31; cf. Plato, *Timaeus* 31a; *Epinomis* 982–86.

unity with infinity in the idea of God. Kabbalah, a mystical tradition still exploiting Plotinian insights, runs more on the tracks of ritual and myth than on those of argument – much as ancient (and even Renaissance) Neoplatonists all too readily succumbed to magic and themselves too often declined into vulgar or sophisticated superstition.

Kabbalistic tropes are popularized and disseminated in multiple hasidic sects, led by rebbes, learned and charismatic in varied measure and not above the temptation to trade upon superstitious appeals to thaumaturgy. Hasidism, like Sufism, is a popular, if semi-esoteric movement. It retains much of the inherited furniture of the Neoplatonic pleroma, but with ascetic exercises called on to replace reasoning to vouch for a vision's credibility, and a deep draught of Gnostic theory, responsive to suffering and tragedy on a personal and national plane, picturing history as tragic and creation itself as a vast, cosmic accident awaiting magical correction by ritual and messianic means.

A reliable guide to the theology hovering over this terrain, or feeding its wellsprings from spiritual heights that often remain unseen, is Louis Jacobs, a rabbinic scholar who took philosophy seriously enough to assay the options and weigh their costs. The kabbalists, he writes, impressed by the case for God's transcendence that Maimonides and other Jewish Neoplatonic Aristotelians had pressed, sheltered divine transcendence under the buckler of negative theology; "yet hungry for the living God of religion," they tried to reconcile transcendence with spiritual access by positing two aspects of divinity:

God as he is in himself is unknown and unknowable. This aspect of deity is called *Ein Sof* ("That which is without limit." – [the Infinite]). From *Ein Sof* ten powers or potencies – the *sefirot* – emanate [but emanation here, lacking the intellectual substance and spiritual energy that fed emanation without loss to its Source, does veer toward the magical], and it is God as manifested in these *sefirot* who is the God of religion, the God whom human beings can know and worship.[74]

Hasidic worship is traditional in form, although perhaps tinged with ecstatic colorations and often marked by the slight liturgical variants and ceremonial twists that can give rituals the branding sectarians may seek as hallmarks of authority and authenticity. All higher knowledge, for kabbalists, is mystical; its goal, like the goal Maimonides pursued and commended, is God's presence. But that goal is sought more by spiritual

---

[74] Jacobs, "God," in *Contemporary Jewish Religious Thought*, 293. In the next three paragraphs, I closely follow Rabbi Jacobs' treatment of kabbalah.

exercises and conning over sacred texts than by the intellectual engagement with nature, culture, and scripture that Maimonides pursued and prescribed. For Hasidism, like other forms of popular pietism, engages with nature more ecstatically than scientifically. Scripture here often becomes a talisman; rabbinic texts, a sort of literary mantra; culture, a kind of magically invested ritualism.

Technically, *sefirot* are numbers, harking back to Pythagorean number mysticism and to the special role Plato assigned numbers, to mediate between the sensory realm and the divine world of the Forms. But *sefirot* are not typically thought of as numbers. Each bears a name and the character of a divine attribute, as if to compensate for the denial of attributes in the *Ein Sof*.

Since the godhead of the kabbalists is conceived as a dynamic organism, each of the *sefirot* has its own role to play in the governance of the universe. *Ein Sof* itself, being utterly beyond human thought, is rarely referred to in the Torah, unless by occasional faint allusions. But kabbalists do allow – indeed advocate – positive descriptions of God, as manifest in the *sefirot*. Such a doctrine easily lends itself to a form of dualism. Indeed, critics have argued that kabbalah comes perilously close to decatheism ... "worse than the Christian doctrine of the Trinity."[75] But kabbalists spring to the defense, using varied metaphors meant to affirm the perfect unity of the *sefirot* with the *Ein Sof* – clear water poured into bottles of different hues.[76] These metaphorical expedients, Jacobs notes, are remarkably reminiscent of Christian attempts to explain how the three persons of the Trinity can still be one within the godhead – an approach equally unconvincing to those not already convinced.

Seeking to embrace God's infinity and unity, as Judaic loyalty invites or demands, kabbalists sunder God's absoluteness from His immediacy, covering the wound with ritual exactitude and a piety more familiarly focused on rabbinic texts than on the ecstatic joy that was often the hallmark of the Hasidic founders in the early days of the movement as a form of pietism. Despite the small deference to argument, ritual practice and rabbinic study preserve the bond of Hasidism to *klal Yisrael*, catholic Israel, a bond that Spinoza, in the end, found himself unable to sustain. His cardinal loyalty, as he explains in the autobiographical opening of his *Treatise on the Improvement of the Mind*, was to the pursuit of truth and understanding, a quest chosen after much close and doubtless painful

---

[75] See Isaac ben Sheshet Perfet (1326–1408), *Responsa*, ed. I. H. Daiches, no. 157.
[76] Moses Cordovero, *Pardes Rimonim* 4.4.17d.

deliberation. His hope, as he confessed, was to share with others such truth as he could reach – and that in a social order receptive to the pursuit of truth and to its retention among those loyal to it and among their children.

Spinoza did not attain those heady goals. Their social side, in particular, remained unrealized. Kabbalists planted more communally rooted, if credally ramified, trees, as demanding in their own ways as the pathway Spinoza dreamed of. The kabbalists lost the logical footing Spinoza had strengthened and sustained. But he lost the moorings in ritual, mythic poetry and popular belief that still keep Hasidic bodies active in multiple communal milieux. Spinoza, in a word, succeeded conceptually where others failed. For few have proved able to sustain philosophy as an open inquiry and an open-ended discourse capable of integrating unity and infinity in their ideas of God, as Spinoza proved able to do conceptually, discovering a unity of thought with extension, where for most modern thinkers down to our own times they remain warring twins, the Jacob and Esau sprung from Descartes' bold but uncontrolled experiment in hyperbolic doubt, the experimental failure that fostered the idealism and materialism that continue today to contest the terrain of human understanding.

Spinoza's organic and dynamic conception of unity in diversity and diversity of expression in the efflorescence of divine unity allowed him to reunite the seemingly disparate worlds of matter and form, thought and extension in Descartes' terms, not as substances but as mutually irreducible attributes of God. The same philosophical brio that allowed Spinoza to see matter and mind as two ways in which God's infinite perfection expression reveals itself allowed him to preserve God's oneness and transcendence without compromising His perfect unity. Recognition of the ultimate unity of those rivalrous but inseparable expressions of divinity is profoundly biblical. Rabbi Johanan (ca. 180–279) marked a like unity when he found scripture balancing exaltation of God with affirmations of His humility:

Wherever you find scriptural reference to the greatness of the Holy One, blessed be He, you also find His humility, whether in the Torah, the Prophets, or the Holy Scriptures: In the Torah, it is written, *The* LORD *your God is God of gods and Lord of lords* (Deuteronomy 10:17) – and what follows: *working justice for the widow and the fatherless* (10:18). Again in the Prophets: *So saith the High and Exalted, who dwelleth in eternity and whose name is Holy* (Isaiah 57:15) – and what follows: *with the crushed and abject of spirit* (57:15). And thirdly, in the Scriptures: *Exalt in Him who rideth the clouds, whose name is* LORD (Psalms 68:5) – and then: *father to the orphan and defender of the widowed* (68:6). (B. Megillah 31a)

In cosmic terms likewise, when Isaiah (6:3) overhears the Seraphim proclaiming God's transcendence, *Holy, holy, holy, LORD of hosts*, he hears the balancing hemistich recognizing God's immanence: *The fill of all the earth is His glory* (Isaiah 6:3). 'LORD' we say, in deference, but what Isaiah heard was the explicit name, echoing the *I AM* that Moses heard. God is transcendent to the highest degree, as the angels' song declares. We repeat the words of Isaiah's epiphany, reaching ever higher, as it were, as if straining after His transcendence. And we emulate that reaching when we chant Isaiah's words, rising on tiptoe to express bodily what we reach for intellectually. But God's transcendence is matched by His immediacy: God's transcendence finds its counterpart in His immanence. And the language of that immanence, uniting *there* with *here*, is what Spinoza saw and argued for when he saw that God's unity is not belied but confirmed by what he called God's infinite attributes.

Respecting nature at large, the species of things, and every particular and individual, reverent toward the human body, as the Torah is, Spinoza, like Maimonides, steered ethics away from self-abnegation and theatrical asceticism. In so doing, he never gave up the moral core of monotheism and held fast to the moral fruits of his metaphysical rigor, preserving *hesed* at the core of ethics, when he equated *pietas* with *humanitas*.[77]

Spinoza boldly captured the monotheistic idea of God as the ultimate cause of all things, through which all things exist and by which they are to be understood. Indeed, he fulfills Maimonides' ideal of seeing God's unity as absolute even conceptually. His God is at once transcendent, being in no way reducible to any mere particular or combination of particulars, yet immanent, in all things: The more we know of nature, the more we know of God. Spinoza's affirmation of unity in God/nature might have found yet more evidence, Harris observes, had he known more of what we now know of the intricate physiological systems at work in any organism. Likewise, had he known what is now known of ecology – or cosmology.[78]

Harris, indeed, relates Spinoza's holism to the "implicate order," that the physicist David Bohm finds "enfolded within each region of space (and time)." As Bohm put it, "whatever aspect we may abstract in thought, this still enfolds the whole and is therefore intrinsically related

---

[77] Spinoza, E2p29s; 3p29s, def 43; 4p18s, 4p41, p51s, p72, 5p4c; cf. 2p49s. 4p41, 72, p51, = Gebardt 2.135–36, 162–63, 202, 248, 223, 265, 283.
[78] Harris, *Substance*, 33–34.

to the totality from which it has been abstracted."⁷⁹ The more we know of nature, as Spinoza saw, the more we understand how intimately each particle and subparticle is integrated in and in its way inseparable from the Whole. Leibniz enshrined a like point in his own philosophy when he proposed unity in each of the monads of his metaphysics and proposed that each monad "perceives" all the rest in a preestablished harmony. For where the atoms of Democritus and Leucippus re-echo the unity of the Parmenidean One, each Leibnizian monad reflects the totality of the universe yet preserves its individuality in the uniqueness of its perspective. The monads of Leibniz, notoriously, "have no windows." But Spinoza's modes are in constant interaction with one another. And God's infinite attributes, for Spinoza, are all of them distinctive expressions of the same creative Unity.

---

⁷⁹ Bohm, *Wholeness and the Implicate Order*, 172.

3

God and Science

Each morning, observant Jews bless God for making light and creating darkness, making peace in the cosmos and creating all that is. We celebrate God, as the world's ruler, for His mercy in giving light to the earth and all its denizens, "each day, in His goodness, renewing the act of creation." Lest it seem extravagant to say that God renews the act of creation daily, the liturgy offers a poetic prooftext: "As it is said, *To the Maker of great lights, for His favor is everlasting* (Psalms 136:7)."[1] The great lights here are the sun and moon (Genesis 1:14–16). For all life on earth depends on sunlight, and the moon regulates the tides and marks the seasons and the passing of the night. But the psalmist, playfully, takes *everlasting* to mean continually, making the rising sun an emblem of the new creation accomplished in each dawn.

The steady rhythm of *seedtime and harvest* is promised (Genesis 8:22) but should not be taken for granted. The constancy of time and the steady cycle of the seasons weaves themes of providence into the idea of creation itself. And holding fast to the same fabric, the evening liturgy embroiders thoughts of design into its images of the passing day: God is blessed as the world's ruler, who at His word brings on the twilight, wisely opens the gates, and with discernment (*tevunah*) lets time pass and causes the seasons to yield one to the next. He marshals the stars in their watches in the sky and creates day and night, rolling away light before darkness and the dark before light. As the days pass, He brings on the night, we say, and divides each day from the next. Rightly is He called LORD of

---

[1] Morning liturgy, *Siddur ha-Shalem*, ed. Birnbaum, 71–74; Koren Siddur, 88–89, 94–95.

hosts.[2] God's hosts here are the heavenly bodies, not gods but creations of the one God, as the eighth-century Sabbath hymn *El Adon* calls them, treating them as God's honor guard, obeying their Lord's command in awefilled joy. Their steady courses show that their Maker still orders their progress by His law, lest there be any fear that the stars retain divine powers of the own.[3]

Discernment, not accident, rules the world, the hymn affirms, a design that declares God's wisdom. What, then, of cannibal galaxies, black holes, earthquakes, hurricanes, and tsunamis? Storms, in the Psalms, manifest God's power:

> *His lightning lights up the world.*
> *Earth trembles at the sight.*
> *Mountains melt like wax before Him,*
> *Before the Lord of all the earth.*
> *The skies declare of His justice,*
> *And every nation sees His glory.* (97:4–6)

In the same spirit:

> *The earth stands firm. It will not be moved.* (96:10)

Linking providence with creation, the psalmist finds reassurance even in the storm wind: The same forces that light up the cosmos will preserve it.

> *Let the sea roar and all that is in it,*
> *The fields and all that they hold!*
> *Then shall every tree in the forest sing joyously*
> *Before the* LORD *– for He is come!*
> *He comes to judge the land.*
> *He judges the earth justly,*
> *And will treat its peoples in His good faith.* (96:11–13)

If mountains skip like rams and hills like young lambs, if the sea itself flees and Jordan River reverses course, it is at the presence of the God of Jacob, who turns a rock into a pool of water and flintstone to a flowing spring. (Psalm 114). How do nature's patterns and convulsions bespeak God's role as Creator and the faithful justice of His rule? Constancy is our

---

[2] See Birnbaum *Siddur*, 191–92, 244–45.
[3] As Birnbaum explains (p. 339), in the hymn's last line *Shevah notnim lo kol tsevah marom* (All the heavenly host pay Him tribute), each word opens with the initial letter of the five visible planets' names: *Shabbatai* (Saturn), *Nogah* (Venus), *Kokhav* (Mercury), *Tzedek* (Jupiter), *Ma'adim* (Mars).

answer. Nature's regularities, and even the stunning disruptions that reset its rhythms reveal not just God's power but His care, as the psalmist sees when he makes a sheep his persona and notes how it finds reassurance in the touch of the shepherd's rod or staff (23:4).

Descartes, in similar thought, binds thoughts of creation to further thoughts of providence when he credits to the light of nature, even before he is fully free of hyperbolic doubt, the sense that existence attests a commitment, moral in Stoic thinking, conative in Spinoza, but perhaps even more immediate in Descartes' finding, a reach for futurity in the very fact of being, a reach answered cosmically by the opportunity to persist: Anatomizing and atomizing time, he reasons: "from the fact that I was in existence a short time ago it does not follow that I must be in existence now, unless some cause at this instant, so to speak, produces me anew." Then generalizing, he argues, that every being, to be conserved moment by moment, has need of the same power and action as would be neededto create it anew. So in the unforgiving light of nature, the distinction between creation and conservation is exposed as a mere distinction of reason.[4]

Many worlds, the midrash proposes, were lost long ago (Genesis Rabbah 3.7; B. Rosh ha-Shanah 31a; Sanhedrin 97a), as prodigal a destruction as is imagined in the planet-destroying violence of *Star Wars*. Nothing, we must realize, was made for our sake alone.[5] But if species replace species and stars replace stars, the grace that drives cosmic change flows forth unexhausted. So we may yet trust in God for new days and new hope – and reflect that the uniqueness of each moment whispers silently to eternity that nothing is ever wholly lost. Every smile and kindness, every generous act or self-deception remains unique, its very transience rendering it irreplaceable.

What, then, of design, the sinew of continuance in nature? Even atheists pay lip service to the idea, so long as design is assigned not to God but to chance or our own projective imagination.[6] The same atheists who spatter mud on pious protestations that nothing here could have begun without divine wisdom to kindle the world's lights do not hesitate to pass judgment on the world they see. Hence their affinity for the Epicurean dilemma. Here, for them, at least dialectically, values count and are allowed to make what sound like objective claims: The dinner is tasty, but the portions too small. Pleasures are delectable; pain and death,

---

[4] Descartes, *Meditations* II, tr. Haldane and Ross, 168; cf. *Guide* I 69, 90a.
[5] See *Guide* III 13.   [6] So Daniel Dennett, *Darwin's Dangerous Idea*, 67–70.

unacceptable, even absurd. Friendship and fellowship are real goods. Even love is accepted, if loosed of moral constraints, as if love made sense in a world where values are arbitrary or subjective (and affections readily turn – or remain – exploitative). In a world of otherwise gray facts, value judgments are now permissible, so long as they stay self-assessed and self-serving. Even anthropic moves pass muster, so long as the world is taken to be made for us – or even *by* us, as per the pseudo-Kantian elenchus once bruited by the race theorist Bernhard Rensch, who argued that if human minds impose the categories that transform a welter into cognizable or recognizable experience, we must be the creators and rise to the task by assuming the mantle.[7]

A humbler version of anthropic idea is advanced by Stephen Barr, pursuing insights of Brandon Carter and others. "Evidence abounds," Barr argues, that supports the hypothesis that life was built into nature's plan from the beginning, leading on to creatures like us.[8] Human hopes, we can say, may or may not touch the apogee to which that plan may point. Much depends upon us; not least, on our moral resolve. That, perhaps, was the caution conveyed in the midrashic tales of lost worlds. For any world, like every individual, is on trial each day in the conduct of the life it has. That makes every day a day of judgment, its events not just eternal but eternally consequential. But is there, in fact, a plan? Barr answers in the affirmative, arguing that unless key parameters and constants had structured the cosmos as they did, human lives and anything that might be called a world would have been impossible.

"ANTHROPIC COINCIDENCES"

Genesis invites us to picture what things might have been like without God's energy and grace. We cannot picture nothingness. Even sheer emptiness would seem a mere expanse of some sort. The biblical poet, as we've noted, wields the words *tohu va-vohu*, translatable perhaps as "welter and waste." If images can conjure an idea, those words might suffice. But today's physics, outpacing poetic imagination, can posit an account of what might have been had specific routes not been taken. Barr lists eleven pertinent counterfactuals, all of them pointing to a plan.

---

[7] See Rensch, *Homo Sapiens*; cf. Freeman Dyson's Gifford Lectures, *Infinite in All Directions*, 119.

[8] Barr, *Modern Physics and Ancient Faith*, 117–57; Carter, *Confrontation of Cosmological Theories with Observation*, 291.

1. If the strong nuclear force that bonds the protons and neutrons in a nucleus were just 10 percent weaker than it is, those nucleons would not hold together, and there would have been no elements beyond hydrogen and thus no sun or sun-like stars. But were that force just 4 percent stronger, the linking of protons in deuterium (with the conversion of one proton into a neutron) would have been far too rapid, and stars would not have lasted the billions of years needed to "cook" the heavy elements of a world like ours, let alone those needed in the rise of living beings.

2. The Big Bang produced vast quantities of helium, atoms of two protons and two neutrons, so-called alpha particles. Such particles tend to reject a fifth particle. They also fail to fuse in an octet. But two helium nuclei do connect, for about 10^{-17} seconds, "about a hundred-millionth of a billionth of a second." If a third helium nucleus arrives during that brief encounter, the three can combine, forming a carbon12 nucleus.

Alpha particles strongly exclude a fifth nucleon that would allow a group of five. Nor do they readily conjoin to form eight-nucleon particles. And the chance of three alphas fusing is so rare that the carbon12 they might form would have proved exceedingly sparse in the universe, far less than the quantities found in nature. Carbon production, as Fred Hoyle explained, must have been boosted by a resonance effect, each triadic union raising the likelihood of another.

The energy level of carbon, at 7.66 MeV, was critical here, in allowing the resonance effect that facilitates the forming of carbon12 from helium triads. Had that energy level been as low as 7.5 or as high as 7.9, precious little carbon would have formed, and the rise of higher elements would have been stymied. But helium is chemically inert, and hydrogen can make no world: "Life based on chemistry," Barr writes (123), "would have been impossible." That outcome, not as graphic as the Genesis poet's *welter and waste*, would have been at least as devastating.

3. Protons, Barr writes, are remarkably stable. They are known to last "much longer than the age of the universe" (123). That stability was fortunate. For without protons there would be no hydrogen. Neutrons, unlike protons, have a half-life of about ten minutes. They rapidly decay, usually into a proton, an electron, and an anti-neutrino. But that is only in isolation. Within an atomic nucleus they can be quite stable. Yet isolated neutrons, having no charge, do not bind, as protons do, to form atoms. Protons are stable only because they have a bit less mass (thus a bit less energy) than neutrons – by about one-seventh of 1 percent. So they lack the energy to decay. But if protons had even a fraction of a percent more mass than neutrons, they would be unstable, and there would be no

hydrogen. There would still have been helium, residual from the Big Bang; and helium stars would have "cooked" the heavier elements. But without hydrogen there would be no water and no organic compounds.

4. The electromagnetic force, familiar to us in the form of light (visible and invisible), radio waves, magnetism, and electrical conduction and induction, depends for its strength on a "fine structure constant" of about 1/137. The parameter controlling the strong nuclear force has a strength of about 1, a force roughly a hundred times that of the electromagnetic force. So two protons close to each other are held together by a force about a hundred times stronger than the repulsion caused by their like positive charges. That is why the protons in a nucleus don't just fly apart. But the strong force is effective only at very short range. In a large nucleus, the protons are held together only by the strong force of other nearby nucleons, but still repelled by their like charges. Uranium, with ninety-two protons, has the largest nucleus found in nature. The strong force holding its protons together is appreciably counteracted by their mutual repulsion. Hence the element's instability: It tends to lose protons, given the rather marginal hold of the strong force alongside the repulsion of all those like charges.

Were the fine structure constant on the order of 1/25 rather than 1/137, there would be only about twenty natural elements. More than half of the twenty-five elements found in the human body would be lacking. There would be no calcium, potassium, or iron, so critical in the composition of bones, the action of nerves, and the functioning of blood as a carrier of oxygen. With a fine structure constant of 1/10, few of the elements we know would persist, and both oxygen and nitrogen would probably be absent in nature.

Were the fine structure constant just double what it is, Barr adds, protons would outweigh neutrons, rendering the nucleus unstable, with the results we already know: There would be no ordinary hydrogen or water, no organic compounds, and no sun-like stars fueled by the fusion of hydrogen atoms.

5. A parameter called v is critical in determining the masses of almost all the basic particles found in nature. In nature as we know it, v needs to be pretty close to 1. But for that condition to be met, the many variables thought to determine the value of v would have to balance. Without such mutual checks, v looks far more likely to have been 10^{17}. Were v to exceed 1.4, there would be no deuterium. And if v were 1.4, the range of the strong nuclear force would be about 20 percent shorter than it is, and deuterium would not hold together. "That would choke off the production of elements heavier than hydrogen" (127). Were the value of

v still higher, the range of the strong force would diminish yet more, and the neutrons in a nucleus would grow increasingly unstable. If v exceeded 5, they would be too unstable for nuclei containing them to exist. So the only element would be hydrogen. If v exceeded 500 there would be no neutrons or protons at all. The only particles possible would not form nuclei, and the only element left would be helium, the chemically inert matter of a sterile universe.

Had v been less than it is, the outcome would have been "just as disastrous for the chances of life" (128). Indeed, Barr argues, the tolerances for variation of v are probably much finer than once thought: "For example, it is likely that a change of v by only a few percent would shift the energy levels of carbon by enough to wreak havoc" with the resonance needed to support much carbon production.

6. The cosmological constant Λ is deemed critical in Einsteinian theory. Its value is thought to be zero or very small (less than 10^{-120}). Were its value modestly negative (say, equal to -1), Barr explains, the universe would have "gone through its entire life cycle of expansion and collapse in the incredibly short time of 10^{-43} seconds" (130). From start to finish the universe would have lasted only a ten-millionth of a billionth of a billionth of a billionth of a billionth of a second. With a negative value for Λ of about one millionth, the duration of the universe works out at about a ten-thousandth of a billionth of a billionth of a billionth of a billionth of a second. For the universe to last several billion years, as we think it has, given the evidence of the red shift and the time needed for life to evolve, Λ would have to be less than about 10^{-120}.

If Λ proves to be positive, other egregious outcomes result. If it were $+1$, the universe would have lasted forever but doubled in size in every 10^{-43} seconds. With Λ at $+10^{-48}$, the doubling would be complete in the time it takes an electron to orbit a nucleus just once, and atoms would have been ripped apart by the expansion. Even with Λ at 10^{-80} the expansion would have been too fast for living organisms to survive, let alone evolve. To allow the gradual expansion over the billions of years necessary to the emergence of life, Λ would have to be near or less than 10^{-120}. So whether Λ is positive or negative, it must be close to zero – "one of the most precise fine-tunings in all of physics" (130). Yet, as Barr argues, there is no intrinsic necessity in so precise a value.

7. Similarly, space would have to be quite close to "flat," that is, rectilinear. We know from Einstein's theory of relativity, that gravity warps space. But the relative curvature, Barr argues, "is not, as far as we know, a fundamental parameter in the laws of physics themselves."

With $\Lambda < 10^{-120}$, as it seemingly must be for the universe to last as long as it has (some fifteen billion years), the curvature of space one second after the Big Bang must have been less than 10^{-35}. Otherwise, the whole would have expanded and collapsed long ago.

8. Again, Barr argues, there is no logical necessity that space be three-dimensional. But clearly the wiring of a nervous system (or the functioning of a circulatory system) would be impossible in a two-dimensional world. And basic physical laws would be radically different in a world of more than three dimensions: electrical and gravitational force would not decline (as they do in the world we know) with the square of the distance but with the inverse (N-1) power, where N is the number of dimensions.

Vanished would be the stability we take for granted in the orbiting of planets and other satellites, where gravity is balanced by the "centrifugal force" attributable to inertia. That point was made, Barr notes, by the much-maligned William Paley, of watch-on-the-heath fame. But the case has broader impact. For, as Barr notes, the same argument applies to the orbits of electrons. They too follow an inverse square law: In a world of more than three dimensions, electrons would "plunge into the nucleus and remain there. Atoms would collapse, so chemistry would be impossible" (134).

As for time, a world with no time dimension would be wholly static. But in a cosmos with more than the one time dimension that we take for granted (although it is not a necessity of logic), the notion of linear processes would make no sense at all – nor would sequences of thought and discursive argument.

9. Quantum physics, Barr argues, is no arcane corner of cosmology relevant only in refined or speculative domains. "Indeed, in all likelihood, life itself would not have been possible in a non-quantum world" (135). Quantum perspectives, he explains, produce the "graininess" unseen by classical physics: Light energy and the energy present in an atom prove not to be continuous but made up of discrete quanta. So the energy of an electron does not diminish continuously until the particle spirals into the nucleus. If it did, atoms would collapse in billionths of a second and so would their nuclei. "In fact, all matter would collapse to infinite density" (135).

In reality electrons are at their lowest energy level when "safely orbiting well outside the nucleus" (136). Indeed, Heisenberg's Uncertainty principle, Barr explains, is just a formal reflection of the world's quantum graininess: Viewed in terms of classical physics, the electron would indeed have a definite position and a definite momentum at once. But that would be when it came to rest in the core of the nucleus. In reality, "the fact that matter, and all the atoms of which it is composed, does not rapidly collapse down to infinite density is due to the fact that the world is governed by quantum principles" (136).

It is because the world is built on quantum principles, Barr explains, that there are specific types of atoms, the elements of Mendeleev's periodic table, each with its own stable chemical properties. Logic does not require that matter be of discrete types rather than a muddy, murky continuum. But the world is not welter and waste. Its matter has the order of discrete varieties, bestowed through the quantum distinctions among atoms. Again, Barr argues, were that not so, "it is highly doubtful that living structures might have evolved."

10. Barr's tenth point is electromagnetism. The core laws of physics do not demand it nor does logic require it. But without electromagnetic forces there would be no atoms or molecules, no light – and indeed, although Barr is too polite to say so, no radio or TV.

11. Finally comes matter itself, its seemingly ultimate particles, leptons and quarks – leptons being a class of particles that includes electrons and neutrinos. The absence of the basic particles would entail no breach in the mathematical consistency of physics. The standard model of physics as we know it today would still need Higgs particles and other particles and anti-particles. But such particles and anti-particles would have annihilated one another in time, leaving only electrically neutral particles. Not much from which to shape a living world.

Thoughts of particles and anti-particles and the edge that being has over nonbeing, given the penchant of particles and their anti-particles to annihilate one another, puts one in mind of a fanciful cover published years ago on the popular science weekly *Science News*. Addressing the speculative idea that nature might have arisen from the segregation of sheer nothingness into matter and anti-matter, that cover showed William Blake's image of God the Father, deploying a great compass or divider to separate nothingness into matter and anti-matter to create a world. Above the bearded Father's while-haired pate rang out the words: "I got plenty o' nothin' – and nothin's plenty for Me."

Aristotle agreed with Parmenides that nonbeing is unthinkable and therefore unreal. But *pace* the Stagirite, it's easy enough to think that there might have been nothing. So the precedence of being over nonbeing gives us a twelfth thought as we read the Torah's account of what might have been without God's act. The actual world is full of a great many things, ordered, as Barr shows, in ways that logic and even the core laws of physics do not require. And all is tuned in ways critical to the possibility of physical and chemical complexity and the rise of life from critically necessary precursors. Such thoughts give all the more depth to what Isaiah (6:3) heard the angels proclaim to one another: *The fill of all the earth is His glory!*

NOT A POCKET WATCH

College students are regularly confronted with the myth of Gilgamesh, perhaps in hopes that they will see in the biblical story of Noah's flood just another ancient myth – and perhaps not notice that God brought the flood that wiped out Noah's generation in disappointment at mankind's moral failings, whereas the flood in the Gilgamesh story was brought on by human noisiness disturbing the gods' sleep. The pagan gods swarm like flies around the savory sacrifices offered them. But the Torah's God bestows a covenant when mankind makes a new start, granting new privileges and duties, and pledging no more to bring destruction on the world for human failings, but to preserve the natural order: *I will no more curse the earth on man's account ... and no more smite all living things as I have done. While the earth endures, seed time and harvest, cold and heat, summer and winter, day and night will not cease. This is the sign of the covenant I establish between you and Me and between you and all that liveth, for all their generations forever: I have set My rainbow in the clouds as the emblem of the covenant between Me and the earth.* (Genesis 8:21, 9:12–13).

With motives all too similar to the students' being confronted with the Gilgamesh story, they are exposed to Paley's parable about a pocket watch found on the heath. They are meant to learn how pallid Paley's reasoning was alongside Darwin's findings and Hume's critique of the argument from design – although, in fact, Hume's *Dialogues concerning Natural Religion*, published posthumously in 1779, long antedated Paley's *Natural Theology or Evidences of the Existence and Attributes of the Deity collected from the Appearances of Nature* (1802) and Darwin's *Origin of Species* (1859).

Paley's thought experiment is not all that weak, of course: No one who found a pocket watch on the heath would think it had just happened there or grown like the gorse and heather. Paley is recruited as a strawman for freshmen and sophomores to knock down. Yet, if the world was created, it was not in the way that a timepiece is. God as a supersized watchmaker is a weak image, expected to dissolve before students hurry to their next class. But what would any of them think if they stumbled upon a cell phone as they crossed the campus? And how like a watch, or cell phone, is the natural world?

Design arguments have always faced rocky terrain, partly because anthropomorphism and anthropocentrism are so readily attached to them. Even Barr's examples look beyond chemistry and physics to life in general and human life specifically. The label "anthropic" more than hints at that. If the laws of nature show evidence of a plan, does that suggest not just divine intelligence but intentions that bore or bear us in mind? Genesis sidesteps that question, remaining as silent about God's motives as it is about God's features. The opening verses do suggest that God is good. For what He made was good. And we are given to understand that He considered human needs. For there was edible fruit in the Garden, although the fruit trees bore seeds that had purposes of their own (Genesis 1:12). God knew, before acting to solve the problem of fellowship and friendship, that it is not good for a man to be alone. But the narrative in Genesis does want us to see that. It does not say that the Garden – let alone the world – was made for our sake.

Isaiah may seem less cautious when he reports: *So says the* LORD, *Creator of the heavens, God Himself who fashioned and framed the earth: "Created it not as a waste but fashioned to be dwelt in: I, the* LORD, *and none other!"* (45:18). Yet Isaiah, too, does not say that God made the world for us alone. The stress in what he hears is on God's unique creative work, not assignable to some mere idol (cf. 48:3–7). The caution is lest Israel again fall, as the people did at Sinai, crediting their liberation from slavery to the calf they'd seen made from their own jewelry (Exodus 32:4). God's words to Isaiah echo the language of Genesis: The world is not the waste (*tohu*) one might have pictured absent God's creative act. The earth and its waters, even the air overhead, afford places for living beings of all sorts – birds and beasts, grasses and trees, insects and reptiles, fish and the great creatures of the seas. None of these exist for our sake alone. God charges them to be fruitful and multiply (Genesis 1:20–30) – the command, at once, compactly, a blessing and a law of nature. The psalmist (104:11–30) celebrates the richness of life that argues God's creation and His care, just as Barr does not ignore the rise of life forms or the rich array of elements that made life possible.

The Stoic philosophers built their idea of design using stones salvaged from what they took to be no longer habitable structures built by Plato and Aristotle. Balbus, cast as the Stoic speaker in Cicero's *De Natura Deorum*, makes nature a great house, a gymnasium or other public place, built by a power whose orders are obeyed and who made sure the place was welcoming. Far more clearly than in any house or public facility, Balbus argues, nature's vast forces are sensitively managed and thoughtfully marshalled. Tracking the movements of the heavenly bodies, undeviating through the ages, he asks, how can one deny that a superhuman, indeed divine, intelligence gave them their order?[9]

Echoing Chrysippus, Balbus argues that only a god could account for the heavenly order, so far beyond human powers of design. No one would think a beautiful building was made by weasels and mice. But just as a fine edifice must have had a fine architect, the world reflects a rational design. One would have to be mad to call mere humans the lords and masters of the heavenly mansions we survey. But divine wisdom and sovereignty are immanent within us: Our bodily heat and moisture, the solidity of our flesh, the breath of life itself reaches us from the air, and reason, too, must come to us from the world in which we live. The world, in its totality, could hardly lack this best of things. The cosmos must have reason and impart it to us along with its other gifts.

The harmony we observe in nature, Balbus argues, must spring from the divine spirit that animates it: As Zeno, the Stoic founder, argued, nothing is more perfect than nature. So the cosmos itself must be both alive and rational, able and willing to share its wisdom with us. The fiery power of reason permeates and rules the world: Nature itself is divine, bestowing reason on us just as it gives life to every plant and animal.

Nature, Balbus urges, is no blind machine. The whole is alive. More like an animal or a tree than a mere mechanism, it animates itself in much the way that souls move bodies, with a subtlety beyond the power of human art – evident in the way seeds germinate and grow, find nutriment, and produce new plants of the kind from which they came. Much like an artist, divine creativity pursues perfection. The artful intelligence that enlivens animals and plants gives them patterns of growth and action no less intricate than the movements of an army. But no smaller harmony is as complete as the harmony that sustains the whole. Many an obstacle may confront lesser beings. But nothing can thwart nature itself, where the divine fire pursues its creative work.[10] Every natural gift bears witness to the divine.

Balbus stumbles over the fallacy of composition when he argues that there would be no art or design in any part of nature without perfect art, life, and reason in the whole.[11] But the Stoic appreciation of design remains a worthy theme, no less than when Aristotle chided his students to squelch their squeamishness about dissection and recognize that even

---

[9] Cicero, *De Natura Deorum* II 15, tr. after Horace C. P. McGregor, 129.
[10] Cicero, *DND* II 16–22, 29–32, 34–35, 42, 57, 81–83, 86.   [11] Cicero, *DND* II 85.

in sea creatures far below the splendor of the stars that Plato had made his stepping stones to the Forms, there is beauty to behold. Why should one prize the representations of natural things more highly than the originals, Aristotle urged. For here, too, as Heraclitus told his visitors, there are gods.[12] To the Stoics, living creatures remain the handiwork of nature's artistry.

No one, Balbus argues, can fail to see how a ship at sea follows a charted course. No one would miss the fact that a sundial tells time by design. So how could anyone fail to recognize the intelligence that steers nature as a whole? Even the savages of Britain or Scythia would hardly miss the craftsmanship of the orrery designed by Posidonius. To ascribe the natural order to the work of chance is to presume, in effect, that Archimedes used more intelligence in modeling heaven's movements than nature itself reveals in their pattern. The encouraging metaphors of Aristotle's coaxing have grown rather harsher here. Debates with Skeptics and Epicureans have sharpened the Stoic claims, rendering more combative Aristotle's talk of nature as an artist: Someone lives in the house we call the world: The master who owns and orders it is, in fact, its architect.[13]

Studying a clock, Balbus asks, can one doubt that it was made to serve a purpose? A fortiori the motions of the heavenly bodies, on which all below depends. Are these not the work of a higher reason, far enough beyond our own to prove it divine? Splendor, regularity, and purpose, bound up with variety and beauty, frame a habitat for us, its stewards. If we could take in nature's panorama at a glance (as reflection, in its way can do), we could hardly doubt it was God's work. How could the constellations that lend beauty to the sky result from merely random atomic motions, as the Epicureans propose? Could forces without mind or purpose devise a system that taxes human intelligence even to decipher? Could random motions give the cosmos the balance and coherence that assure and undergird its stability? (II 97–99, 115–16).

The Stoic elenchus sets nature against divinity even as Stoics proclaim divine power and intelligence within nature. So Stoic appeals to design turn about to play false to the naturalism that bred the Stoic pantheism. Turning to rebut Epicurean reductionism, the Stoics set up a rivalry between divine and natural causation, even while discovering in nature the embodied divinity they celebrate. Rather than find order in the

---

[12] Aristotle, *De Partibus Animalium*, I 5, 645a.   [13] Cicero, *DND* II 87, 90.

seeming play of chance and recognize in natural powers the expressions of a deeper plan, the Stoics have pitted the naturalism of their rivals against their own posit of divine immanence. The result is to polarize the debate and give up scientific explanation to their Epicurean rivals. A good part of the fault here lay in Stoic anthropocentrism and the spurious assumption that nature could not have a plan unless it centered on humanity.

The rhetorical questions that Balbus mooted are tendentious. The argument they pose is a *reductio ad ignorantiam*, challenging an adversary to explain things he is presumed unable to explain. So the Stoic appeal suffers from the flaw fatal to any such appeal: Someone may find ways of constructing the naturalistic explanation that the Stoics challenged their hearers to devise. That, in fact, has been done, as science has advanced. And the success of the natural sciences has put wind in the sails of deniers. So today's materialists make Darwin the poster child of mechanism and broaden that salient to make any notion of divine design appear otiose and unscientific. The fault here lay in the rivalry evident or latent in the dichotomy that Stoic polemics foolishly opened up. The resultant split widened over time to a crevasse and then a chasm, between scientific and religious modes of explanation and even description. The Stoics, of all philosophers, should have seen the false dichotomy: If nature is God's handiwork, nature's forces would be God's tools, and the constancy of nature's laws would be the hallmark of God's work.

The permanence of nature, to which Balbus appeals, was denied, in fact, by mainstream Stoics, who predicted periodic, all-consuming conflagrations. And what would Stoic sages say were they indeed to see the cosmos at a glance and realize that the constellations, whose poetic descriptions Cicero had translated into Latin in his youth,[14] viewed from some other vantage point than ours, prove to have far less connection in their array than the patterns anyone might trace in the clouds? How far, then, can we ride the Stoic mount? Clearly, we need to dismount before the fallacy of composition throws us: That there are minds in the world does not entail that the world has a mind. The risk of that bad inference counsels caution even about Spinoza's giving Nature itself a mind until one sees just what can be meant by any proposed equation of God with nature. All the more do we need caution about the anthropocentrism that haunted Stoic thinking. Here it is Spinoza who offers sage advice: Not

---

[14] Cicero, *DND* II 104.

every purpose found in nature is there to serve our wants and wishes, let alone flatter our fears.

Balbus does not avoid the anthropocentric trap. For whose sake, he asks, was the mighty work of world making undertaken? Surely not for trees and plants. That would be absurd. Vegetation, although sustained by nature, is devoid of sense or feeling. All things serve a purpose, but only beneficiaries capable of appreciation, it seems, are worthy of the ruler's gifts. Are animals, then, the intended beneficiaries? Why, Balbus presses, would the gods have undertaken so vast a labor for creatures lacking understanding? The world and all that is in it must have been made for gods and men.[15]

Human anatomy and physiology are prime cases of the gifts we enjoy: We can walk upright, with eyes on the heavens. We have the gifts of speech and reason. All things in the world, indeed, were made for us.[16] And since we alone can study and appreciate the motions of the heavens, the stars, too, were made for us (a thesis that Maimonides finds absurd)[17] – as were the fruits of the earth. Flutes and lyres, Balbus argues, are made for those who can play them. And the crops we cultivate are for human use. Animals may steal some, but it's not for them that fields are tilled.[18] Here the Stoics' wholesome inclusion of culture within nature is pressed to serve the claim that nonhuman creatures are mere casual beneficiaries of nature's bounty. For, as the self-flattering argument is meant to show, whether humanly cultivated or left to nature's artistry, only humans can properly appreciate her fruits.

Animals, Balbus presses, were made for human use – to give us their fleece and flesh, the labor of oxen, and faithful service of the dog. Swine, as Chrysippus said, have souls only to keep their flesh from going bad. And it must be for our sake that minerals and metals are buried in the earth, where we alone can find and mine them. Divine care reaches every race, near or far, and touches every human being, in every age. But providence, Balbus adds, is general, not trivial. It inspires virtue and poesy, courage, heroism, and statesmanship. But it is not tied to small matters like the fields and vineyards of some humble farmer.[19]

Anthropocentrism here invokes the distinction of general from personal providence to stave off the challenge of the Epicurean dilemma but only by an unseemly appeal to invidious class distinctions. Is there, then,

---

[15] Cicero, *DND* II 133. [16] Cicero, *DND* II 140, 148, 151–53.
[17] *Guide* II 11, 23b; III 14, 28a. [18] Cicero, *DND* II 154–58.
[19] Cicero, *DND* II 159–68.

we ask, a way to disentangle the idea of creation and the allied ideas of providence and nature's sustenance without tripping into anthropocentrism and worse? Does appreciation of nature's bounty and beauty allow one to make sense of the idea of design without projecting human wishes onto our image of divine intentions? For, surely, it's quite different to hold that God made human beings, male and female, in His own image, each of us unique and irreplaceable, without presuming ourselves the cynosure of the cosmos and arrogating to ourselves the power to fashion gods in our own image. Can the Torah help us here?

WHAT THE HAMMER?

The Torah announces the act of creation "majestically," Leon Kass writes[20] – but "baldly," the Midrash admits.[21] For, as Maimonides explains, the immensity and sublimity of creation situate that act beyond human comprehension. That is why the Torah, reaching to express divine wisdom in its verses, broaches the topic of creation "obliquely and poetically" in words on the face of it, "quite baffling."[22] We are not told how God created. And only by inference do we learn why, since God saw that what He had made was good – very good once humanity was in the mix. We can infer that God is good, not in the same sense that God's creations are good but as a giver is.

Among the many questions unanswered by the opening of Genesis, Kass raises several: the beginning of what? "Of time? Of everything?" The latter may seem more likely. And thinkers who see time as relative to nature's workings will include time itself along with the trees and plants and heavenly bodies as included among God's acts. For they agree with Aristotle that time is relative to motion but do not agree with him that the motions seen in the cosmos, from the heavens and down to the air, water, soil, and flames seen on earth are themselves eternal. Philo and Maimonides, accordingly, reverse Aristotle's argument that since time is eternal so must be the movements in the cosmos, of which time is the measure. On the contrary, they agree, quite independently of each other, that time, belonging inextricably to nature, can be no older than nature; so, they argue, since the world and its bodies in motion are not eternal, neither is time.[23]

---

[20] Kass, *The Beginning of Wisdom*, 28.   [21] Midrash Sh'nei Ketuvim, Batei Midrashot 4.
[22] *Guide*, Introduction, 5ab.
[23] See *Guide* II 30, 66b; Philo, *De Opificio Mundi* 26, LCL 1.20–21; cf. Runia, *Philo of Alexandria and the Timaeus of Plato*, 215–19.

The idea of creation, embraced by Philo and Maimonides and other scriptural monotheists including Christians like Philoponus and Muslims like al-Ghazali, brings in tow two weighty issues, first raised by Parmenides, in support of the eternity of all that is, the view favored among Greek philosophers from Aristotle to Proclus and Simplicius. Parmenides' argument boils down to two barbed questions still raised by critics of the creation idea even today: Why? and How? How, it is asked, did your God create the world? And why at this moment rather than any other? The two-pronged challenge, as Parmenides put it: "What birth will you seek for it? How and whence did it grow? ... What need would have driven it later rather than earlier .... Justice has never loosed her fetters to allow it to come to be or to perish .... How could it come to be?"[24]

Cicero puts both challenges into the mouth of Velleius, cast as the Epicurean in *De Natura Deorum*. Targeting the "likely story," of Plato's *Timaeus*, Velleius asks:

> How could your friend Plato in his mind's eye comprehend so vast a piece of architecture as the building of a universe and how God labored to create it? How did he think God went about it? What tools did he use? What levers? What machines? Who assisted him in so vast an enterprise. How came air and fire, earth and water to serve and obey the will of this creator? And whence sprang those five archetypal shapes of his from which all else was derived, so neatly devised to appeal to the mind and rouse the senses.[25]

Plato had derived the five elements of his world from the five solid figures now named in his honor – the pyramid, cube, octahedron, dodecahedron, and icosahedron, whose geometry, according to Proclus, was first celebrated by Pythagoras. Well theorized by Plato's mathematician friend Theaetetus, the five are demonstrably the only regular convex polyhedrons in three-space. So it was natural, if nature was to derive from mathematics for Plato to make geometric realities the archetypes of his elements: fire, earth, air, aether, and water. Velleius scouts the scheme: How could mere geometrical figures turn into bodies. "All this is the stuff of dreams, not the search for truth."

Velleius' rhetorical questions as to the tools and implements of the gods resonate in Blake's Tyger poem:

---

[24] Parmenides, Fragment 8, ap. Simplicius' on Aristotle's *Physics* 78, 5; in Kirk, Raven, and Schofield, *The Presocratic Philosophers*, 249–50.
[25] Cicero, *DND* I 19, LCL 22–23, tr. here after McGregor.

> What the hammer? what the chain
> In what furnace was thy brain?
> What the anvil? what dread grasp
> Dare its deadly terrors clasp?

Blake's eye was on the problem, and the power, of evil. But behind his freighted questions lie ancient wonderings as to the mechanics of creation, an issue the rabbinic Sages had finessed with a midrashic trope, listing the first tongs among the items created by God in the twilight of the sixth day – "for tongs are made with tongs" (M. Avot 5.8; see B. Pesahim 54a). The Sages' aim: to scotch an infinite regress, not just about blacksmithery but about any creative work: The ultimate Initiator must be God.

Velleius presses on impatiently:

> But this tops all: Plato first gives us a world that not only began but is even manufactured, but then claims that it will last forever! Can anyone with even a smattering of natural science imagine that anything with a beginning will not also have an end. What is put together that cannot come apart?[26]

The assumption that any composite will ultimately decompose is rooted in Plato's own reasoning (*Timaeus* 27–29). But Plato commutes that sentence in the case of the world at large, arguing that the same divine generosity that gave existence to lesser beings will favor their sustenance. As his creator god puts it, "whatever has come to be by my hands cannot be undone but by my consent" (*Timaeus* 41ab). Maimonides will adopt the same solution, appealing to God's creative grace to sustain the world.[27] Stoic reasoning underscores that thought, appealing to the virtues of responsibility and concern: Divine goodness would not abandon what it had created.

Cicero's Epicurean waxes vehement in rejecting that inference. For the promise of dissolution anchored the Epicurean denial of an afterlife and thus offered confidence in one's immunity to otherworldly judgment and set personal decisions just where Epicureans held them rightly to belong: in personal hedonic judgments, well guided by prudence as to the long-term impact of one's choices. So Velleius presses his attack with multiple rhetorical questions as to the mechanics of divine control. Only then does he press Parmenides' question, "Why now?"

> Why did these creators of the world suddenly wake up, after ages of sleep? For even if there was no world, ages must still have been.... So I ask you, Balbus, why that 'Providence' of yours stayed still through that great lapse of time? Was it

---

[26] Cicero, *DND* I 20, LCL 22–23.   [27] *Guide* I 69, 90a; cf. II 29.

work-shy? Work makes no difference to a god. Besides, all the natural elements, sky and fire, earth and sea, stood by awaiting the divine nod.[28]

Eternalists down to recent times have made an issue of slumbering or lazy Gods.[29] And Proclus urges, if God is essentially a creator, He must create eternally, making the world eternal. But an eternal world, came the riposte, needs no creator. Indeed, having no origin and facing no death, it seems itself to become divine, its own necessary being. That outcome was not unwelcome to pagan philosophers, affirming their commitment or hankering for thoughts of the world's divinity. Without creation, the unique and world-transcending God of scriptural monotheism was swept away by an ever-expanding hierarchy of gods. Thus Proclus, who fanned the flame of pagan piety in the fifth century, in his *Elements of Theology*, filled the ontic pleroma between the world and the One by positing an intermediary hypostasis between any two higher and lower "principles." And, building on Aristotle's discontent with the idea that the world began, he marshalled eighteen arguments against creation, all of them anchored ultimately in the two Parmenidean questions: Why? and How? Monotheism, as Maimonides saw clearly, rests on the idea of creation – and, indeed, creation building on no prior substrate.

Recognition that there are alternatives to creation brings into high relief the contours of what Genesis affirms. As Kass writes:

Right from its beginning, Genesis, by speaking about the origins of heaven and earth, denies the eternity and, a fortiori, the divinity of the visible universe: neither the heavens – the lofty celestial vault with its sun, moon, stars – nor the earth, the fertile, teeming source of life, are gods. They are, rather, creatures, creations of God. Perhaps more important, Genesis denies the alternative of *generative* beginnings: the sky did not beget upon the earth; our world is not the result of sexual (or warring) activities of gods and goddesses.[30]

We can see why the days in Genesis are merely numbered and not named and why the sun and moon are called the big light and the little light, and assigned tasks by God rather than honored under their divine names or credited with creative and destructive powers. Biblically, God will judge the worth of His work, calling each constituent of the world good, a judgment we are invited to share. Darwin makes a like appraisal countless times when he assays the parts and processes found in living

---

[28] Cicero, *DND* 21 LCL 22–25.
[29] See Grünbaum, "The Pseudo-Problem of Creation in Physical Science," 373–94; William Lane Craig responds in "The Origin and Creation of the Universe."
[30] Kass, *The Beginning of Wisdom*, 28.

beings as features that serve (or once served) the needs of organisms and their lineages. Yet scientism today professes to disallow value judgments. How did that come about?

Creation

The Torah opens with an enthymeme: *In the beginning God created heaven and earth* (Genesis 1:1). What God created, Rabbi Akiva explained, was the world. For the particle *et* in *et ha-shamayim ve et ha-aretz* signals inclusion: The first *et* implies the inclusion of the sun, moon, stars, and planets, the entire cosmos. The second marks the inclusion of trees and vegetation – the Garden (Genesis Rabbah 1.14), of course – everything on earth. Since the Hebrew words for heaven and earth are both preceded by the definite article, the Sages reason that the terms denote the earth and the sky that we know. The challenge, then: Would the world exist had it not been created? Had it always been? If so, nature would be absolute. The inference, then, implied obliquely: There must be more to reality than the world we know, inhabit, and exploit. Nature does not explain itself. The very fact of its existence invites reflection and points toward transcendence, not just to "a higher being" but to a perfection, an overflowing creativity, beyond the creativity and generosity familiar in our daily lives and not reducible to anything we know in nature itself – yet not alien to nature or divorced from it.

We may not know just what God is, as we may think we know the earth and sky, or our friends and neighbors. But we learn something about godhood from the Torah's opening lines: that only what is worthy of worship could make the difference between the world we live in and the existence of nothing at all or the welter and waste we might imagine as our world's alternative. And only an absolute Creator, Author of all that we know and seek to understand, is worthy of the name of God.

The opening verse of Genesis, then, tells us much, as does the account it introduces, schematized in six days of creative activity and a seventh that God blesses and sanctifies (for our sake, not for His, for He is holy, utterly and blessed and in no need of rest). The sanctity of the seventh day will bear prescriptive impact, practical and symbolic, pointing to the grace of creation itself. For if we think we know the world, we should not take for granted the beauty and the good that it contains. Appreciation is the foundation of devotion and is rooted in the recognition that the world did not arise by its own power, cannot endure by its own force, and is not fully understood solely in its own terms.

Yet the world does constitute a system. Thus, Rabbi Simeon's astonishment that sages of Hillel and Shammai's stature would stoop to dicker over which came first, heaven or earth: The world was created as a unified whole, he argues (B. Hagigah 12a), and so it remains: Heaven and earth, like a pot and its lid. They answered God's call together, as Isaiah was given to understand by God Himself: *I call them, and they rise together* (48:13). Nature is a system and no *tohu va-vohu* but an integrated whole at work under one divinely given natural law. Pythagoras would use the term cosmos with a like force, acknowledging the beauty of nature as an integrated system. Genesis, similarly, tells us (1:4) that God saw that the light was good. For God made that first value judgment before light had any function; and beauty is what is good apart from any use a thing might have.

To understand the idea that the cosmos is a system – heaven and earth together, as Genesis puts it – is to catch a hint of the Torah's answer to the question that Cicero would imagine Veleius pressing: God's tools were the elements of nature itself. Not fire, water, earth, aether, and air, nor the spheres, nor even Plato's quasi-divine numbers but the real elements and their particles and sub-particles, and all the energies that we know, and time and space, light and natural forces: God's tools were the matter, energy, and design, not to mention purpose and conatus that allow all things to be, to strive to become what they are, and to exercise their impact on one another. Hence the force of the midrashic dictum that among the things God made in the twilight of the sixth day was the pair of tongs that made possible all the fashioning yet to be accomplished. For if the world truly is a system, it functions as a system, and that fact is reflected in its coming to be, as is its sustenance.

Heraclitus saw the cosmic order as setting limits to the elements' strife. The Hebrew scriptures make a comparable point when they speak of God's setting bounds to the reach of the sea (Proverbs 8:29, Job 38:8). For Heraclitus, the world order ever was, is, and will be (frg. B30). But biblically the natural order is God's work. Hence the conclusion to be drawn from the Torah's enthymeme: none of this need have been or would exist at all if its being depended solely on itself.

To recognize that there is but one world (not the infinite worlds of the Epicureans or the multiverse of some cosmologists today) is, as Maimonides puts it, echoing Aristotle and Plato, "critical, or most helpful, in proving that God is one. Just as organs cannot exist in separation and remain real organs – liver, heart, or flesh by themselves – the world's parts cannot exist without one another in the world as a whole."[31]

The cosmos has a plan, and the plan bespeaks a Maker. The infinite worlds of Epicurean philosophers form no unified system. Their causal patterns, indeed, might differ radically, for all that we can know, so long as the necessities at work within them remain purely mechanical and signal no divine authorship and thus no authority that might have something to say about the way we humans ought to live. Those cosmologists of today who propose a multiverse betray a similar bias: For them, too, nature has no unifying theme, lest its laws suggest a deep creative rationality at the root of every actual world, unifying the cosmos as a universe.

John Polkinghorne captures the tension between such thinking and the (ever more successful and wide ranging) quest for intelligible pattern that underlies the project of scientific inquiry. He redoubles the impact of the anthropic reasoning that we've seen in Barr's theistic proposals by reading the "fine tuning" of the cosmos not only in terms of the welcome it offers to the rise of life and thought in the world's creatures but also in terms of nature's intelligibility. It is as if the world was made, on Polkingorne's account, not only to be lived in, as Isaiah had it, but also to be appreciated and understood: Emergence here takes on an epistemic and indeed aesthetic dimension, complementing its ontic side. So just as Barr argued that neither logic nor the core demands of physics require that the cosmos should be such as to welcome or even permit the rise of life, Polkinghorne broadens the case, finding "no a priori reason why beautiful equations should prove to be the clue to understanding nature."[32] That thought leads Polkinghorne to what he calls an axiological line of argument analogous to Thomas' "Fourth Way," the appeal to Plato's thought that there must be some cause of the goodness and perfection found in all things[33] – an absolute and perfect good beyond all the relative and partial goods familiar to us.

Polkinghorne quotes the brilliant physicist Paul Dirac, "who was not a conventionally religious man," addressing a question about his fundamental beliefs by striding to the blackboard and writing that a keystone of his beliefs was the idea that the laws of nature should be expressed in beautiful equations.[34] Beauty here was not a subjective notion. Nor was

---

[31] *Guide* I 72, 100b; cf. II 1, 10ab; Plato, *Timaeus* 31a; Aristotle, *Metaphysics* X 1074a31; *De Caelo* I 5–9.
[32] Polkinghorne, *Belief in God in an Age of Science*, 4.
[33] Polkinghorne, *Belief in God in an Age of Science*, 20.
[34] Polkinghorne, *Belief in God in an Age of Science*, 2.

it, in the mind of cosmologists like Dirac, a matter of logical inevitability. The world does not have to make sense. The marvel is that it does. Evolutionary psychologists might dismiss as a matter of mere fit such appreciation as Dirac expressed: Of course, the world makes sense to us because we evolved within it. But physicists do not win their way to the subtle and elegant expressions in which they seek to sum up what they see of nature in the way that infants and toddlers learn the rudiments of causality or object permanence. They, unlike their infant selves, must think creatively about the terms in which to frame their insights and then must test the predictions grounded in their hypotheses against all sorts of phenomena whose relevance they never anticipated – hypotheses, indeed, whose terms were not accessible to them when those hypotheses were first framed – as neo-Darwinism meets the tests of DNA analysis and passes with flying colors, although DNA and even the most basic facts of genetic inheritance were unknown to Darwin and his first followers.

Einstein was elated to learn, in 1907, that all things behave in a like manner in a gravitational field, as he had predicted. It took him eight years to work out the mathematics of that relationship. And that work allowed him to frame the General Theory of Relativity. Nature was speaking to him, as Abram Pais put it.[35] And, at a meta-level, Polkinghorne draws a conclusion of his own. His argument: "There is no a priori reason why beautiful equations should prove the clue to understanding nature" – or, for that reason, why fundamental physics should be possible at all.[36]

The solar eclipse of May 29, 1919, gave empirical vindication to Einstein's General Theory of Relativity: Displacement of the apparent position of the planet Venus confirmed that space-time does, in fact, warp, just as Einstein's theory had predicted. Science is possible. Nature and our vision of nature are not bound by what we might take to be our irrefragable intuitions. And, crucially, as Polkinghorne argues, the possibility of such a finding, and indeed the elegance of Einstein's finding, add structure and stability to the recognition that nature is built to a plan – and, in fact, a plan of remarkable beauty, whose subtlety it would take a brilliant mathematician to appreciate, let alone discover.

The possibility of elegant equations, painstakingly framed on the basis of extensive and creative conceptual work and deep commitment to the consilience of data from highly diverse empirical sources, then stands

---

[35] Abram Pais, *Subtle is the Lord*.
[36] Polkinghorne, *Belief in God in an Age of Science*, 3–4.

alongside the welcoming of life and thought in our strikingly hospitable cosmos. So there are twin pillars to anthropic theism supporting the idea of a transcendent divine intelligence: the possibility of life and cosmic order in nature, and the higher possibility of grasping and appreciating that order, scientifically, aesthetically, or indeed in the hybrid grasp of an elegant scientific vision.

Exponents of the multiverse idea do have an alternative to argue: that ours is an exceptional world, accessible to us and to our thinking just because it is the rare case in which we happen to be alive, but that ours is just one among many alternative worlds that do not prove so welcoming. That option does look rather ad hoc. It champs at the bit of the ontological parsimony usually favored by deniers of divinity. And it slights the demand for evidence called for in any serious hypothesis. Without good evidence, attempts to dismiss our world as the mere lucky draw among alternatives unknown to us – and perhaps unknowable, should their natures prove too exotic for our unriddling – looks increasingly like an a priori Hail Mary pass.

The Epicurean roots of the multiverse idea still show at or near the surface. But multiverse radicalism outdoes the Epicurean posit of multiple worlds. For any Epicurean world would still have natural laws; and those, perforce, mechanical, no nonmechanical principles being admissible in an Epicurean world. But if the multiverse is to have the diversity that would make our world just one of an indeterminate variety of alternatives, it must contain "worlds" that lack the order that makes life possible and lack even the coherence that allows scientific discovery.

As doctrinaire denial presses the multiverse thesis, Polkinghorne observes, the speculative gambits grow "rapidly more rash and more desperate. Maybe laws of nature themselves fluctuate, so that a vast portfolio of conceivable, or (to us) inconceivable, worlds rise and fall in relentless exploration of random possibility – "occasional patches of transient and varied order in a sea of seething chaos"[37] – the very welter and waste against which Genesis contrasts the world we know.

If natural laws in such putative worlds are arbitrary, absent, or transient, science loses its grip. For science, like life itself, demands some measure of stability. If our world is just a random exception to a plethora of otherwise incomprehensible alternatives, then, as Polkinghorne puts it, the denier's "exercise of prodigal conjecture" has "moved far beyond

---

[37] Polkinghorne, *Belief in God in an Age of Science*, 9.

anything that could be called scientific."³⁸ Fear of the God idea has undermined the idea of nature itself, on which the authority of the deniers was meant to rest.

Scientific practice and experience, by contrast, as Polkinghorne argues, confirm cosmic unity. They confirm it in the consistency of the natural laws we know and in the synthetic understanding that proves able to relate the evidence encountered in what may seem the most distant and disparate realms of natural inquiry.

Kant caught a glimpse of nature's unity when he realized that the seemingly blurry stars visible in a telescope were not single bodies but vast, if distant, galaxies, their array attesting to the same laws of physics by which Newtonian physics explained the motions of the planets. The possibility of synthesis of this sort bespeaks a unity, and thus a common plan. It seems tendentious to localize such a plan and parochialize the reach of reason, which has proved itself so well in capturing beauty of this sort. Indeed, when advocates of a multiverse project worlds with as many and diverse patterns of order and disorder as logical possibility might permit, and for no better reason than distaste for the idea that our universe is built to an especially elegant and life-welcoming plan, we need to ask just who it is who's imposing a priori notions on the work of science. Given the nature, or lack of nature, in fanciful projected worlds, it's clear that we can't know them. So we'd have no evidence to support affirmation or denial of their existence. Is the multiverse, then, no better than a *reductio ad ignorantiam*, appealing to the inevitable limitation of human knowledge rather than to any scientific evidence?

In behalf of cosmic unity, by contrast, Polkingham can cite the relevance and consilience of findings brought from natural domains at what seem to be the most distant extremes of the natural universe:

Those who work in fundamental physics encounter a world whose large-scale structure (as described by cosmology) and small-scale process (as described by quantum theory) are alike characterised by a wonderful order that is expressible in concise and elegant mathematical terms .... This use of abstract mathematics as a technique of physical discovery points to a very deep fact about the universe we inhabit, and to the remarkable conformity of our human minds to its patterning. We live in a world whose physical fabric is endowed with transparent rational beauty.³⁹

Nature as we know it is intelligible. We can't exclude a priori the possibility that there are other "natures" (or "anti-natures"?) that we would

---

³⁸ Polkinghorne, *Belief in God in an Age of Science*, 9.
³⁹ Polkinghorne, *Belief in God in an Age of Science*, 2.

find unintelligible. But the fit of explanation to the physical phenomena of our natural world, from the vastest to the most minute of its components, counts against such speculations. The elegance that Einstein rejoiced in when his theory of Relativity found its place in humanity's shared understanding of nature, the beauty that Dirac rightly treasured, and the ever-growing host of synthetic understandings, together reflect the beauty in nature's design that scientists seek to capture – one critical part of what God, in Genesis, proposed His first rational creatures should endeavor to discover when He commanded them, male and female, to *be fruitful and multiply, fill the earth, and master it* (Genesis 1:28).

A BARRIER TO EXPLANATION

Andrew Steane names Hume as the modern philosopher who drew a hard and fast line between the domain where explanations can be sought and any other where causal questions must be barred.[40] The boundaries of sensation marked that frontier for Hume. But even in the days of Democritus, such boundaries seemed porous. For sensations, as Democritus saw, are clearly subjective; and the words that name their causes, as Locke well knew, are projective: The water in the tub is not hot in the sense I use to tell you how it feels when I test it with my toe. The irony is too often missed, bred by the friction between Hume's sensation-based empiricism and any thought of real properties in nature.[41] Hume's reduction of causal necessity to the stuff of anticipation only compounds the difficulty. For Hume went Democritus one better, by treating not just Locke's secondary properties but the causal nexus itself as subjective. The irony is palpable when the project becomes one of building a (Quinean) universe without minds – or demanding means of verifying claims by appeal to acts of observation without leaving room in the natural world for an observer.

Today, Hume's wall between sensibility and nature is meant to be overlooked by strict empiricists, lest they trap themselves in Bishop Berkeley's world, where being is reduced to being perceived. We're simply told to call on physics to teach us what it is that our sensations point to or signal presence of in the world. Hume's wall is then admitted to be permeable. But its portals are picketed by recruits from physics: There will be room for gravity and electromagnetism and even for the quantum

---

[40] Steane, *Science and Humanity*, 176–97.
[41] See Goodman, *In Defense of Truth*, chapter 2.

properties of things if experiment speaks up for them. But access is denied to seeming mysteries like beauty and goodness, or even consciousness. They lack the passwords that only physics is taken to allow. The acknowledgment of facts thought knowable awaits the verdict of a shifting and conflicted coterie of experts, expected to reach a consensus idealized by philosophers like Quine. The members of that priesthood are called on to impose the critical standard. But its locus, like the membership of that body of guardians, ever threatens to move onward toward a utopian ideal not unlike the idealized future to which Marxian priesthoods demand ritual obeisance and timely or unbounded sacrifices in its name.

The effect, as muted struggles rage behind the scrim, is to exclude acknowledgment of value or of any sort of cause denounced as spooky. The sanitized world is now called disenchanted, as though ghosts and ghouls were the only suspect denizens before Humean hygiene made its sweep. We're not to notice that phantoms and apparitions still make their appearance in the subjective world that Hume privileged – habit being one of them. Epicureans once cheerfully acknowledged anthropomorphic gods, in deference to an uncompromising empiricism. In the name of religious experience, an experiential God may yet gain entry to the subjective world countenanced by Humean deference to subjectivity. But the unseen God of monotheism is cast out. Physics guards the borderlands, lest nature seem to point beyond itself, as Genesis invites one to consider.

It's something of a cliché that a world without God looks rather cold and empty, just as morals without God left the existentialists of the last century with a sense of forlornness, as they put it, dramatizing their sense of loss at failing to find a competent moral authority. But things can always turn worse. Without creation, nature starts to take on absolute pretensions. The cosmos may look like the world of Strato, successor to Aristotle's successor Theophrastus. But nature, stripped of its links to the divine, may balk when called on to explain itself. Or it may lurch forward, goaded to fill God's place. Stoic options lurk nearby, naturalizing divinity or divinizing nature in tones that seduce romantics, drawn by the lure of ambivalence and other emotions more readily suffered or enjoyed than critically examined. But the flickering piety fed by such enthusiasms wobbles on its slippery logic, easing toward nature-worship or superstition, or sliding toward a new materialism, making God a thing, large, perhaps, and perhaps unseen, but still a thing, invoked when outsize powers are wanted, for prognostication, predestination, imprecation, or intervention in a crisis. But even allowing for such pragmatic excursions, disenchanted nature still looks rather cold and dreary.

Tellingly, today's Stratonician shackles the bold explanatory project of inquiry. Reaching particles that seem small enough or rules that seem broad enough, many seekers and far more spectators lose sight of the quest for ultimacy that was once the raison d'etre of science, its past achievements now a torso in the sand. Stubborn spirits and sporting passersby may try to re-attach a missing limb or rummage in the debris to find the missing head. But even as they do, delapidators labor to find uses of their own for the scattered parts of the once imposing colossus.

If all causes must be natural causes, as Jaegwon Kim demands, nature is left to explain itself. But it cannot. For the ancient quest for ultimate and universal answers must seek causes of a different order from those familiar to physics, even with an ever-expanding repertoire of etiologies. Fields and radiation are acceptable today, elements of the repertoire of physics. But causes that fail to fit that growing chorus line are debarred. And yet, as Saadiah argued, a cause of the same order as what we seek to explain joins the rest in need of explanation.[42] The retreat mandated in the name of empiricism and its scientistic allies may make sense of many of nature's parts. But much is left unexplained, not least the cosmic entirety of the integrated system. And the piecemeal methods of the special sciences, adequate to account for varied subsystems, leave behind, as if by choice, nature's most dynamic and exciting feature, the fact of emergence, with its varied faces, from the birth and history of stars to the growth of chemistry and the rise of life and understanding. Such phenomena are inexplicable in the terms allowed by the scientific powers that be. For the critical explanatory terms do not resolve to the naming of parts.

Yet what Aristotle once said of thinking remains true of emergence at large, despite all courteous or curt dismissals:

One does not deliberate after previous deliberation, itself presupposing prior deliberation. No, there must be some starting point. Nor does one think after first thinking one should think, and so ad infinitum: Thought is not the starting point of thinking, nor deliberation of deliberation. So what can be the starting point if not chance, leaving everything to come from chance! But perhaps there is a starting point with none beyond it, that can act as it does by being what it is. That would be the object of our search: the source of movement in the soul. The answer is clear: As in the universe, so in the soul, it is God. For, in a way, the divine in us moves everything. The starting point of reasoning is not reasoning but something greater. And what could be greater even than knowledge and reason but God? (*Eudemian Ethics* VII 14, 1248a18–28)

---

[42] For the danger of reducing the quest for an ultimate cause to the term that causes were expected to explain, see Saadiah Gaon, *K. al-Mukhtar*, II Exordium.

The kind of quest for ultimacy that Aristotle points to here regarding thought and deliberation was of a piece with his claims regarding motion, the root of all causality for him. Like questions can still be asked of what we now call energy, just as they have long been asked about the ultimate origin of matter. Hobbled by the strictures that a reductive appeal to empiricism has long placed on inquiry, the quest for ultimacy that science and religion once shared remains unsatisfied. Yet an insistent, childlike voice is still heard asking *Why?* and urging us to renew the larger quest for a higher cause and deeper varieties of causation.

If metaphysics is a search for ultimates and theology is its ancient name, science itself, to be true to its questioning and questing spirit, cannot foreswear its timeless search for ultimate causes. Nor should it deny, as we near the big questions, that the ground we tread on now is holy ground. For the quest for an ultimate reality is not alien to but cognate with the quest for ultimate value.

Without a First to energize nature's dynamic, initiating and sustaining the processes of emergence and evolution that culminate in the lives of persons, there is nothing to explain the evolutionary "groping" found in nature that culminates in what we prize as thought and creativity. Given not just the vastness but the dynamism of natural projects and the diversity of forms and pathways they take, and the increasingly self-directed purposiveness of living beings in general and persons in particular, it does not seem inept to describe as infinite in power the underlying ultimate Cause. Nor does it seem at all apt to rule out goodness in the character of that Cause, if Infinity is to be more than just a very high if fanciful number. Grace and wisdom, on this account, will find a place among the attributes of an infinite being, once being is understood, as it should be, as perfection, and once natural beings are understood by reference to their diverse ways of seeking perfection.

The options we face are pretty straightforward: We can posit a perfect being as the ultimate source of all that is. Or we can trace one finite being to its source or basis in another and march on ad infinitum, perhaps in unending circles of mutually dependent causes. Any such trails will end in time, when the causes start to peter out that seemed amenable to capture or control. Gravitation will be accepted, despite the posit of "no action at a distance," if its workings can be marshaled in equations. Radiation will be accepted, just as magnetism was long ago, if its reach can be corralled in fields of force. But when the analogs and heirs of mechanism give way, a censuring and censorious brand of naturalism is invoked, and scientistic souls draw a line, where they declare that explanation stops, just as

Epicurus barred the search for any cause beyond the motion and impact of his atoms.

MORE THAN AN EXPLANATION

Steane, a practicing physicist, but also a practicing Christian, confronts the proposed scientific barrier by urging that God is no mere hypothesis – not in the way that Newtonian or Einsteinian gravity is. He traces the rejection of a God-hypothesis that he finds in Richard Dawkins, echoed by Daniel Dennett, and with counterparts harking back to Hume – and long before him, to Strato and Epicurus, of course. Thomas Aquinas, Steane observes, heard the now regulation objection to divine design long before Hume's time – and saw the need to address it at the start of his philosophical theology, raising a middle road between the notion that God's reality is self-evident and the contention that Godtalk is nonsense, as the logical positivists once urged – or, as Thomas put it, more courteously in the denier's behalf, that explanation finds its proper province within nature and must end at nature's borders.

Dawkins, as Steane reads him, reframes the old objection, "in fresh language" that displays its force, by constructing a dilemma. In Dawkins' words, "Any Designer capable of constructing the dazzling array of living things would have to be intelligent and complicated beyond imagining. And complicated is just another word for improbable – and therefore demanding explanation."[43] Dawkins' argument aims to put God back into the world of things requiring explanation. It rejects the very idea of an ultimate explanatory principle. Innocent of Saadiah's warning against treating an ultimate cause as just another item to be explained, it ignores Spinoza's insight, too, that a being infinite in every way, far from going unexplained, proves Self-explanatory.

Methodologically, Dawkins assumes that explanations must be bottom-up and cannot run top-down. This, despite the fact that living beings, the focus of his work as a biologist, can do many things not explained by their parts and predecessors, or there would be no meaning to the idea of an organism and no truth to biological evolution. Left unexamined by Dawkins' dismissal of the God idea as needlessly complex is the thesis favored by philosophical theologians of all stripes, that God is an ultimate simplicity, a being of supreme, sublime, and infinite perfection

---

[43] Dawkins, *Climbing Mount Improbable*, quoted in Steane, *Science and Humanity*, 180.

that we human beings try to characterize in terms of virtues that we know and to which we aspire – generosity, wisdom, power, and grace. Dawkins was perhaps distracted by the complexity of thought and language that philosophers, poets, and the poet philosophers that we call prophets use when they seek to convey something of what one must mean if one hopes to speak of God.

Tackling Dawkins by catching hold of the assumption that God is a hypothesis, Steane argues that religion is not a science, not a search for explanations, let alone a misguided search that offers complex and problematic explanations where simpler, more straightforward, and more earthbound explanations are at hand.[44] Steane is happy to accept scientific accounts, say, of the origin of life and the evolution of living species, the domain that mothers Dawkins' objections: "No one knows for sure at the moment," he writes, "but I think probably life got started because the universe was pregnant with the possibility of it and ready with the wherewithal to support it" – a tacit tribute to the approach we saw in Barr. As Steane puts it, "that the natural world has such propensities remains a powerful indicator that it [the origin of life and the rise of higher species] is the outcome, or the expression, of an extraordinarily creative origin or root. This also heightens, rather than diminishes, the sense in which God may have regard for the world, since it makes the world all the more expressive and valuable."[45]

Targeting the assumption that religion aims to answer the same sort of question that natural scientists pursue, Steane draws on Peter van Inwagen's insights, not ignoring the strong claim, so stressed by Kim in the idea of causal closure, that every phenomenon has either a natural cause or no cause at all. This, Steane observes, following van Inwagen, "is not an argument for atheism; it is the premise of atheism."[46] Kim and others in his wake or of his ilk have begged the question.

But pressing on, again relying on van Inwagen, Steane turns to the nature of religious life and experience: As van Inwagen confesses, he does not believe in God because he "made a hypothesis and then addressed the merits of that hypothesis." He arrived at his belief in quite another way, more like the way that he reached the belief that material bodies exist, that other persons have mental lives, or that men and women are intellectual equals. Beliefs that one holds although unable to trace their origins or even to support by way of argument are not for that reason irrational.[47]

---

[44] Steane, *Science and Humanity*, 181.   [45] Steane, *Science and Humanity*, 183.
[46] Steane, *Science and Humanity*, 186.   [47] Steane, *Science and Humanity*, 186.

Drawing an analogy between unargued and perhaps unaccountable beliefs may sound like readiness to give away the store. But Steane has telling examples to help him make his point. To start with the most commonplace and familiar: People may meet by chance, but if they become friends it is not just because they weigh their usefulness to one another – nor even just because they prize one another's interests in much the way that they value their own. For, in that case, they're already friends. We humans make friends, Steane argues, "by paying attention to each other, and allowing parts of our identity to become bound up with another." No one needs a syllogism to be convinced that it would be rational to be friends. Such attitudes may only sour a friendship.[48] Knowing God, Steane suggests, is more like finding a friend than like choosing a bank. That helps. And if we reflect on Israel's relationship with God, the analogy grows all the more telling. For the phenomenon of Israel's relationship with God, although never lacking argument, was for the great majority of Jews far more like a friendship, or the bond between lovers, or the existential commitment between parents and children than it is like being convinced by a geometrical argument that the Pythagorean theorem is true. But Steane's second example is yet more telling.

He speaks of King Lear's pressing his daughters: "Which of you shall we say doth love us the most?"[49] Dramatic irony underscores the anomaly, if we already know or can guess how Lear's royal 'we' will be abased, and how Cordelia, in the end, will prove her love in ways her foolish father is as yet unable to imagine. Even in posing his ugly question, Lear has stepped out of the frame of fable and exposed how little he knows of love, elemental lessons that only life and death will teach him.

Steane's analogies strike home, since they turn toward love, not knowledge of the sort that Kim or Quine, Dawkins or Dennett aims to privilege. But does Steane's brief risk surrendering religion (and love itself more broadly) to the irrational. He rightly presses the recognition that religious choices are existential. Like love and friendship, religious commitments are life-altering; they can, and often should be life-defining. They make moral, social, even ceremonial demands and can lead on to ever higher, deeper, and broader commitments. But they are not, therefore, simply unaccountable.

Partly because he recognizes that fact, Steane leaves space, intellectual as well as moral and spiritual, for the arts and the humanities, and for fellowships and communities of religious practice, where deeper

---

[48] Steane, *Science and Humanity*, 130.   [49] Steane, *Science and Humanity*, 190.

commitments find articulation and lay out trellises on which beliefs can grow and find expression in actions, art or poetry, or charity, and in the symbolic forms of ritual and ceremonial. The existential character of such commitments may yield an outcome not unfamiliar in religious circles and in other domains where commitments have grown up that are existential: Arguments, whether solid or shaky, are often framed secondarily, aiming to shore up or render sensible to self or others the commitments that have taken root in a soul and become a way of life.

Sound commitments, of course, are not capricious. One cannot say that there is never a poor choice of friends or lovers. Here's a place for well chosen, if tactfully stated, parental or peer advice. And, by the same token, it's unwise to pretend that there can be no wrong choice of gods. A god that demands violence, or sexual license (or sexual surrender, as some cult leaders do) is a false god and to be shunned, not followed, to be suspected and exposed as a projection of dark emotions of dominance and exploitation, delusions once ascribed to demons rather than to anything rightly deemed holy. If we follow Aristotle in agreeing that the truest friendships are not meretricious but are anchored in mutual and deserved respect, we should look to the qualities worthy of respect in a potential friend – and a fortiori in a lover, or one's God.

The issue calls to mind Molnar's 1909 play *Liliom* and its Broadway adaptation in Rogers and Hammerstein's 1945 musical *Carousel*. The musical plays on the romantic theme of unconditional love, drawn rather than repelled by the character flaws of the male lead, and egged on by the specious equation of good character with stodginess. Such typings and cliches feed the show's popular appeal. But one need not be calculating to distinguish human goodness from weaknesses – or to see through the specious promises of liberation offered by gods whose images confound holiness with violence, violence with power, or debauchery with freedom.

Steane echoes Alvin Plantinga's brilliant analogy between belief in God and belief in other minds. But if we're to take that analogy seriously, we should not ignore Gilbert Ryle's critique of the very idea of a mind.[50] If minds are, as Ryle urged, best treated adverbially rather than substantively, we need to consider the charge that the very idea of God, like that of the mind, rests on a category error. Steane opens himself to such a charge when he (rightly) links the idea of God to one's choice of a way of life. Is God too a category error, standing in for forms of social

---

[50] Gilbert Ryle, *The Concept of Mind*.

engagement and moral or even ceremonial commitment but not a living being whose actions matter in the world?

If God does make a difference, shouldn't there be some domain where His presence can be seen? The light that shines through this chink in Steane's well-polished armor suggests that there may indeed be some good reason to think of God as the answer to a question. For it's only a real being, and not just a sense of belonging, or commitment to what may prove just a lonely child's imaginary friend, that can address questions about life's meaning or explain why there should be a world at all, and why the world takes the form it does.

Steane's thesis that God is no mere hypothesis leads him to a proposed detente between religion and the sciences. That possibility may help motivate his thesis. He cites Stephen Jay Gould admiringly in another connection[51] but goes on to follow Gould in proposing that the humanities and arts, and perhaps the varied realms of human ritual engagement, afford ample room for relating to God without encroaching on the domain of science, where hypotheses are tested and (as Karl Popper argued) discarded if found wanting. Gould's well-known proposal that religious commitments and the natural sciences rightly occupy "nonoverlapping magisteria,"[52] although irenic in spirit, is all too reminiscent of Pope Alexander VI's bull of 1493 dividing the New World between Portugal and Spain – or Descartes' declaring that the Church best serves to show men the way to heaven, leaving nature free for the work of science.

Neither of these old lines of demarcation proved lasting or effectual. Doubting believers today freely argue against the evolution of species by natural selection – macroevolution, as Steane calls it, echoing the doubters' language.[53] But the compelling evidence for neo-Darwinism grows stronger daily and cannot fail to have an impact on the varieties of belief accessible to thoughtful theists. Evolution hardly makes atheism intellectually respectable, as Dawkins urged. Indeed, the warfare that Gould hoped to stem, promoted by sectarian interests on both sides, is exposed as a false struggle by the deep complementarity of evolutionary biology with the religious recognition of the ways in which value pervades

---

[51] Steane, *Science and Humanity*, 189.
[52] See Gould's posting "Nonoverlapping Magisteria," dated October 12, 2009.
[53] For the motives underlying Christian polemics against neo-Darwinism and use of the notion of macro-evolution as a polemical redoubt, see Goodman, *Creation and Evolution*, esp. chapter 1.

nature. To cite just one revealing dimension of that complementarity: Darwin's work transformed the Aristotelian idea of adaptation from a mere biological given to a process with causes and a history. Teleology, as a result, became more central than ever in the life sciences. As Darwin's son Francis put it:

> One of the greatest services rendered by my father to the study of Natural History is the revival of Teleology. The evolutionist studies the purpose or meaning of organs with the zeal of the older Teleologist, but with far wider and more coherent purpose.[54]

By making teleology central, Charles Darwin made the search for value and its sources, traditional provinces of religion, not less relevant but strikingly more relevant in the natural sciences, undermining the embattled barrier between science and religion. Galen's classic work *De Usu Partium*, On the Uses of the Parts of the Body, following up systematically on Stoic and Aristotelian ideas of physiology, had long forged a bond between biology and teleology. But Darwin's work set the teleological account of anatomy (and life processes) into the context of history by showing how critical any heritable adaptation can prove to be in the struggle of living beings to survive and perpetuate their lineages. Indeed, Darwin's work confirmed in biology what Spinoza had urged with metaphysical universality: that the essences of things are dynamic rather than static – and conative rather than fixed.[55]

Evolution, then, proves highly relevant in religion as a result, inter alia, of Darwin's work, and not in the sense that anti-Darwinists have feared. Gould's NOMA proposal, meant to defend science and religion from one another, proves not only unnecessary but counterproductive. In cosmology no less than in biology, as we've seen in reflecting on anthropic questions, science and religion have much to say to each other.

---

[54] Francis Darwin, in his introduction to Charles Darwin's *Autobiography*, 308; see Goodman, *Creation and Evolution*, 138.

[55] Spinoza himself bears much of the blame for his lingering reputation as a foe of teleology, given his outspoken condemnation of such thinking in the Appendix to Part I of the *Ethics*. But, as he stresses there, his target is anthropocentrism in teleology: "All the prejudices that I here undertake to expose depend on this one: that people commonly presume that all natural things act as they do with an end in view and in fact hold it certain that God Himself directs all things to a definite fixed end. For they say that God made all things for man, and man that he might worship Him." Gebhardt 2.78 *ll.* 1–6. Maimonides rejects the same anthropocentrism (*Guide* III 13), arguing that it trivializes God's intent and magnifies man's status by purporting that all things exist to serve human needs, wants, and vanities.

For evolution itself is just one special case of emergence – albeit a case of special concern to us, since we humans are interested parties. Any religion worth its salt cannot afford to turn its back on nature, as if the world we live in and share with one another and with all sorts of other creatures told us nothing about the divine, which the scriptural monotheist regards as its Creator, Ruler, and Judge.

Working scientists, we can add, need not fear and should not self-censor their religious awe at nature's intricacy and magnificence. They need not eschew the sense of glory that springs up at the uncovering of some natural mystery. And least of all should they give up the childlike curiosity that prompts the question, *Why?*, so natural and unstoppable in biology but no less pertinent when one wonders why anything should exist at all.

Still, if religion and science are to speak with one another and not just talk past each other, there has to be the possibility of disagreement. God, to take just one example from Maimonides, did not halt the setting of the sun at Gibeon (*Guide* II 35, 77b). And it is not science but politically charged ideology that pronounces human beings just another animal species no different in desert from the rest (See Genesis 1:27, 2:7, 9:3–7).

NEW METRICS

The scientistic project is more a task of barrier building than of constructive, creative, or heuristic work. But its Achilles heel is the collapse of explanation altogether when it fails to reach (or at least point to) some ultimate explanatory term. Inquiring minds may have begun their quest in hopes of explaining some phenomenon, familiar or arcane. But the train of explanations stalls for lack of explanations deemed acceptable unless cut down to accepted proportions and dimensions. The once bold exploratory, explanatory project runs out of steam when inquirers are told to curb the global curiosity that first fired their inquiries.

Scientism, under the more anodyne name of naturalism, reveals its sterility when the train pulls up at the barren field left uncultivable by a blanket spraying of disenchantment. One can't help thinking of Hilary Putnam's well-placed jab at the clumsiness of attempts to use atomic physics to explain why it's so hard to fit a square peg into a round hole. A plumber knows better than to tackle a problem with the wrong tools. And similarly, when causes on the order of the mechanical or electro-chemical, and their latest surrogates and substitutes, are found wanting and causal regularities stand silent, unable to explain themselves, we may need to recognize that the sort of causes we need to acknowledge may be undetectable by the instruments we've brought to the explanatory workbench. For ultimate explanation, as Saadiah saw, must be of a different order from the factors left behind to be explained. Yet the causes to be invoked at such a juncture are not, therefore, as if by default, the stuff of magic.

If it's the totality of nature that we wish to understand, or its beauty, or the welcomes it tenders to life and understanding, we may need to move beyond the limitations imposed by scientism. The need to expand one's categories if one hopes to address hard cases has been a challenge recognized (or willfully ignored) for as long as we humans have sought to understand the world we live in. Magnetism, we had to learn, could not be ruled fanciful because it does not bow to the mechanist's rule of "no action at a distance." The same is true of gravity. Descartes' reduction of matter to geometry proved no more successful in arraigning nature before the court of reason than did Plato's derivation of all solids from the five shapes studied by his friend Theaetetus. Cartesian geometry cannot give bodies their impenetrability, nor their elasticity. Mechanism, as a study of impact, carom effects, and ricochets, does not explain why all physical actions yield an equal and opposite reaction. So Newton found his Third Law of Motion empirically, and it was only empirically that he could test it. It's not an a priori truth. Nor is the existence of electromagnetic fields or phenomena like electrical induction. Still less "intuitive" was the impact of Einstein's realization that it's the speed of light that must remain constant, even if that means that space is not quite so rigid as one might have expected.

Evolution, just as strikingly, does not fall to the critique made in its early days by Darwin's teacher Adam Sedgwick, that Darwin had "deserted the inductive track, the only track that leads to physical truth" – since he had not derived his theory by generalization from particular cases.[56] It was the scientific method itself that needed to fan out in the wake of Darwin's work and that of William Whewell. Consilience and what we now call inference to best explanation (or, in Peirce's terms, abduction) were the pathways that needed more overt attention if induction was to be framed widely enough to cover Darwin's reasoning (and that of many a previous investigator, as Whewell's historical studies had shown him). Explanation itself proves to have a historical dimension,

---

[56] See Goodman, *Creation and Evolution*, 113.

alive in Darwin, and in the book of Genesis, but less at home in the works of Aristotle (unless in the *Politics*), given Aristotle's discontent with myths of origin and his commitment to cosmic eternity and the constancy of species.

If inquiry is to continue in pursuit of ultimacy, windows must be opened to the realm or realms of value: Beauty, goodness, even utility at times, have been shaved away and shed from the modes of permissible scientific discourse. So science is left to labor under the delusion that (with the embarrassing exception of the quantum realm, left open to thoughts of indeterminacy and indeterminism that make it easy prey to mystery mongers) only properties measurable and manageable by physical means are such that the sciences need acknowledge and address them. Beauty, goodness, and other values, we are assured, are subjective – as though what cannot be weighed or measured, priced and packaged, or registered by a Geiger counter or other instrument can lay no claim to objectivity.

But can we afford to strap moral claims into the same procrustean bed as the one on which aesthetic judgments have long been presumed to fit? The voices making such demands sound rather harsh and scratchy when they seem to set a work by Rembrandt onto the same pan or dissecting table as a Margaret Keene or a Thomas Kinkade and leave the matter of quality up to personal or communal taste, or link them to sales records and market prospects?

On the contrary, the standards guiding theory choice in the sciences often prove to be in good part strikingly aesthetic. Values like coherence, breadth, economy, heuristic fruitfulness, and that odd hybrid known as elegance are critical in the sciences. Does appeal to such standards, in their varied blends, render theory choice subjective? That would be a hard case to make – and harder to hold onto. The choice between Copernicus and Kepler, on the one hand, and Ptolemy, on the other, is hardly a matter of subjective preference – any more than subjective preferences would suffice in choosing morally between Mother Theresa and the Marquis de Sade. It seems wiser to admit that there are facts about values than it is to pretend that moral and aesthetic values leave nothing to guide a choice beyond personal or communal preferences. And it seems pretty clear that the same is true in theory choice in the sciences: The critical criteria include value notions that are hardly subjective at all.

It's problematic (to put it nicely) to pretend that since beauty can't be weighed or measured it can't be real. But what about utility, a notion foundational in economics, which makes serious claims to status as a science? And isn't there a version of utility that proves critical in physics, in making sense of the idea of entropy? For differences in energy levels are crucial in the Second Law of Thermodynamics. And the index or outcome of such differences is the ability to do work. Just what counts as work depends pretty gravely on what kind of work one has in mind and how it is to be allocated. But entropy is no less real for that. It's entropy that explains why every organism is mortal and why the Patent Office won't patent a perpetual motion machine. Notice here how a core law of physics opens up onto questions of value in the appraisal of work of any kind.

Biology, as we've noted, clearly makes no sense without the idea of organs and their functions. Nor is there any concept of evolution without the ideas of adaptation and adaptability. All three notions – function, adaptation, and adaptability – involve values that can be measured, in the health of an organism, the relative fertility of a population, and the chances of survival and futurity for a lineage. But none of these numbers exhausts the meaning of what's at stake in such cases. In a way, they barely touch it. For what's at stake is the life and health of an organism, the survival (and potential rise) of a lineage – or, indeed, the sustenance of an econiche, or an ecosystem.

Physiology is empty without the idea of function; and medicine is helpless without that idea. Evolutionary biology is empty without the concept of adaptation. And evolution itself has no future without adaptability. But all three phenomena – function, adaptation, and adaptability – rely on notions of the good. The goods here are local and relative. Indeed, such goods are themselves adaptive. For the term 'reproduction' is a misnomer: Procreative success cannot be left to mere replication, as if living beings and the lineages they project into the future were mineral crystals with no more to them than copying. Anyone who expects offspring to be clones of the self is doomed to disappointment. Evolution depends critically on variance. Only so can evolutionary success allow the lineage of dinosaurs to give rise to birds – or that of simians, to human beings.

Goodness, then, in its protean forms, is not so readily shelved as subjective and dismissed from the domain of science. The dynamism of goodness in its varied forms is part of what makes it real and wins it a rightful place in science. If emergence is a fact of nature, with biological evolution as a paradigm case, value needs to be part of what a scientist needs to keep track of alongside the more familiar "pushmi-pullyu" brands of explanation. So it's worth comparing how the Torah holds up to the light of language the beauty and worth of things that scientism relegates to the unscientific dust heap. God inspects each constituent of the world He has created and sees that it is good in itself and relationally. For each phase of the creation schematized in Genesis anchors the next. Plants make way for animals, wind and water make way for the rise of life, and thought, and even work (Genesis 2:5).

Reductionists, in seeking explanations, face the same sterile end game whether the causal series they trace leads them to ever smaller particles or ever more basic kinds of energy. All along the way, at every phase of their narrative, the source of the drive toward higher modes of being – toward elements, molecules, and compounds, and toward the shores life and thought – the energy behind the local energies is slighted, if not smothered under the blanket notion of complexity. But complexity is not an explanatory term but only an all too generic renaming of a host of trends. Here lies the ancient and original sin of reductionism, treating an outcome as if it were a cause and ignoring the fact that complexity in nature is never uniform but always channeled and never value neutral but always directional and ever more purposive.

What grows increasingly clear, if we dare to press inquiry beyond the limits set by scientism, is that we need a change of register. We need, a broadening if we seek a universal cause, as Genesis challenges us to do. Our quest must be for another kind of cause, not the kind sought or intercepted by our instruments or registered for retention by our sensuous imagination. The causes we need to seek lie beyond those whose action we can map and anticipate as we might chart the results of throwing a switch or casting a spear. Are we well equipped for such a search? Clearly, human psychology is rooted in sensation, anchored in the sight brain, if not more deeply still, in the sense of touch. Are the tools we have of the kind we need if we're to press our inquiries in pursuit of their highest quarry? The causation to be hunted for, if our quest is for a universal cause, must be nothing too specialized and specific. It must be universal. For the vastness of things looms saliently in the vastness of their variety.

Here the Torah's account of creation proves strikingly relevant: We need to look for the source of the good in things, the good that Genesis tells us God saw in all that He created. Good is not something to be assayed with our usual lab tools. Yet the Torah invites us to see it, as God did, in all things. How would so universal a good be recognized in the world's welter? It must lie in a complementarity of the kind we've begun to study when we trace the complementarities in an ecosystem, where the conflict manifest in the diverse species of things, including in the many that are inimical to us, invites us to perceive higher order harmonies.

And how would value of so universal a kind be imparted? Spinoza can help us here again. For the most general character he could name as the universal essence present and particular in anything real is manifest in things not as a *this* or a *such* but simply (or not so simply) as a being, the conatus that Spinoza finds in all things real, their striving to preserve, express, and promote their being. And how would such a good be imparted? By the empowering of things, granting them capabilities not just to be but to persist, to act and express their natures, and (insofar as the universe of other beings around them gives them room and resource) to develop and perfect that nature and raise it to higher phases of reality and expression.

The causality discovered by such thoughts is not (or not wholly) of the sort found in mechanical interactions. We do catch sight of it, of course, in physical resilience and impenetrability. Spinoza saw it even in inertia, as newly understood in terms of persistence. But the conatus of things shows itself more overtly in phenomena like growth and nutrition and, more revealingly, in procreation. We see it in fuller flower in evolution. The underlying causation at the root of creation is all the more prominent when the laws of nature take on the directionality of providence, where the gift of conatus becomes empowerment. It's most strikingly evident in persons. But it's present too in species and in the lineages to which they give rise. For nature is everywhere dynamic in the energies of its constituents, even those that are "inanimate." All things everywhere, at every level of complexity, are active and expressive. Nothing is merely static.

No particular, and a fortiori no species or lineage, is fully defined by its origin or its parts. All beings are, in fact, inchoate, seeking expression, interaction, and development. And higher things, increasingly, as we scan the living taxa, are increasingly self-defined, until we reach the plane or the plateau of persons, where minds come to be and come into play, not just alive to but conscious of the call toward self-expression, self-definition, and self-perfection.

There's complexity, to be sure, in a mud puddle, discernible to any chemist or biologist, and to the keen eye of many an artist. But the capacity that allows persons to reach for self-definition, to *become* a chemist, biologist, or artist, is critical in making persons something higher than the planaria alive or thriving in the still water.

We see hints guiding our attention to God's special kind of causal action in imparting the conatus that is the birthright of all things when we read in Genesis of God's telling the waters to teem with life, birds to fill the air (1:20), and the earth to produce and sustain all sorts of living things (1:24). The same creative grace is celebrated biblically when God charges the animals at large, and human beings specifically, to be fruitful and multiply (1:22, 28). The causality at work is poetically portrayed by metaphors of instruction. God initiates His world by way of words and inaugurates the laws of nature not by magic but by direction, an imperative, as it were. Neoplatonists conceived of providence and creation as effectuated by ideas. For intelligence is an energy undiminished by sharing, but specifying a rule and a role, enriching each recipient without loss to the Giver. But in Genesis the words voicing the creative call are also a blessing.

BEYOND MECHANISM

Maimonides may help us find our way past the barriers of self-censorship erected or respected by naturalists hoping to confine their thinking (and that of others) to the categories of mechanism and its avatars. With his penchant for drawing out the generalizations implicit in categorical judgments, whether in law, in medicine, or here in metaphysics, Maimonides recognizes the global thrust of the biblical imagery of God's inspection of His work, and His finding it good. Being itself is good, he writes: God, he writes, "produces only being, and all being is good." (*Guide* III 10, 17a). Notice the language of the prooftext, presenting the goodness of all that is as though it were a discovery: *God saw all that He had made, and lo, it was very good.* (Genesis 1:31).

Reminding us of the Sages' dictum that the Torah speaks in human language, Maimonides writes that in human terms 'good' means answering to one's purpose. So in reporting that God called the completed world *very good*, Genesis must mean that "all that came to be met God's purpose flawlessly. For a thing might be good and suit one's purpose for a time but later fail. Yet the Torah tells us that all that God made met His purpose and intent and did not fail or break down." (*Guide* III 13, 25ab).

Maimonides' gloss opens up two questions for us: What can we take to be God's purpose, and what has the phrase *very good* to do with permanence? We should tackle the first question first. For the second will lead us on to consider the fuller force of what we might understand by divine causation.

A classic question that the ancient Sophists taught their trainees to pose whenever words like good came up, was "Good for what, and to whom?" Such questions are not out of place here. And it's worth recognizing that the ideas of value most apposite in the sciences are, at least in the first instance, local. Without paradox, that thought is part of the force of the Torah's having God see that *all* that He had made was good. The judgment was metaphysical in scope. It applied to all that God had made, and God had made all that is. How is it that God could see all things as good? The best answer we can give is that some of the most basic properties of things are those that impart stability and allow creatures, animate and inanimate, to interact with another, to bond or keep their distance, to retain the character they have, and even to strike out in new directions. For God does not keep all His creativity to Himself.

God, we observe, did not just declare good what He had made. Still less does Genesis demand that we find good what God made just because He made it. The terms the Torah uses here are objective: *God saw that it was good.* So this is not the goodness of theistic subjectivism or what is sometimes called divine command theory, where the moral weight of what God commands derives simply from the fact that God commanded it. On the contrary, God's commands embody and specify His wisdom, generosity, justice, and grace. It is for this reason that such commands can be scrutinized and found wise and just, even by observers who are not existentially or covenantally committed to them (Deuteronomy 4:6). It is in just such a sense that we are told that God *saw* the goodness in all that He had made: It was a God-given goodness, but manifest to the most objective of external observers, God Himself.

What, then, was God's purpose? Maimonides treads cautiously here. A verse in Proverbs tells us that *The* LORD *made everything for His/its sake* (16:4). The pronoun is ambiguous. If God is the antecedent, the verse is saying that God made all that exists for His own sake. But God has no needs. So was the act of creation a sheer act of will, expressing God's absoluteness? God, I submit, is not so truculent.

"God's will," Maimonides reminds us, in the light of radical monotheism, "is Himself" (*Guide* III 13, 25a). But if God has no needs, why should He find satisfaction in Self-expression? In Isaiah we read that God created all things for His glory (43:7). At first blush those words might seem to bring us full circle. For "God's glory," Maimonides finds, can be another way of referring to God Himself (*Guide* I 64, 83a). But Isaiah's words shed more light than may at first appear. Since God has no needs, His glory would not come in making things for His own satisfaction. Still, Maimonides argues, God's purposes do not lie in making things just for one another's sake – and pointedly not just for ours:

> If you study the book that guides every seeker of truth and so is called the Torah, you will plainly see the point I'm making: In the Account of Creation, from beginning to end, it never says that anything was created just for something else's sake. Of each part of the world, it says that God brought it to be and it met His purpose. That is what it means by *God saw that it was good* (Genesis 1:4) ....
>
> Don't be misled by its saying of the stars, *to light the earth and rule by day and by night* (1:17–18), as if it meant that they were created for that. It is just telling us that this was the nature God chose to give them, shedding light and governing, the same as it says of Adam, *and rule the fish of the sea.* (1:28) – not that we were created to that end, but simply to apprise us of the nature God gave us. (*Guide* III 13, 25ab).

Maimonides finds it especially inept to say that God found value in all that He had made because all His works met our human wants and needs. For there are many things in the universe that we humans do not need, or want, or even know. Maimonides is careful to avoid assuming that our notions of God's presumptive purpose do not become presumptuous and trap us into assuming that the world revolves around us as individuals or as a society, species, or race. That kind of thinking reflects a particularly insidious form of idolatry. So it might be best, with such thoughts in mind, to speak of purposes in the plural: our own and those of others, including other beings, some beyond our reach and perhaps beyond our ken.

Still the use of terms like good in Genesis cautions us not to set aside the idea of purposes altogether. But the purposes here would be universal, pointing to the goals and aims of creatures in much the way that justice and generosity call on us to recognize the creative and expressive purposes of other beings in general and persons in particular, who seek to build their own identity, character, and understanding.

Taking aim at those theologians within or under the influence of the Ash'arite discipline of kalam, Maimonides writes:

> As for the school of thought of those who claim that God does not do this for the sake of that but deny cause and effect and say that He just does as He pleases with no end in view, ours not to ask why: He does what He will, not pursuant to wisdom – they class God's acts as pointless. (*Guide* III 25, 55b)

But nothing in creation is pointless, Maimonides holds, agreeing with Aristotle, that nature does nothing in vain.[57] Pressing the point until it glistens sharply, reflecting the debates between Neoplatonists and Stoics,

---

[57] "God and nature do nothing in vain," Aristotle, *De Caelo* I 4, 271a32, *Politics* I 8, 1256b16, cited at *Guide* II 14, 31a; cf. III 13, 25.

Maimonides draws the conclusion that all things exist, at least in the first instance, for their own sake and only secondarily for the sake of others, as constituents in the harmonious and integrated system of the cosmos (*Guide* III 25, 55ab). Nature is an integrated causal system, and one does not honor God by making Him the sole cause of all events. Such an outlook, in effect, denies the beauty and wisdom of creation itself: God gave all things their own natures. So plants have seeds, and trees bore fruits to propagate their kind before there were any humans to enjoy them (Genesis 1:11). Nature thrives by the use of God's gifts, and God need not be called on to create each tree or plant anew.

We humans are guests at nature's table. But nature does not exist solely and simply for our sake. God, the psalmist says, *feeds the raven chicks when they cry out* (147:9) – but this God does by way of the parents that bring the chicks their food. Springs water the beasts of the wild, and grass is there to feed them, just as there is vegetation to meet our needs, oil for the skin and bread for nourishment. God does not plant, hoe, weed, thresh, mill, knead, or bake our bread. Yet we bless Him for it since He is its ultimate Creator. We have wine to gladden the heart, the Psalmist says. God is not the vintner. Yet we bless Him for creating the fruit of the vine. God provides trees for birds to nest in, hills for the wild goats, rocks for the badgers (104:10–18). We bless God not so as to omit or overlook the proximate causes found in nature but to celebrate Him as the Creator who initiates every such cascade of causes, natural or human, or in the collaborative interplay of the natural with the human.

The psalmist who speaks of God as his shepherd finds reassurance even in the master's chastening rod (23:4). He lets the persona slip slightly; and, reversing the imagery, as if turning around a mirror, voices his delight at the rich table and brimming cup set before him, as if to spite his enemies. Then he turns his eyes back to the sheep that graze under his watch, not fearing the wolves that may watch hungrily nearby. There's a complex of purposes here: The meadows don't exist just for the sheep, and the sheep don't exist just for the shepherd.

The purposes found in nature have not vanished since Maimonides' day. And today's positivist, who abjures teleology, lands in much the same slough as Maimonides' occasionalist bête noire who proves unable to acknowledge such salient natural facts as the uses of bodily organs (*Guide* III 25, 56a). But if we seek the good in the purposes of things, Maimonides urges, the wise answer is to turn to God's grace, His favor directed not just toward us but toward the flourishing of all things: "God's whole purpose was to give being to all that can be in the world we know" (*Guide* III 25, 55b).[58] Each being and each natural kind exists for its own sake and plays its part in nature's larger harmony and economy.

Where, then, is the goodness that Genesis tells us that God saw? Clearly it was present in all God's works, the same that are called perfect in the song of Moses as the Mosaic Torah reaches its climax (Deuteronomy 32:4). Part of what we learn from Maimonides and from the Neoplatonic philosophers whose works he studied is that when it is asked for whose sake God created the world, the best answer is that God created all beings for their own sake (*Guide* III 13, 3.24b). But mere existence would be an empty gift: God empowered His creatures to express their natures and advance in the ways those natures make possible.

Nature, we find, is dynamic throughout: Even what seems to lie most still shows a stalwart drive to persist and express its nature. That is why it makes sense, in my theory of deserts, to speak of mountains, waterfalls, and desert arches as monuments of nature. There's a striving in everything. That is how emergence becomes real: Particles become atoms, atoms join together as molecules, molecules interact to form compounds. But long before chemical processes began, new elements were arising in the stars. And once there were compounds, the powers they received gave them new properties. And just as compounds manifest properties not present in their constituents, living beings can act in ways not describable in terms of the behavior of their constituents: They pursue interests.

Chemical compounds arise and biological evolution results not from any conscious recognition of a goal by the players in those processes but from the conative character of the agents and reagents in their milieu. God's grace is manifest in the welcoming milieu, pregnant with the possibility of life, but most tellingly in the fact that living beings *have* interests. The very concept of an organism reflects that fact. What we see

---

[58] God created not every conceivable being. For "nature followed His wisdom's decree" (*Guide* III 25, 55b). Plotinus anticipates the point, making special reference to the problem of evil: The Reason-Principle, he argues, cannot desire that all things will prove welcome to us. The divine will ordains the world we know: "An artist would not make an animal all eyes; and in the same way, the Reason-Principle would not make all divine ... all is graded succession, and this in no spirit of grudging but in the expression of a Reason teeming with intellectual variety." *Enneads* 3.2.11, tr. MacKenna, 170. As Lovejoy noted, Plotinus here links the principle of plentitude to the idea of the great chain of being. Lovejoy, *The Great Chain of Being*, 82. The celebratory tones of the philosopher are by no means muted here and by no means unechoed by many successors.

here, in emergence, and specifically in the rise and increasing richness and relevance of the idea of interests, is a paradigm case of the kind of causality we need to be alive to if we're to pursue the quest for ultimate and universal causality that religion and science undertook from the outset of their most serious and thoughtful inquiries.

4

God and Value

That truth is a value is clearly signaled when God is called the Truth.[1] The value-ladenness of truth is evident in another light as well, when postmodernists speak out against objective truth, and its cousin right, as ghosts of God. Here was what Nietzsche meant by asking, "Have they not heard? Can it be that they have not heard that God is dead?" Atheism could be taken for granted, Nietzsche assumed. But he painted Zarathustra's dismay at the thought that moral realism survived: People still seemed to see objectivity in values. They failed to see that without God everything was permitted and that they were now the moral arbiters.

That, as Maimonides reads the drama of Genesis, was just what the serpent promised Adam and Eve – although the serpent, being a serpent, of course spoke with forked tongue. Symbolically, the serpent was imagination, and what he promised those archetypes of our humanity in telling them that they would be like gods was that they would now be moral arbiters. But in reaching for that brass ring, taking our human preferences to be self-validating, we humans are not elevated or divinized but degraded, learning to spurn the counsels of God-given reason and pursue the specious goods of appetite, passion, and – perhaps most fatally – convention (*Guide* I 2).

More recent theorists readily drop mention of God and sever the arteries of moral realism by saying simply that there are no values without a valuer, as if that bit of grammar somehow proved that there are no moral facts. For these recent theorists can now see many who take it for

---

[1] See Jeremiah 10:10; cf. Saadiah, on Job 34:17, *The Book of Theodicy*, tr. Goodman, 359–60.

granted that God is dead and need no Zarathustra to inform them of the implications. Some existentialists shed crocodile tears about forlornness, bathing publicly in the grief they suffer at the absence of a moral guide, be it Kantian or canonical. Others, of pragmatist background, speak longingly of an ideal observer. But even as they do, they reserve to the regency of private (or social) conscience, however self-serving or manipulated, the decisions they deem consequential, whether regarding alcohol or drugs, abortion, sexual orientation, gender choice, military service, civil and uncivil disobedience.

But realism about values, the hard-won lesson of the binding of Isaac, does not mean making God the arbitrary arbiter of value – as in the familiar strawman version of Divine Command Theory, better described as theistic subjectivism. That is why Abraham can be welcomed for his piety (and called God's beloved, *ohavi*, Isaiah 41:8), even though – and indeed because – he has *not* sacrificed his son. It was at Mount Moriah that God's true character was seen, as Abraham proclaimed when he gave the height to which God had led him the name Har ha-Moriah, the Mount where God revealed Himself (Genesis 22:14). For it was there, at that critical juncture, that God revealed to all capable of grasping Abraham's discovery, that God and His justice, as Maimonides put it, are inseparable (*Guide* 3.35a).[2] The equation of justice with truth is a core theme in our biblical and rabbinic texts, perhaps most prominent in the epiphany to Moses when God declares Himself *abundant in grace and truth* (Exodus 34:6). *Grace* here is *hesed*, favor beyond desert; and truth is justice.

Moses, as we've seen had a practical goal in seeking to know God. He needed to understand God's governance, so as to model his own leadership on the pattern of God's rule:

"Look, You told me to bring this people up to the land. But You have not told me of anyone You will send with me. You said, 'I singled you out by name', and told me that I found favor with You. But now, please, if I am truly favored by You, teach me Your ways, that by knowing You I may keep Your favor. For this nation is Your people." (Exodus 33:12–13).

The guidance Moses seeks is that of a statesman. He wants to know God's ways of governance. God had indeed singled Moses out, called him by name. And He had called Israel His people (3:4, 7). He had charged

---

[2] There is no "teleological suspension of the ethical" here. See Goodman, *God of Abraham*, chapter 1.

Moses to lead Israel to the land long promised to their ancestors (3:8, 6:8), and God has confirmed that Moses has His favor (33:17). But to deserve continuance of that favor, Moses now needs God to teach him how to lead. He asks God to make known to him concretely the ways by which He governs. Hence the content of the new epiphany. God, Moses is told, has no face that any living man can see (33:20). But rather than reveal any putative essence that might invite idolatrous reduction, God proclaims His presence by the renewed utterance of the name Moses had heard at the burning bush, giving voice to His absoluteness. But now that name is swiftly followed by the attributes that mark His rule:

LORD! LORD! *A God Merciful and gracious, slow to anger and abundant in grace and truth, preserving grace thousandsfold, bearing with wrongdoing, sin, and evil, but not leaving guilt unrequited.* (Exodus 34:6–7)

Along with those words comes the epiphany biblically called seeing God's back (33:23). God, of course, no more has a back than a face. Hence the gloss Maimonides proposes: Moses was shown the panoply of nature, what follows in God's wake, as it were. For it is in the governance of nature that God reveals the tenor of His rule.[3] Grace is the core theme of that governance, most visible in the wisdom of nature's design by which creatures are enabled and empowered to survive and advance their interests – and, indeed, to have interests to advance. But in the words Moses hears and reports, grace is coupled with justice under the gentler name of truth. For God's grace in nature is abundant but not boundless. Creation is an act of grace to every creature. And truth is what we recognize in the claims of any creature, affirming but also setting limits to the gift of being and the claims to be made in its name, as justice must acquit them, lest any creature (as all seek boundlessness) overwhelm the world and destroy itself and all the rest. The instruments of God's natural justice, like the gifts of God's grace, come in the bounties creatures open to one another and the limits creatures set to one another's claims.

It is at the core of the equation of truth with justice, the pivot point, as it were, on which that equation spins, that we find the idea of deserts: All beings deserve to be treated in recognition of what each being is. The essence of a being is its conatus, its project and its striving to be and to persist, to project, express, and perfect itself as the being that it is. So the practical recognition that most matters in morals lies in the treatment of a being as what it is. Such recognition won't imply or permit passivity in the

---

[3] *Guide* I 54; cf. I 21, 25b-26a; and *MT* Laws of the Foundations of the Torah 1.10.

face of onslaughts from beings that are what they are by harming or destroying others. So we have no compunction about combating the deadly bacteria or viruses that live or reach for life by attacking us or what matters to us. Justice as truth does not mean making our dwellings a home for termites, or our blood vessels a habitat for filarial worms. Nor does justice bar us from containing, restraining, indeed executing others when they have so strayed from their humanity as to negate it by making a blight or a danger of their powers. "No fool is more fatuous," Maimonides writes, "than one who claims that it is humane to abolish punishment. That would be the height of inhumanity and the ruin of civil order. Real compassion is what God commanded: *Judges and magistrates shalt thou appoint in all thy gates*" (Deuteronomy 16:18, cited at *Guide* III 33, 75b).

We rightly abhor wanton destruction in nature and in our civil and social millieu, and we rightly avoid imposing undue pain and suffering on other creatures. Such concerns are the least of justice, but they are its leading edge. For to flout or violate such minima gives entry to cruelties that can grow to more general and vicious varieties of injustice. But the positive side of justice has a life of its own, calling on us to support and sustain the life and development of other beings and the self-expression of our fellow human beings.

We have both perfect and imperfect obligations toward any moral subject: Perfect obligations not to harm or thwart the innocent lives of other persons and their innocent self-expression and open-ended (and thus imperfect) obligations to support and sustain the physical, moral, intellectual, and spiritual development of others – our children and spouse, in the first instance, as unique individuals who become our charge by nature, in the case of offspring, and by covenant, in the case of the person we espouse. Due recognition must be tailored to the needs and aspirations of those we hope to help. It can extend well beyond the immediate family to others with whom we have bonds of kinship, fellowship, and formal or informal reciprocity. And there are comparable obligations, if less deep and lasting, of teachers toward their students, of doctors and other caregivers toward their patients and the patients' loved ones, and many another category of advisor or helper. Even customers and clients in a working or commercial relationship can expect comparable consideration of their personhood – minimally in the form of civility and courtesy and some level of presumptive trust. All such relations command and, typically if tacitly, elicit a commensurate response. One of the pervasive tasks of any culture is to modulate and regulate the informal bonds without which none of the more readily articulated and more typically formalized or ritualized channels of human relationship would be workable.[4]

None of these moral obligations spring simply from a divine fiat. Yet all of them are readily recognized as ordained by God. For these obligations are existential, reflective of the social nature of our species, our interdependence, not just for the niceties and necessities of life but for the framing and flourishing of human identities and personalities. Our most basic duties and the corresponding rights, in other words, belong to us because of who and what we are. They are deepened and elaborated by the actions we undertake and the relations we establish. So, like any right or obligation, they stand under God's eyes. We can read of them in the Torah, not least in the Decalogue, where murder, kidnapping, adultery, and even covetous thoughts, desires, and intentions are forbidden; but also in Leviticus (19:11–18), where we are commanded not to curse the deaf or set a stumbling block in the path of the blind (or play upon another's weaknesses) but commanded also to reprove others (tactfully and privately, the Rabbis advise) when we see them embarked on an erring course. It is here, in grounding our obligation not to indulge ourselves in schadenfreude when see another slipping morally, that our broader duty is invoked: to regard and treat the interests of others as our own, or, as the Torah puts it, to love one another as we love ourselves. It is not because God or the state or society imposed such duties on us that we have these obligations.

Nor is it because we have agreed to do so. It is because of what we and those others are, to us and in themselves. Social mores and societal strictures and structures do seek to regulate our natural and existential obligations. But that is a task, or a system of tasks, that rules and mores, including the formal norms of law and ritual, may perform well or badly. Such variance (and the resulting ability and need for societies to learn from one another) is clear evidence that society is not the ultimate source or judge of the rights and duties of persons. For corrigibility, as Plato's Socrates so often showed, is the clearest proof of the presence of an objective truth of the matter. What moral corrigibility points to here is the fact that our deserts and those of others are not conventional but existential.

None of our most basic obligations can in practice be merely imposed or dissolved by the state, by social agencies or conventions, or even by

---

[4] See Goodman, *On Justice*, chapter 1.

personal choices. Rather, our most basic obligations, to ourselves and to others – to beings of all kinds and those most intensive and enduring obligations owed to our intimates and our offspring – arise in what we are. They come from God in the sense that God is our ultimate Author and is thus the metaphoric Guardian and Legislator of the obligations that we, as moral subjects, bear toward one another and toward all beings: our obligations to act in recognition of what each being is.

Appeal is often made to God when a need is felt to invoke a higher – that is, more objective – standard than those seemingly on offer by merely temporal authority. But the real source of our deep existential obligations (and the mutuality they engender) is the moral logic of subjecthood itself. And since our being is both social and dynamic, it is in and through our identities as persons and thus as social beings that the unfailing judgment of divine justice most readily strikes home: The innocent may suffer and indeed may die. But they suffer and die as innocents. The vicious may seem to profit and prosper through their vices. But they live in moral squalor, having damaged or destroyed within themselves what was most precious in their humanity long before any external accountancy may overtake them or even find them out. For they have made monsters of themselves, and no one would choose to live with a monster. But that is the sentence that every moral monster imposes on himself.

Not all values are moral values. Political values stand nearby, leaning on moral values. And there are aesthetic values too. Truth, I hold, anchors all of these. For all deserts, moral, political, and aesthetic are rooted in the being of things, in what each being is, in itself and in its context. Truth, as I've suggested, is not to be found among the sensations from which a strict empiricism seeks to construct an epistemology and a world. Since truths can be recognized, we may say they can be seen. But truths are not sensations, despite the warm feelings adduced by the sentimentalist school of the Enlightenment era. For sentiments are corrigible, and truths are not. By the same token, today's fashionable deference to empathy as a moral gauge comes no closer to building a moral meter than Bentham did in proposing the pleasure-pain calculus as an empiric gauge of right and wrong.[5]

Truth is a tree with many trunks. But all of them, like the branching trunks of Deborah's palm tree, spring from a single body. My hope in this final chapter is to trace the linkage of artistic, moral, and political truth to

---

[5] For a modest deflation of the empathy balloon, see *Love Thy Neighbor*, 3–5.

one another, anchored in truth itself in its fullest, richest sense. I'd like to start with truth in art. For artistic truth may seem the most elusive, partly because convention, deferentially, even obsequiously, but overconfidently marks artistic appraisals as subjective, as if they were, somehow, territorial rivals to truth itself. My own thoughts here lie closer to those of Keats. I see no mere romantic effusion or aestheticist manifesto but a profound insight in the lines that close his Ode on a Grecian Urn:

> Beauty is truth, truth beauty, – that is all
> Ye know on earth, and all ye need to know.

ARTISTIC TRUTH

The easy way out in disputes about truth in art is to concede that beauty is in the eye of the beholder. If so, it would seem that no taste can be mistaken and no aesthetic judgment can be wrong. But that outcome would yield a gaggle of paradoxes. In cases of disagreement, a would-be aesthetic realist might be tempted to call on others to confirm his aesthetic judgments. But that would soon mean retreat to some variety of cultural or class-based relativism at odds with the realist's intent and at risk of narrow and dogmatic, perhaps chauvinistic appeals smacking of some tribal or elitist affinity.

A wiser option awaits in the approach that John Dewey learned from Albert Barnes and that Barnes himself had learned when his childhood friend, the painter William Glackens, taught him how to look at a painting. Rather than project judgments of aesthetic success on the object or introject them into the mind of the beholder (as though it hardly mattered just what an artist had done or tried to do), Dewey locates aesthetic value in the aesthetic experience, a relational place that remains empty without reference to an actual artwork and its means and matter, in dialogue with the sensibilities of a beholder.

Such an interactive approach resonates with the relational metaphysics mooted by C. S. Peirce and developed in ethics, with broad appreciation of the Judaic roots of such ethical concerns, in Martin Buber's I-thou strategy. Here human relations are placed, even ontologically, ahead of both subject and object. Ulric Neisser, used his presidential address to the American Psychological Association to introduce his colleagues to Buber and help wean them away from the scientistic dogmas of Behaviorism.[6] The relational approach speaks to our questions about truth in art

---

[6] See Neisser, "Five Kinds of Self-Knowledge."

because it sees art in terms of communication. And communication always needs and seeks a medium. But the medium in artistic expression is not just the paint and canvas, stone or bronze, or the performance on stage or on the printed page. It comes to life in the mind, giving color to subjectivism – but only if one ignores the creativity of the artist and the centrality of the vehicle that any artist must use to share artistic impulses or inspirations and bring them to birth in a world beyond the inner world that first gave them life.

Here's what Dewey wrote on what he called the delicate topic of the connection of aesthetic effect with the qualities of all experience:

> I would ask how art can be expressive and yet not be imitative or slavishly representative, save by selecting and ordering the energies in virtue of which things act upon us and interest us? If art is in any sense reproductive, and yet reproduces neither details nor generic features, it necessarily follows that art operates by selecting those potencies in things by which an experience – any experience – has significance and value. Elimination gets rid of forces that confuse, distract, and deaden. Order, rhythm and balance simply means that energies significant for experience are acting at their best … there is a definite sense in which art is ideal …. Through selection and organization those features that make any experience worth having as an experience are prepared by art for commensurate perception. There must be, in spite of all indifference and hostility of nature to human interests, some congruity of nature with man or life could not exist. In art the forces that are congenial, that sustain not this or that special aim but the processes of enjoyed experience itself, are set free. That release gives them an ideal quality. For what ideal can man honestly entertain save the idea of an environment in which all things conspire to the perfecting and sustaining of the values occasionally and partially experienced?[7]

It might help to gloss a few words here. By 'reproductive' I suspect that Dewey meant what others might call mimetic. But the core idea comes through: Art, as Aristotle taught us, aims to reflect or represent things – or, in the terms that Dewey favors, aspects of experience. It's in choosing the facets of experience to be represented that much of the expressive contribution of a creative mind typically finds its first domain of choice. 'Elimination' is another term to gloss here. I think Dewey means abstraction. And when he speaks of order, rhythm, and balance, he seems to be reaching for the formal dimensions that make an artwork identifiable as art and allow the painter, poet, musician, sculptor, or novelist to use (and show off) artistic skills and talents to shape how the representation will be presented.

---

[7] Dewey, *Art as Experience*, 185.

Beyond those glosses, in fairness to Dewey, I think one needs to read his use of the word 'ideal' here with rather less gingham print colors than he may seem to give it. He acknowledges that "sentimental and popular use" has cheapened the term; and he charges that its apologetic use among philosophers, as he puts it, has made it a way of disguising discords and cruelties. I don't think it's fair or productive to read Dewey's appraisal of art, meant to register in the most general and generic terms he can muster, as requiring that all art must be cheerful. If art is to explore experience and capture its varied aspects, any facet is fair game. Suffering is no more foreign to artistic capture than delight. A still-life may contain a memento mori, and Primo Levi is no less an artist than Rosa Bonheur. A pollyanna-ish cast can make any work ring false.

Perhaps the rule of charity might permit replacement of Dewey's 'congenial' with terms of broader reach. Not all art is or need be edifying or instructive. But neither are representations meant merely or mostly to shock or offend well qualified as art. Yellow journalism is borderline as journalism, and pornography sidles away from artistic values toward more exploitative interests. Surely not all art need be uplifting, but an artwork does seem to pass an important test if it provokes some sort of YES! That thought fits well with our contention that art has value in part because it can convey a truth.

Stephen Pepper, an established writer among specialists in the philosophy of art (a guild to which Dewey did not belong before writing *Art as Experience*), tells in the Schilpp volume devoted to Dewey's philosophy of the letdown he felt on reading that book when it appeared in 1934. He had tried himself, he writes, to anticipate what a pragmatist philosophy of art might look like and found "that all of the features I had thought important were emphasized by Dewey, together with others along the same line revealing further insights that I had not previously noticed." But Pepper was disappointed and dismayed "to find Dewey saying many things which I had deliberately excluded from my tentative pragmatic account" – thoughts that seemed "contrary to the spirit of pragmatism." They were, in fact, "things which an organic idealist would have said, and which I should have thought Dewey would rather have bitten his tongue than to have said."[8]

---

[8] See Pepper, "Some Questions on Dewey's Esthetics," 371. Dewey, we should recall, began his encounter with philosophy through an engagement with Hegel, reflected in his 1897 lecture on Hegel at the University of Chicago. John R. Shook and James A. Good reflect on Hegel's lasting impact on Dewey in *John Dewey's Philosophy of Spirit*, which reprints that lecture.

Dewey's heresies, Pepper finds, had turned him inconsistent, affirming "a view he has often vigorously repudiated."[9] He had so dwelt on "the organic character of art" as to lead to the suspicion that he was "reverting to Hegelianism in his later years." Convinced of his own correctness about the thrust of a pragmatist aesthetics, Pepper concluded, "it was Dewey who had here gone astray." Much that Dewey had committed to the page, Pepper felt sure, "should not be said by a pragmatist." For "an organistic esthetics cannot be harmonized with a pragmatic esthetics." Moreover, "much of Dewey's polemic against Platonic and materialistic theories loses its force, unless he comes to terms" with the muddle produced by yoking together inconsistent esthetic theories.[10]

Citing Bosanquet as the accredited exponent of an organicist view, Pepper calendars six theses of the offending view:[11]

1. Experience in general is coherent or interconnected. So we adequately apprehend an experience when we discover and make explicit the implicit coherence of the fragments in which experience is originally found.

Pepper's reference to the fragmentary character of experience echoes William James' famous "blooming, buzzing confusion" characterization. So Bosanquet's premise parallels James' rather Kantian assumption that it is up to us (that is, to one's consciousness) to find or make coherence out of what might otherwise seem sheer disorder. 'Experience' thus becomes a success term, as it was for Kant, marking the differences between, say, dreaming and waking, or between sanity and madness.

Applied to art, Bosanquet's view would make an artist's work much like that of a scientist: In different ways both are trying to make sense of life. But Bosanquet's offense, in Pepper's eyes, it seems, was to assume that coherence was there to be discovered, even before such work was done. Dewey had sinned by following Bosanquet into a kind of realism, as if ignoring the fact that there is no order in experience until one puts it there.

2. Value in a finite or fragmentary experience is proportional to the degree of coherence achieved in it.

Here the "organicist" compounds the initial sin of his first assumption.

---

[9] Pepper in Schilpp, "Some Questions on Dewey's Esthetics," 371.
[10] Pepper in Schilpp, "Some Questions on Dewey's Esthetics," 372.
[11] Pepper in Schilpp, "Some Questions on Dewey's Esthetics," 372–75.

3. Value depends entirely on the organization of materials. So truth would be "an organization of judgments," moral goodness, "an organization of acts," beauty, "an organization of feelings."

Pepper seems to cast the organicist as a sort of Platonist – or a Platonist manqué, lacking Platonic forms to allow truth its reference to the higher reality that Plato found in the forms. The organicist, as a result, becomes a coherentist of sorts. Pepper's critique does lay bare a feature of Kant's Socratic expectation of coherence in morals. But that feature becomes a weakness only if one boosts coherence to a sufficient criterion of moral rightness rather than a necessary condition of it.

The fault Pepper finds in an organistic aesthetics lies in the formalism he imputes to Dewey's account: It ignores the *quality* of an experience, he writes, as if echoing the term 'qualia' introduced by C. S. Peirce in 1927. Pepper seems keen to call attention back to the material, sensuous dimensions of an aesthetic experience, which he corrals under the (Humean) term "vividness," as contrasted with the formal dimensions of an artwork, suggested by the term organization. He uses the words extensivity, immediacy, and depth to name key dimensions of such an experience, which, he writes, may reach a climax of sorts in what "may be called a 'seizure.'"[12] The three terms do register rather vague, not least against the call for aesthetic vividness. But Pepper's final phrase, seemingly meant to clinch the case, echoes Stoic hopes that katalepsis can protect judgments from doubt once they are firmly grasped as "apprehensions." Such language may reflect the high drama of the most gratifying aesthetic experiences. But it does ring rather personal and idiosyncratic if meant to reach the generality one might have expected in a general theory.

Still, to assume that theorists who accept Pepper's organicist strawman must ignore the material side of an artwork or the sensuous dimensions of an aesthetic experience seems simply untrue. I can't help recalling Kenneth Clark's fine response to the notion that if a nude elicits any erotic response at all, it is false art or bad morals. Clark's reply: "No nude, however abstract, should fail to arouse in the spectator some vestige of erotic feeling, even if only the faintest shadow – and if it does not do so it is bad art and false morals."[13] Does an "organicist" who thinks Clark had a point somehow contradict his commitments? I don't think the experience of art is quite so regimented as Pepper would have it.

---

[12] Pepper in Schilpp, "Some Questions on Dewey's Esthetics," 375.
[13] Clark, *The Nude*, 30.

4. One more organicist heresy: "The greatness of a work of art is judged by the degree of imaginative construction it contains." The artist "draws materials together out of experience and exhibits their coherence" whereas a good appreciative critic "follows the coherence" that the artist has achieved.[14] Again, everything depends on organization.

It's worth passing over the final two bolts in Pepper's pillory. His charge is that "organicists" are single-mindedly committed to a coherentist, thus formalist, conception of what artists do, how they do it, and how they succeed when they do. The alternative Pepper offers seems to aim for the more contextual, more situated, more sensuous, qualitative, even material side of art. But much of his animus is entrusted to rather murky claims about the "fusing" or "funding" of "certain of" the "relational phases" of an experience, aiming for an immediacy bearing degrees of vividness. "In a broad sense," he writes, "(and perhaps in a final sense) the esthetic field can be identified with that of the qualitative phase of experience."[15] It may grow increasingly hard for passing generations to say just what this might mean as the code words here have lost the glow that once gave them meaning.

Surely the sensuous side of art was not lost on Picasso or Matisse, Pissarro, Gauguin, Cezanne, Degas, Renoir, Monet, or Van Gogh. What Monet could see in a rocky coastline, a cathedral exterior, or a haystack, Van Gogh could discover in the play of light on a terrace by night, and Degas could find in the steamy flesh of a bather drying off, or the sweat of women ironing clothes. Nor is it likely that the material context in which artistic works or performances are produced was unknown or ignored in the aesthetic that Glackens imparted to Barnes and Barnes to Dewey. If Dewey learned to look at an artwork in broader terms than Pepper's pragmatist constraints permit, so much the worse for any narrow orthodoxy that attempts to prescribe what art shall be or shall have been.

Perhaps the most self-betraying phrase in Pepper's polemic is his describing artistic experience as "an enduring historical process with a past sloughing off, a central present, and a future coming in."[16] One of the beauties of art as such is the power an artwork has to transcend the limits of its immediate cultural or historical context and reach beyond its moment to other times and places. It's in that sense that art can be

---

[14] Pepper in Schilpp, "Some Questions on Dewey's Esthetics," 374.
[15] Pepper in Schilpp, "Some Questions on Dewey's Esthetics," 375; he details his critique in the pages that follow.
[16] Pepper in Schilpp, "Some Questions on Dewey's Esthetics," 374.

timeless and may even become, in some ways universal. So it was a revelatory moment when Monet or Van Gogh first saw ukiyo-e prints and equally revelatory when Hokusai first saw postcards bearing scenes using vanishing-point perspective, a convention not then in use in Japan. But Hokusai was a natural. He immediately saw what those Western artists were about and recruited the new device into his own repertoire.

There are truths in human experience and in the world itself; and part of the magic and mission of art is to discover them, lest, in life's urgency and haste, one might have missed them. The historicist dogma that the past is somehow sloughed off betrays a parochialism sustained in part by notions of unilinear progress or lockstep progression in artistic tastes, techniques, and idioms. That sort of outlook weakens the vision of those critics who fail to see Andrew Wyeth's greatness as a painter, more in Albrecht Dürer's league than in David Hockney's. Picasso knew better than to closet himself in Montmartre. He was open to discover the energies salient to his sensibilities in the African masks on display as ethnographic exhibits in the Trocadero. Gauguin, similarly, found aesthetic and spiritual energies in Tahiti that he had missed in Europe. Rembrandt sees beyond his moment when he paints Aristotle, wearing the chain and medallion given him by Alexander, as the philosopher contemplates Homer's bust and reflects on what he learned from the *Odyssey*, about the chasm separating civil and civilized human beings from the Cyclopes, who live without the humanizing institutions of the polis. Here were insights Aristotle could set forth in well-argued lectures, where Homer had counted on the vivid (yes, vivid) fantasies of epic poetry.

Was it Dewey's sin, as Pepper sees it, to presume that structure and coherence are already present in experience or even in the matter from which experience is constructed? Had Dewey presumed that an artist, like a scientist, does not just impose structures or invent coherence on the tattered cloth but discovers them? If so, how was Pepper any less an idealist than he charges Dewey with becoming or remaining? If the pragmatist's boast is to have sidestepped metaphysics, is it less metaphysical to deny that nature, or experience, or life itself has a meaning, or meanings, to be discovered, than to deny that meanings are present before an artist puts them there?

My daughter Allegra Goodman is a pretty well-known novelist. Once, when giving a talk, she was asked where her sense of humor came from. She answered, "From paying attention." That makes sense to me, and I can testify that in her case it's true. Back at 30,000 feet, where philosophers are meant to fly, one can say that if there are elements of coherence in experience and even truths latent in nature or in life, it will make sense to wonder where they came from and to see some sense in the very old idea of inspiration, especially if we can strip it of Bullfinchery. Maybe some of the sense of things comes from the way things are. Consciousness, as James argued, would not have evolved, were that not so. For it would have had no adaptive value.

ART AND TRUTH

Artists and their advocates protect their artistic independence jealously, given the long history of efforts to shake off subservience to the Church and other patrons of painting, music, statuary, and the architecture of public spaces. Aesthetic values did survive; and they often flourished under such patronage, whether by gladly offering up the fruits of virtuosity as gifts to a higher echelon and its arbiters and servitors or by allowing the buds of creativity to peep out in muted expressions of artistic freedom. For not every value is so readily subsumed under the presumptive dominance of the highest.

Modern aesthetes prize expressions of artistic independence, celebrating their emergence in insouciance or satire, aesthetic tours de force, or subtle ambiguity. We can see that in the joy that critics take in Chaucer or Bocaccio, or in the brilliant detachment of Hamadhani, or the wine poems of Abu Nuwas. But the welcome given and deserved by art for art's sake or music for music's sake need not trap us in the illusion that sacred art was somehow merely trammeled or inevitably insincere. Nor should we let aestheticism cordon off from the rest artistic work that finds or seeks a calling beyond the liens of church or state. Great artists are not deaf to the varied calls of truth itself, sometimes found within a contractual mission and sometimes declaring spiritual independence of them

Isaac Levitan (1860–1900), a Russian Jewish artist, seems to me an exemplary exponent of truth in art, painting a truth that he could see, not so panoramically drawn as Homer's truths, or Shakespeare's, but no less skillfully captured in the keen aperture opened by an artist's eye. Growing up dirt poor and, as a Jew, long barred from life in Moscow, Levitan grew to a major talent as a landscape painter. His intensive work ethic was grounded in a love of the Russian outdoors and sparked by the talent he was able to hone by diligent training and personal exploration. He came to win artistic recognition and the support of patrons with a keen aesthetic eye of their own. His lifestyle was bohemian; his love life, Byronic –

but without Byron's title or wealth. He died before turning forty, apparently from aortic infections caused by tertiary syphilis. His close friendship with Anton Chekhov, dating from their student days, was fired by their mutual recognition of the kindred sources of their artistic power. For, as Levitan and Chekhov understood about each other's art, Levitan's empathic response to nature had its counterpart in Chekhov's power in reaching the interiority of the figures he brought to life in his stories and on the stage.

Landscape painting was not a highly esteemed genre in Russia during Levitan's formative years. Genre painting was seen, conventionally, as more relevant, as it was in Victorian England, for its ability to capture human foibles and to convey Dickensian moral and social messages and critiques. But Levitan's eye caught something in the Russian landscape that held his gaze. What he saw has its counterparts in some of the work of Winslow Homer and more particularly in the paintings of Thomas Cole and George Inness: something spiritual that spoke to him and that he was moved, almost to the point of compulsion, to convey to others.

The power of a Levitan landscape, like that in an Inness, springs from the subtlety he used in sharing something of what he saw in the birch woods and frigid ponds of Russia. The emotions that such vistas awakened in him and that he (like Inness) worked successfully to communicate, belonged to the artist and to those with whom he shared his work. The values that work conveyed came from the scene itself that had inspired him. But his apprehension and retention of those values and his skill in expressing them in paint gives those who view his work a redoubled pleasure in his virtuosity alongside the memory of their own encounters with a landscape no longer quite so familiar.

The diligent work of artists and thoughtful focus of viewers is what makes such sharing possible. The play of light and memory, the stillness of the grass or rustling in the trees, the vibrancy of life and the visible reminders of the moment's brevity were all present and visually conveyed. Painting here was not just a matter of reducing the three dimensions of lived space to the two projected onto a canvas. It was the sense evoked by an objective correlative: There was something real here that the artist had seen and felt and that he had the skill meaningfully to invite others to share.

In his dual biography of the friendship of Levitan and Chekhov, Serge Gregory tells of Chekhov's several stories committed to the presumptively impossible task of translating into words something like a counterpart of Levitan's vision. Chekhov's "masterpiece," a story titled "The Steppe,"

Gregory writes, "written quickly in January 1888," was a bit of a publication breakthrough for the young doctor. It "resembles not so much a landscape painting as a landscape film, a long tracking shot of the unfolding expanse of the steppe as seen by the nine-year-old Yegorushka from the back of a slow moving wagon . . . .

> The steppe moving before his eyes is rendered in ever-changing colors that create a succession of moods. In the early morning, the far hills are 'lilac-hued'; sunlight first appears as bright stripes and then completely drenches the grassland in dew. But by mid- day, he writes, "the air grew still and the disappointed steppe took on its despondent July appearance. The grass drooped, the life went out of everything. The sunburned hills, brown-green and – in the distance – violet colored, with dark hues of peaceful shade… now seemed endless and numb with misery. Toward the end of the day "submissive nature became stunned into silence." As the sun set, "fed up and losing patience, the hills and the air could no longer stand the oppressiveness and tried to cast off its yoke. Behind the hills, a curly ash-gray cloud unexpectedly appeared. It exchanged glances with the steppe, as if to say, 'I'm ready' and frowned."[17]

In the anthropomorphizing of nature and its changing moods, Gregory finds a key to Chekhov's empathy with Levitan, and to Levitan's empathy with nature. "In this most 'Levitan-like' story," Gregory writes, "Chekhov found a way to use his imagination and precise observation to make the natural world reflect human feelings."[18] There is anthropomorphism here but no pathetic fallacy. Quite the contrary. Rather than project human passions onto nature, here it's nature that evokes the passions of the artist.

Writing to Chekhov of his response to the vista of the Volga, Levitan departs far enough from his usual metier to put into words the emotions that came to life in his art:

> I've never so loved nature, never been so sensitive to her, never have so strongly felt this divine something, suffusing everything but not visible to everyone that you can't even name because it isn't subject to reason, analysis, and is only comprehensible by love. Without this feeling it's not possible to be a real artist. Many people won't understand; they'll call it, if you will, romantic nonsense – so what! They are being sensible. But this insight of mine is for me the source of deep suffering. Can anything be more tragic than to feel the eternal beauty of everything that surrounds you, to comprehend a deep secret, to see God in everything and to be unable, recognizing your powerlessness, to express this deep feeling?[19]

---

[17] Gregory, *Antosha and Levitasha*, 50–51. [18] Gregory, *Antosha and Levitasha*, 51.
[19] Gregory, *Antosha and Levitasha*, 51.

Levitan, as Gregory explains, had absorbed from a well-read friend the sense of something false in Romanticism, perhaps because romantics pretended to present something too vast and profound for mere art to capture – even as they showed off the pelts of their quarry. But we need not share the snobbery of Levitan's friend. There is profundity in Keats and pretentiousness at times in Shelley. But there's truth, too, sometimes confessional, sometimes celebratory, often satirical in, say, Byron's *Don Juan*. We should take truth where we find it, as Aristotle advised in surveying his own intellectual landscape. No one will capture truth entire and bring it home alive, as Peter (with some help) brought home his wolf. Levitan caught a basketful. His tragedy lay not in the impossibility of communication nor in the inevitable limitation of the powers he felt so keenly but in the early death resulting from a medical and moral ignorance that his friend Chekhov did not quite so fully share.

Beauty as truth or truth as beauty has many voices, as many as the aspects of all things in nature and beyond it. So it was with due humility that Dürer wrote, "I know not what the ultimate measure of true beauty is, and cannot describe it aright." He had a keen awareness of his own eye's keen vision. But along with this came a fitting humility before nature's vastness and what he sensed must lie beyond it. So he added, "I believe no man alive can grasp the whole beauty of the meanest living creature. God alone knows such things."[20] Dürer could see beauty in the truth of all things, although always convinced that God could see more. For an artist must choose the objects to let his eye fall on. But the primary Artist saw all, beholding and appreciating the inmost workings of all that He had made, and delighting in His creation, when he called the whole of it *very good*.

Beyond the work of Levitan, consider another landscape artist's masterpiece, Frederick Church's *Twilight in the Wilderness*. Painted in 1860, the scene is dominated by a vast and portentous sky. Color is the key to the work's power, and Church carefully chose the colors that gave his work its power: madder lake, stone yellow, Indian red, lead white, vermillion, red lead, strontium yellow, chrome yellow, cadmium yellow, chrome green, green earth, umber, ultramarine, and Prussian blue. Prussian blue, the first modern synthetic pigment, was invented in the early eighteenth century, its presence usable today to detect counterfeits among supposedly medieval Persian miniatures. The pigments Church

---

[20] Dürer, *Literary Remains*, 224–25.

ordered and deployed were critical to the impact he hoped his work would have: He wanted his sky to be truthful to the scenes he had seen and to the emotions those experiences had aroused in him. I've been privileged to see Dürer's home in Nurnberg and the room he devoted to mixing his colors. He too was committed to truth in conveying what he saw and felt, whether his subject was a young woman, a hare, a clump of weeds, an emperor, or a saint.

Truth need not be attractive. But its portrayal (or betrayal) is always aspectual. Anselm Kiefer can give us, almost verbatim, visually, the strafed fields of his homeland. But he did not find the means to bare the backstory of that devastation. There's greater depth, if no less real emotion, in his more recent efforts, to bare the reveries that *Finnegan's Wake* aroused in him. There's a gentler truth in the messy loveliness of his semi-abstract River Liffey that these more recent paintings convey. Neither suite, the all too visceral strafed fields, nor the muted tones that stand in for the Liffey would mean much to viewers without the textual lines from Joyce that surmount the new Kiefers or the contextual cues provoked in the earlier works for those who know much about the German War and the Holocaust that Germany perpetrated. But any artwork needs its context. And if truth is a fair and faithful measure, the Liffey paintings work better as art than Kiefer's strafed fields. Perhaps the artist's passions have cooled enough to make these later works less literal than the earlier series; and his subject is not so painfully close to home, although still close to Kiefer's heart and artistic mind.

Otto Dix and George Grosz had a bitterness of their own to project. But their passions clouded the eye and turned their vision astigmatic. Max Beckmann, by contrast, once given the objectivity of distance, could paint as a prophet, able to gain greater distance, both geographical and semiotic, by recourse to his own iconographic mythography. Something similar might be said of Mahler's music, prophetic in its own way, of the storm not yet broken when he died in 1911.

Part of the resistance to the idea that works of art aim to express ideas or emotions and to link them to other places in experience is fed by a wholesome distaste for reductionism. No one needs to visit a museum or gallery who fancies he has understood a work once he can name what he thinks it represents – as if one might replace a work by naming or reframing in words just what the work aims to express or portray. Such reductions are bizarre. If artworks mean to communicate something, it matters materially why they did so in the form, medium, and manner chosen. Rituals, similarly, must be performed in the received way if they're to have any chance of bearing the received meaning. And even then faithful witness remains most difficult.

Yet, despite the pitfalls of literalism and reductionism, analysis remains fruitful, elementally, to help a witness, viewer, or hearer read a work and parse its syntax; and, more thoughtfully (but with greater risk) to try semantically to unriddle its poetry and touch just what it was that an artist was reaching for. Such unriddling, although it cannot be complete, is not an idle exercise. But not every interpreter or critic does it just as well as any other. There's not much use pedagogically or exegetically in R. C. Jebb's famously dismissive remark that the meaning of the *Oresteia* is the *Oresteia*. Jebb's impatience was doubtless piqued by plowing through a few too many over-interpretations by professionals and facile student readings. But one learns more from F. M. Cornford's profound reflections on the close of the trilogy at the close of his *Timaeus* commentary,[21] where he ties the word 'persuasion' to the love of peace and reason and marks how Athena has pacified the Furies and given them an honored place beneath the Hill of justice, finally ending the cycle of vengeance that her favored city could never have survived.

There's poignance, too, in Cornford's plea for peace, all too visible when we recall the date of his consummatory words. His commentary, crowned by the epilogue where he makes his impassioned plea for peace, appeared in 1937. Those who had lived through or knew too well the sufferings of the Great War hoped and prayed for "peace in our time." But Cornford's judgment as a scholar was ill matched by Neville Chamberlain's judgment as a statesman. Hitler's furies were not to be silenced by the gray-eyed goddess' persuasion. Peace, a goal devoutly to be wished, is not won by wishing, and least of all is it to be won by persuasion of those who are too passionate for persuasion. Athens and its Spartan enemies did, in the end, destroy the world that had bred their rival virtues. The completion of that destructive task was left to Alexander and his successors. Greed and power-lust could accomplish that without much help from the Furies of the *Oresteia*. Rome could muster to pick up the pieces. Committed Nazis and Jihadis are not persuadable. Their heritage is destructive, first of their enemies and victims and then of the perpetrators they have seduced.

So we can learn from the *Oresteia* something of what Aeschylus hoped his first audiences would glean. But the love of peace that Cornford hoped

---

[21] See Cornford, *Plato's Cosmology*, Epilogue, 361–64.

would make the trilogy a dramatic achievement for all time did not make it quite the recipe needed for Cornford's own time. A tragic cycle, no less than a proverb, demands wisdom if one is to know where and when and how to put to its insights to work. Interpretation, for that reason, remains in a very real sense a critical art, both necessary and sensitive: One still can profit from knowing, say, if Plato's *Menexenus* (or Thucycidides' earlier reconstruction of Pericles' Funeral Oration) is to be read straight or as a satiric parody. And likewise with any work: Is it jovial or serious, ironic, hyperbolic, playful or tragic, or somehow a hybrid best rediscovered in borderlands between such modes. Contextual cues matter. But these too, like the criticism that hopes to quarry them, can read hints, clues, or tropes well or badly, appositely or foolishly.

Some thoughts are worth hearing more than once; some are worth remembering. Much depends on the needs and expectations, skills and background of the intended or the present audience. Some art is about art itself. That's often true in music. But it's certainly a key aspect of what's going on in Picasso's *Demoiselles*, which is in part a manifesto.[22] An artist can change in outlook or in tack, technique or medium – as Picasso clearly did, between that work, say, and *Guernica*. Mondrian, for one, shifted from abstractions on the subtle angularities and tones he saw in cathedrals to the hard right angles and primary colors of his best-known work. The shift toward abstraction for its own sake lost him the support of Helene Kroller-Muller, a warm and enthusiastic early patron, who had seen a deep spirituality in the earlier work and regretfully found herself unable to sustain her interest in the later work, where he clearly felt he had come into his own.[23] No one can blame the artist for his shifting interest. But neither can one blame a key early collector for her inability to follow him where his eye had led him. It would be churlish to say that Mondrian's mature work was trivial. Fashion designers and printers of packaging were not slow to catch on to and exploit its vibrancy. But their take-offs on Mondrian's designs expose just how close to trivial his late discoveries and self-imposed canons had proved to be. If there was a truth grasped now, as there surely was, it was not a subtle, nuanced truth of the sort that Kroller-Muller had found so uplifting in Mondrian's earlier steps beyond Monet's facades of French cathedrals.

There's a similar difficulty with Josef Albers' extended series of paintings in his *Homage to the Square* project. Where the Bauhaus color

---

[22] Goodman and Caramenico, *Coming to Mind*, 234–35.
[23] See Troy, "Telling Tales," 40–41.

theorist Johannes Itten was able to show his students how color interactions affect our perception of even the simplest and purest seeming color fields, and to illustrate how the perceptual genius of a Rembrandt or a Van Gogh could use such color relations effectively in eliciting an emotional response,[24] Albers devoted the last twenty-five years of his life to repeated variations on the same color experiment, begun in 1950. The work he did at his teaching perch at Black Mountain College and elsewhere was perhaps a sublimation on his experiences in Weimar Germany and thereafter. But it was also, and by that token, perhaps, a form of escape. If Levitan had to confess the powerlessness he felt in contemplating the landscape he so loved in Russia, Albers may have found a refuge in the ever-expanding complexity of the simple puzzle he had set himself and set before his public. Here was no candid or hesitant confrontation with God or history or nature. That, perhaps, was part of the point, as it often became in abstract expressionism. If the id displaced the ego in the work of the exponents of that school, the superego displaced the id in the work of Albers or Mondrian.

My contention here is not that Van Gogh or Rembrandt is a greater artist than Mondrian or Albers. That seems pretty obvious, if only in the depth and range of feeling that those earlier artists proved able to convey and evoke. My point is a simpler one that does not demand descent into the trenches of art criticism: that art of any kind aims to say something, to confront and express a truth. So to take seriously an artwork and the artist who stands beside it is to look to or listen for what the work communicates. Without that kind of attentiveness, the work is merely decorative (at best). There's beauty in truth and truth in beauty. But the worth of an artwork rests on the range and depth of the truth it proves able to convey.

Since music (even more than painting) is an art form that almost militantly demands its independence, having been so long and so mercilessly and tellingly exploited to stir up a mood in fighting forces, or bodies in the pews, or to lull disquiet in a baby or distress in a companion, I'll end this section about truth in art with thoughts from my late friend Roger Scruton, who knew far more of music than I will ever know and who

---

[24] See Itten, *The Art of Color*, especially 54–144. Itten's cosmopolitan study is a masterful exposition of the expressive impact of colors and the varieties of impact in color contrasts. The discussion on p. 44, with its accompanying plate, reveals the seriousness of Mondrian's color experiments.

wrote what I think is the most serious and wide-ranging philosophical study of music in his hefty volume, *The Aesthetics of Music*.

In the sciences, Scruton writes, the organizing concepts function like a window. They are "world directed." So I improve my scientific understanding by improving my knowledge of the world. Similarly, Scruton explains, in moral education, I must come to know what a person is and how a person should be treated. A metaphor, he goes on to explain, is to be understood by reference to its literal sense. "But what happens when concepts are removed from their justifying context, and applied in a systematic metaphor, like the concepts that deliver the intentional realm of music?" Here, as Scruton notes, there is no orienting framework. That would be too literal (or too literary) to describe what's going on in music: "I do not understand what life is by hearing life in music; rather, because I know what life is, I can hear life in music. Any improvement in my understanding of this concept is an improvement in my understanding of *life*."[25]

The idea that the experience of music is a mere by-product of other perceptions is the outlook that defenders of musical autonomy reject with understandable vehemence. For such a posture "would seem to imply that the organization of music is of no intrinsic significance." We need to recognize, Scruton presses, that there is something essential and un-abstractable about the fact that values and ideas were expressed in music: "Just as we learn about the human face from painting, so do we learn about movement and life from music ... we come to see movement and life in another way, to sense its inward meaning, and to respond to it as in a dance. Our own life is transfigured as we listen, sensing the movement in ourselves."[26] Watching children move as they listen to music, one can see something of the truth in Scruton's point.

The metaphor that animates our experience is not founded in a bare comparison: it involves an imaginative shift of attention comparable to that which occurs in the appreciation of painting. In listening to music and experiencing its inner organization we are also encountering as a pure appearance something which, seen through the window, is not appearance at all.

And here, I suggest, lies the importance of aesthetic experience in general, and of the imaginative act in particular. Our ordinary intentional understanding is subservient to our goals: the order that it discerns is one that opens to the world of our projects, dividing it not at the joints, but in the way most useful to moral and practical existence. But there is another way of seeing the world: the way that

---

[25] Scruton, *The Aesthetics of Music*, 234.   [26] Scruton, *The Aesthetics of Music*, 235–36.

opens to us when our projects are set aside. Another order then spreads through the realm of appearance, an order that we actively create through our imaginative perception. In perceiving this order, we employ our ordinary concepts, but obliquely, to describe appearances. In a mysterious way, this oblique use of our concepts purifies them, and reconciles us to the world that they describe. It *shows* the meaning of the world, by translating the world into appearance. Imagination cleans the window of perception.[27]

What Scruton says here of music, and of art more largely, is also true of prayer, when prayer is real. It's because he felt music so deeply that he could write about it not just with an expertise honed by dedication, study, and practice, but also with emotion not deadened but enlivened by familiarity, and to speak of the bond of music to movement in terms of dance. It's because music connected him not to a higher world but in a different way to the world we already know, that he was able hold and regard music as something sacred – as prayer is at rare moments for the rare congregant, and as paintings became for Barnes, explaining why he so hated the thought of Philadelphia Main-Liners sipping cocktails and exchanging gossip with an artwork in the background at a fashionable exhibit opening. Chit-chat was a desecration, as bad architecture was for Scruton – or bad philosophy was for Aristotle.

Art relates to truth, as I see it, in the same way that thought and language in general relate to being and the good. The best way I know of to characterize that relation is by using Aristotle's expression *pros hen*: All beings reach for the good in their own ways. They don't all pursue the same project, but all beings *have* a project. All modes of artistic expression, similarly, reach for something – sometimes mimesis, sometimes autonomous expression. But all, in their diverse ways, reach for what might be called perfection. Perfection for one life form might be very different from what it proves to be for another, perhaps even, in some ways antithetical to the perfection or expression sought by another – although we should not discount the critical ways in which even antitheses can prove constructive, as any ecologist, or dietician, knows. Likewise in the arts: All artists reach for truth in some form, although for different facets of it, and by different means. The history of art reveals repeatedly that new forms are seen by their creators, critics, or appreciators as displacing or subsuming, rediscovering, transcending, or reinventing the truths pursued by others and the varied means and media by which those truths and the vehicles to express them are sought.

---

[27] Scruton, *The Aesthetics of Music*, 236.

So diversity in the arts, like diversity in nature, forms a mosaic whose tesserae coalesce in larger patterns that individual practitioners and partisans may not always perceive. For truth has different facets just as living beings find different ways of flourishing or surviving.

Can art not lie, then? Of course it can – not that the portrayal of horrors is itself a lie. It's a profound truth when a Goya or Manet exposes the horrors of war, or when a Cervantes uses hilarity to expose the folly of what Auerbach more directly called the grisly business of chivalry and its false ideal,[28] or when a Melville uses darker colors to expose the tyranny of obsession, or an Orwell, with a sterner vision, holds up to the light the ugliness and mendacity of tyranny. Chaim Soutine, inspired in part by Rembrandt and by life itself, can bring one into the abattoir, and Thomas Eakins can bring viewers into the surgical theater of the Gross clinic. Here too are momentary glimpses of parts of life itself. But when Francis Bacon or Lucien Freud pretend that their perverse portrayals picture life itself, exploiting the confrontational vividness of their images, they have used their skills and talents to perpetuate a lie. If the business of art is expressive, then art can be used to frame a lie. Not every painting must be a Fragonard; and, indeed, a Fragonard, with all its flowers, and even a Watteau, with all its seductive charm, may tell a lie, by what it hides beyond the picture plane. But one must say here, of Francis Bacon and Lucien Freud, what I say consistently about the problem of evil: that evils would not be evil were it not for the goods they prey upon. It's the concealment and denial of real goods that make lies of the paintings of Freud and Bacon, expressions of the very sort of generalized alienation that we witness in the carnage perpetrated by mass killers: The ugliness is not in nature or in being itself but in the anomie of the offenders, a denial, all too pointed, of our shared and social humanity.

Truth, I argue, plays as prominent and essential a role in art as it bears in politics or morals. Truth here is not literalism. Nor can artistic truth stomach the cheap emotivism of kitsch or propaganda. What makes kitsch distasteful to a refined sensibility and what makes propaganda revolting to thoughtful spirits is the way that both ring false when tested: propaganda, for its trade in stereotypes; kitsch, for its pandering with

---

[28] Writing from his refuge in Istanbul as the Shoah was reaching its peak, Auerbach, in his *Mimesis*, touches more delicately on the truth about knighthood: "The courtly romance is not reality shaped and set forth by art, but an escape into fable and fairy tale. From the very beginning, at the height of its cultural florescence, this ruling class adopted an ethos and an ideal which concealed its real function." 138. Auerbach wrote the work between May 1942 and April 1945. V-E Day was May 8, 1945.

emoticons in place of insights that respect the depth and complexity of experience and the greater depth and complexity of nature and life itself.

MORAL AND POLITICAL TRUTH

Norms, as I see it, are grounded in the claims that beings make. This approach obviates idle questions about whether rights and wrongs, goods and ills, are natural or non-natural properties. Deserts reflect the very essence of beings. In that sense deserts are existential. They're not properties at all. They arise in what it is for a thing to be what it is, not statically but dynamically. For all being is dynamic. Were there just one being in the universe, that being's deserts would be absolute. That might be true, in a sense, of God. But there are, in fact, multiple beings. So one can even speak (although rather misleadingly) of their claims upon God. What makes the most sense, however, all the sense in the world morally, are the claims that beings make on one another – and, specifically, on those beings in whom personal consciousness and agency render relevant an active and thoughtful (considered and considerate) response.

The prima facie deserts of any being are the claims of its conatus. But the full deserts of any being are what I have called its equilibrated deserts, that is, its deserts reconciled with the rival and complementary deserts of other beings.[29] Rights and dignities are those special cases of deserts that pertain to persons. All persons, I have argued, stand on a moral plateau: No person's existential deserts outrank those of any other. That is what we can and should mean when we speak of human equality. But any individual's deserts are scaled relative to the deserts of others. A smoker's need for a cigarette does not outrank the need of others for clean and wholesome air.

Baseline personal deserts are existential and thus inalienable. Here we encounter the most fundamental human rights. But many of the entitlements that we familiarly call basic rights are in fact presumptions, defeasible by bad actions. So punishment is not rightful harming of a person in proportion to the harm that person has done but the scaling back of presumptive privileges based on actions that have defeated some customary presumptions – so trustworthiness is presumptive but defeated by proved acts of embezzlement.[30] Core existential deserts are inalienable: It is never just to torture a person. But it's merely bad rhetoric to speak of

---

[29] See Goodman, *On Justice*, viii–x, 6–10, 23–34.
[30] See Goodman, *On Justice*, chapter 2.

animal rights. Nonhuman animals have deserts, and so do plants, species and biological lineages, econiches, ecosystems, and monuments of nature and of culture. All these deserts are intrinsic in the first instance, based on what these beings are and (secondarily) on their usefulness or aesthetic or intellectual, historic, or ritual interest.

One strength of our ontological theory of deserts is that it is not contractual at its base. Indeed, it helps anchor claims about the legitimacy and prescriptivity of contracts and other undertakings and does not try to suspend them from a skyhook. Because our theory grounds deserts in what beings are, its reach is far broader than that of a contract theory, be the contract historical or putative, explicit, tacit, or (like Rawls' social contract) virtual at bottom. But nonhuman deserts are not rights properly speaking. For animals, plants, and the rest are not the existential equals of persons. Persons alone stand together as equals on an existential and therefore moral plateau. But if there are nonhuman persons, biologically different from our own human kind, their moral standing is equivalent to ours since they too are subjects.

A skeptic about deserts might argue that the mere existence of a thing has no implications about what ought to be the case, let alone about entitlements. But even facticity, I argue, makes claims on us – centrally, to demand that we face facts, and minimally, to acknowledge the truth when we can know it. But how do the claims of one being gain prescriptive purchase on the actions or intentions of another? Traditionally, moralists sift such demands prudentially. So in Hobbesian or Lockean terms, we rationally refrain from aggression against others lest they retaliate or strike out against us preemptively. And the demands of charity, similarly, are pressed prudentially: Who knows that one (or those one cares about) might not stand in need of help or even protection some day.

But such prudential appeals, the notional linchpin of Rawls' equality principle and the rhetorical force behind many a counsel to put oneself in another's shoes, although often efficacious emotively, do not effectuate a strictly moral claim. Those addressed might care enough for "number one" to bracket, downplay, or slight the claims of others. They might feel confident, or just prefer to take their chances. Some might even welcome suffering, affront, or assault. It's not because slavery, or fraud, or unprovoked attack might happen to anyone that slavery, fraud, or random battery is wrong but chiefly because such acts violate another's personhood.

Likewise, as I've argued in behalf of an ethos of stewardship, it's not, in the first instance, because a cancer cure might lie hidden in the rainforest that we have duties to preserve such ecosystems. The moral claim rests most squarely on the intrinsic, not merely instrumental, worth of the creatures that inhabit such domains and the econiches they sustain. It's in just such a spirit that Mishnah Avot (5.10), focusing on human deserts, pushes the claims of moral duty beyond appeal to a tacit contract and calls for cultivation of an ethos of generosity (*middat hesed*).

To justify concerns for other beings, and for other persons most pointedly, one might argue by analogy: Just as our self-awareness can convince us by analogy that there are other minds like ours, in the same way recognition of our own needs, it might be said, should convince us of the like urgency of the needs of other creatures and other persons. That's a rather limp argument. I doubt it would do much to move a staunch egoist, or even a libertarian who favors his own wants and needs above those of other persons, seeing selfishness, perhaps, as a law of nature and thus an anchor of natural right. His reasoning: Just as you have no right to one or both of my kidneys, you have no right to call on me for help, let alone collect taxes to sustain a common good. A bolder egoist might turn to Bernard de Mandeville's *Fable of the Bees* and urge that selfishness will redound to the common good. Epicureans long ago reduced justice to a contractual convention and even suggested that do-gooders are busy-bodies, likely to annoy or interfere in others' affairs or infringe on their autonomy. Everyone profits, the argument goes, when people leave each other alone, or rely, at most, on a close circle of friends who need no formal undertakings to come to each other's aid.

Such arguments are riddled with holes, not least on their own prudential grounds, as Spinoza clearly saw, when he found nothing more useful to man than his fellow man.[31] But a larger issue lies outside the envelope of prudential suasions: What does an egoist's outlook make of one's character? "What's mine is mine, what's thine is thine," we read in Avot (5:10), was the ethos of Sodom. The Torah invokes an ethos of *hesed*, kindness, grace, and generosity. We need to consider the impact of our acts and choices on our character as individuals as well as on the social ethos.

Even where our core concern is legitimately first-person focused, we cannot ignore what our maxims make of us. As the Ramban, Nahmanides, put it, underscoring the call to *middat hesed*, the law is stark indeed when stripped bare of other-regard: One can be a wretch

---

[31] Spinoza E4p18s, Gebhardt 2.223.

(*naval*) within the strictures of the law.³² A body of such wretches will be wretched multiply, not a community. The friction and inefficiency that result from lack of caring and a sense of shared worth cause even the barest of transactions ultimately to run aground.³³

A higher calling, to one's higher self, than that of the egoist or mere contractualist is voiced in the Torah's commands to walk in God's ways and make ourselves holy (Leviticus 19:2, Deuteronomy 8:6, 10:12, 11:22). Israel is called to become a holy nation, a nation of priests (Exodus 19:6), a people whose character can make them worthy to serve as a model and a guide to others. For an isolated saint is no sufficient model of human flourishing. Most human virtues find their theater in the community – perhaps most tellingly, at the juncture between personhood and society, in the family. It is in here that an ethos becomes effectual, with the aid of natural relations built up over time by example and emulation.

The ultimate model calling humanity to the exercise of grace and graciousness is God, who gives without expectation of return. We requite God's grace not by repaying it but by sharing the goods we receive. That's one reason why, in Jewish law, even the recipients of charity must contribute. Beyond that, the recipient belongs no less to the community than those best able to contribute.

An ethos of *hesed* can be justified even without appeal to divine imperatives and their moral themes in simple recognition of what we are and what we hope to be and to become. Virtue ethics asks us what kind of human being we hope to be. I've always been struck here by Cicero's suitably rhetorical argument in *De Officiis*, that a solid reason for not stealing is that if one does too much of that sort of thing one becomes a thief.³⁴ It's not just a matter of what others might think of one (although social and societal roles do matter to us all, as they did with special force in Cicero's own case). The question as to what one is making of oneself strikes hard against fraud and prostitution and many another crime and vice: The perpetrator all too readily becomes a secondary

---

[32] Nahmanides, on Leviticus 19:2.
[33] Thus, the opening argument of Goodman, *On Justice*, chapter 1.
[34] See *De Officiis* III 76. Following Panaetius and Posidonius, Cicero argues that nothing unjust can be to one's advantage. At III 82, he characteristically mingles his argument with concerns as to one's reputation. But repute is not irrelevant in seeking a fair appraisal of one's moral worth. At III 84, Cicero adopts the conclusion Plato had argued *in extenso* in the *Republic*, that scarcely anything could be less advantageous than to win political sway (and plaudits) by unjust means.

victim, a wretch (*naval*), in the strongest sense that Nahmanides called out. Vicious or even thoughtless habits build us into a cage of our own construction, ever more difficult to climb out of and escape.

If we turn that line of argument from vice to virtue, still reflecting the dynamic of personhood, we see a case for generosity that reaches beyond the merely prudential, although still self-oriented: Practice can make one a better person. We can witness the possibility of moral transformations when troubled youths, or adults, are given responsibility, say, for horses or other living creatures. Generosity and caring become a mode of therapy, at least for those not yet too scarred and constricted to absorb their rewards. There's a suggestion of such thoughts in Philo's take on the biblical cities of refuge: Those sheltered are meant, he suggests, to absorb the ethos of the Levites living there, strikingly different, we can say, from a prison ethos as we know it.[35]

A comparable transformation is said to have taken hold among the British convicts transported to Australia in its early days. The sense of a common plight and tacit, perhaps tactful, recognition of like histories allowed convicts to build new identities and a new ethos, a sense of "mateship." New songs and new idioms were born, a folk culture recognizable even today, folded into the cultural contributions of newer arrivals who did not share the backstory of that earlier generation. The challenges of life on the American frontier similarly built a new ethos there. But no wholesome ethos can endure without continued cultivation and new energies responsive to new challenges. The dynamic is powerful, but it remains constructive only if not washed away by self-indulgent impulses of the sort that Nahmanides warns of, and others less familiar to him but strident in our own times since they grip their victims with unanticipated suddenness and even fiercer tenacity than those that Nahmanides might name.

The evidence that still speaks to us from ancient times is all the more telling in our own. It speaks of the sensitivity and need to build a new ethos atop the old, that one might be tempted too passively to count on. Jeremiah (30:18) hears God address this need when He promises a new city to be built on the ruins of the old. For the ruins of ancient settlements,

---

[35] See Philo, *On the Sacrifices of Cain and Abel* 4.128–29, LCL 2.186–87. Philo reads the ordinance of Numbers 35:9–29 sending those guilty of manslaughter to dwell with Levites in the Cities of Refuge, in hopes that some of the holiness of the Levites will, as it were, rub off on those "reckoned unholy" since they had committed involuntary manslaughter.

become the kind of *tel* that casual passersby took all too readily for mere features of the terrain, a gentle hill and not portentous ruins of lost cities. It's just such thoughts that are brought before us when we joyously embrace the challenge every household knows, of the need for constant rebuilding, echoing Jeremiah's words in *Lekha dodi* ("Come My Beloved"), the happy epithalamion of Shlomo Alkabetz (ca. 1505–84) that welcomes each new Sabbath as a virgin bride:

> Don't be shy, or shamefaced!
> Why all this grief and moaning!
> My hardpressed people
> Will find shelter here!
> And a new city will be built
> Atop the ruins of the old![36]

The story of Israel's second founding, the building of a new state in 1948, is the latest response to the ancient challenge of rebuilding. The revitalizing of Hebrew as a spoken language, establishment of the Hebrew University and National Library, founding of the Knesset and of Israel's Defense Forces, and many more new institutions from labor unions and political parties to airlines, yeshivot and synagogues, hospitals and health plans, public parks, sports arenas and athletic leagues, theaters, symphony orchestras and museums, art institutes like Bezalel, dance troupes like Inbal and Batsheva – all contribute to the building of a new state and full complement of civic and social institutions but also of a new ethos and new identities on the foundations of the old. Many of the strengths of Diaspora culture survive. But the defeatism and fatalism bred by oppression are in retreat and defeated, just as Jeremiah urged.[37]

The first founding of Israel as a commonwealth, with the entry of the nation into the land that God had sworn to give their ancestors, after their durance in slavery in Egypt, was an even more radical enterprise: For now there was a new law built on the quarry rock of Abraham's moral monotheism, its broad principles now given fuller, richer articulation in the Mosaic Torah and its detailed rabbinic sequelae, marking the measure and modalities of the practices that would transform its themes and principles into actionable prescriptions, given ritual precision to transform them into the doable good of which Aristotle spoke. The newly emergent ethos, like the creation itself, was built on grace.

---

[36] Lekha Dodi, in the Siddur, ed. Birnbaum, 245–46. The translation here is my own.
[37] See Goodman, *Judaism*, chapter 6, "Regrouping."

It's in the challenge of self-construction, whether for a person or for a people, that we find our answer to the skeptic's challenge demanding the grounds for the prescriptivity we see in the call to recognize the claims of all beings and those of all persons par excellence. That affirmative answer is well anchored in historical experience, both ancient and recent: We make more of ourselves not through domination or acquisition but by moral growth, cultivated by the exercise of regard for others. Caring opens pathways to human flourishing.

It is in generosity that we find our clearest, surest route toward self-development and self-perfection. But, how, it might be asked, are we to warrant the call to self-perfection? On the face of it, the question rings captious. How can one argue with an interlocutor who doesn't seem to acknowledge his own deserts. One could make a case dialectically, finding as Socrates often does, tacit recognition of some interest that the questioner is not ready to abandon or openly reject. He does want, clearly, to be understood, accepted, and find agreement. Plato, a wrestler in his younger days, could readily appreciate Socrates' skill in using an adversary's weight and postures, or even his grip, to topple false pretensions. The moral skeptic might not have asked his question without hopes of some Thrasymachean eclat, recognizing its cleverness or originality. So there's a glint of self-interest even in the raising of the issue that betrays a certain hollowness in the question.[38]

But if the question about self-expression and self-perfection is asked in earnest, it seems to demand a broader inquiry as to just what interest is and why it matters. Even captious questions may mask the stirrings of an appetite for understanding – and so an appetite for self-development. Some smattering of earnestness may lie behind a mask of cleverness, a yen for self-perfection behind the sophomoric mask.

God, we find, if the Torah is our guide, commands and invites all forms of life, including human beings, to be fruitful and multiply (Genesis 1:22, 28). The mandates are at once blessings and duties, prescriptions, privileges, and natural laws. So are the drives of every being to maintain, sustain, express, and where possible perfect itself. Our human callings to self-direction and self-perfection are cases in point: at once demands of nature and commands of God, blessings and privileges, as palpable and prescriptive as any other natural law. But in the human case, the

---

[38] Aristotle has not forgotten Plato's logic, when he notes that one who challenges the law of contradiction has reduced himself to silence since he is committed to the contradictory of his own thesis.

commands are explicit and in good part needing conscious appropriation – the full range of opportunities they point toward, protean, refracted through the prism of each person's unique talents and creative bent.

One needs to find one's skills and indeed one's tastes if one is to acquire the capacity and the appetite to hone and develop them. Wise teachers and thoughtful parents can help. So perhaps, can a Rousseauvian freedom to explore – and, for those who hope to offer guidance, a sharp, firm line between wholesome encouragement and mere projection or exploitation. For projection is among the subtlest (and thus the most insidious) forms of emotional exploitation. Spouses, parents, siblings, teachers, friends, and peers need to remember that another human being is not a surrogate or catspaw but a unique individual of intrinsic worth, deserving of support in any worthy project but ultimately in the self-chosen projects of that person's own life.

Deserts spring from the conatus. So it's worth remembering that the Latin *conor*, to strive, from which 'conatus' is derived, is a deponent verb, passive in form but active in force. For although human energies are a gift, funding and fueling the potentials present in every human being, the creative or expressive project or enterprise in which a person's striving will take shape, is unique to that individual. We humans strive in varied ways to exercise our capacities and realize our natures. Minimal, if critical, among those ways are the means and modes in which we respond to facts – recognize them and determine how and when to accept or seek to modify them, or perhaps just to appreciate, say, the solidity of a rock or its mossy carapace, the endurance and emblematic self-assertion of a mountain's mass, the refreshing torrent of a waterfall. Morally, what matters most are the strivings and sufferings of living creatures and those human beings whose projects we witness as their lives unfold and their generations spin out.

The projects of living beings become social in all animals and plants that breed sexually, although in many predators the need for territory limits the duration and extent of the sexual bond. Symbiosis, whether in corals and their zooxanthellae or in the relations found in larger creatures, such as those whose teeth or fins or fur are cleaned by smaller fish or birds tolerated, instinctually, for the services they render. Here we see instances of interdependence, highly specialized and sharply limited but no less necessary in communities. Animals that hunt in packs and those that graze and migrate in herds form communities in their own ways, for predation, seasonal sustenance, or protection. But in animals that are social in a stronger sense, such as hive bees, ants, termites, and naked mole rats, reproductive competence is centralized, and behavioral adaptation is routinized. In social insects, as Teilhard explains, a surrender of individuality is necessitated because the weight of the exoskeleton limits body size and therefore brain size, restricting the possibilities for individual behavioral flexibility, confining complex behaviors to the realm of communal instinct and rendering much of learning otiose and individuality an irrelevance.[39]

But in the human case, evolution allowed and fostered the rise of immense neural complexity, making communal life no longer dependent on the mechanisms of instinct and reflex. Here behavior is no longer quite so mechanical. It now makes sense to speak of actions and activities and no longer resort solely to the generic and rather reductive term behavior. Projects grow far more complex, varied, and ambitious than a beaver dam or termite mound. Individuality and mental flexibility render human undertakings creative and often personal and personally expressive. For humans, and humans alone, among the species known to us on earth, have become persons. On our present planet, we are the only living beings to have taken that step, the advance that makes us moral subjects. It is for that reason, Maimonides explains, that the Torah can represent God as issuing commands to our archetypal ancestors (*Guide* I 2). We humans act. We can choose our own course. Our freedom renders us responsible for our choices and, through our choices, for our character. Our friendships and fellowships too are, in some measure, of our own choosing and, as Mishnah Avot (1.6) reminds us, of our own making. Even our communities, although we are born into them, whether at the level of the family, clan, tribe, or nation, are in some measure self-chosen. For they can be left behind, albeit with some pain or difficulty – or altered, albeit at some cost.

Our human intellectual potentials can but also must be cultivated.[40] And it is our cultivated potentials that give us our most specialized and flexible capacities for self-expression and self-development. We see a hint of the higher order moral charge that comes with subjecthood emblematically in the placement of Adam and Eve in a garden, not a wilderness, and given charge of other creatures, not one of which is mankind's counterpart (Genesis 1:28, 2:19–20). We humans, represented in the

---

[39] See Teilhard de Chardin, *The Phenomenon of Man*, 153–55.
[40] Maimonides makes the point in glossing the Torah's saying that Seth was begotten in Adam's *image and likeness* (Genesis 5:3), *Guide* I 7, 17b–18a.

person of our first ancestors, are to tend the garden, our first habitat (Genesis 2:15). For even in Eden work is necessary, and responsibility is human (cf. 2:5). We will name the creatures that surround us (2:20). But to name them we must know them. We will have dominion over them (1:28). But knowledge itself begets responsibility.

Granted the first couple's life in that virtual place, the garden, is meant to contrast with the lives that the earliest Bible readers knew best, a life of sowing and reaping, threshing, winnowing and milling, mixing, kneading, and baking was onerous by comparison. But the imperative of stewardship grows all the more pointed when God commands Noah to save the animals of every kind (6:19–20): Humanity, all of Noah's descendants, must preserve God's other species. And that charge persists when God renews His command/blessing to His living creatures to be fruitful and multiply (7:17). For the same command (along with the instincts that underwrite it and the understanding that guides it) charge humanity too, compellingly and lastingly, with the care parents must give their offspring, and the aid to that and other ends that they owe each other – imperatives that mirror in anticipation the caring that offspring will owe their parents and that whole communities will owe the elders among them (Exodus 20:12, Leviticus 19:32) – models of the more universal love and care that all human beings owe each other (Leviticus 19:18). For the ethos of care and caring reaches broadly beyond the family and the proximal community. Maimonides, keenly alive to the Torah's moral and spiritual themes, presses beyond the minimal demands against polluting the neighborhood or endangering passersby to the call of virtue at large, a paradigm case being the shared responsibility to heal the hurts of all who are broken (*Guide* III 53, 131a).

No less lifegiving or empowering than the rearing of a child or the heroic gift of a kidney, perhaps to an unknown recipient, is one's commitment to another's intellectual growth. We find a paradigm case in Samuel Clemons' decision to pay the room and board of Warner McGuinn, a Black student at Yale Law School, who went on to graduate first in his class and to become the mentor of Thurgood Marshall (1908–93), who successfully argued the case against racial segregation in American public schools in *Brown v. Board of Education*. The decision of the Warren Court in that landmark case overturned the inherently invidious "separate but equal" precedent of *Plessy v. Ferguson*. Marshall himself went on to become a Supreme Court justice, and the Thurgood Marshall Scholarship, established in his name, has awarded over $300 million to Black students and their schools and has helped thousands of beneficiaries, in keeping with the Maimonidean thesis that generosity can beget further generosity as its flow broadens, helping unknown others to self-sufficiency. As Ben Azzai said, "One mitzvah leads on to another" (M. Avot 4.2).

To sustain, enable, and constructively empower any being – especially a conscious being, capable of profiting from intellectual, moral, and spiritual support, is to contribute to God's project. So it's here that we see the fullest moral applications of the idea of truth. Where an artist seeks to express a truth and communicate the beauty and truth he sees, the morally responsive and responsible person takes up the charge by extending further the beauty or goodness, or truth of which a being is capable, not by expression alone but by support.

If being is dynamic, some of its varieties will need to be restrained or cropped, lest they destroy or subvert others – and then destroy themselves for want of resource. But there are many whose inchoate claims merit the support and collaborative sustenance that will allow them to discover and fulfill their potentials and contribute to the world's betterment.

Gandhi, like the biblical authors, saw a moral truth in the nexus of political rights and duties with human dignity. It was with such thoughts in mind that he gave the name *satyagraha* to his aspirational project. Political independence for India was a vital part of that project and, in practical terms, its leading edge. But the moral truth he exercised in requiring the members of his ashram give massages to one another, regardless of race or caste, and the self-reliance he championed, that found its tool in the spinning wheel and its banner in the homespun dhoti, sought a higher, broader goal. The same can be said of Booker T. Washington and his educational work and of George Washington Carver, who made a tool of education. Seemingly humble crops like soybeans, peanuts, and sweet potatoes, he found, could rejuvenate soils depleted by cotton monoculture. And the hundreds of products that his discoveries showed could be made from soybeans made them at once an emblem and a means of self-determination and economic self-realization for individuals and their communities. Much the same is seen in modern Israel, where technical innovation and intellectual creativity have made a desert bloom, and the land that I can remember Harvard economists once condemned as fated to live on remittances to become a source of prosperity for many others.

CONCLUDING THOUGHTS

In my 2001 book, *In Defense of Truth*, I took up the Aristotelian idea that "truth," like "good," is a cross categorical, a term with broad application across all the Aristotelian categories: There can be a good time for planting or for writing fiction, a good body-mass index, a good swimmer or basketball player. The title I gave that book reflects the climate of the times in which it took shape: The very idea of truth was under attack from skeptics, relativists, phenomenalists, post-structuralists, postmodernists, and others. Such attacks are less prominent or less flashy now, perhaps. But, sadly, that is not because truth has gained doughtier defenders. Deflationary ideas of truth and Quinean notions of ontological relativity persist, although mostly in the recesses of academic conferences. Public discussions of truth have grown politicized and involve the angry and presumptive selection of favored attitudes, dressed up as truth claims among polemicists who count on their siloed hearers to know little of the values or insights behind the shibboleths of their rivals. The nature and the task of truth itself are rarely touched on, let alone the nexus of truth to the other values in which its recognition plays so critical a part. Truth, it seems, still needs defenders, not least among those who are alive to the demands it makes.

Truth, I have argued here, makes its demands in the dynamism of being at large and in the claims beings make individually and collectively for a place and space and a moment and opportunity to flourish. Its paramount occasion arises in the primacy and potential of persons, moral subjects, whose personhood demands respect toward the claims they make and concerted, ideally collaborative efforts to integrate those claims in the larger social and societal spheres where complementarities can be realized in collaborative, constructive, and creative enterprises.

Spinoza wrote, insouciantly, to the enduring frustration of professional epistemologists, that truth is its own sign. And Aquinas, who saw truth not just in sentences and judgments but in things as well – an insight he ascribed to the early Jewish philosopher Isaac Israeli (ca. 855–955) – saw the truth of every being as the cause (although not the ultimate cause) of the truths that might be known about it. The truth of things, for Thomas, is their reality as what they are. So it encompasses their goodness, unity, and beauty. For, as he wrote, "Nothing exists that does not participate in beauty and goodness. For each thing is beautiful and good according to its own form" – a likeness, "of the divine beauty, in which all things share."[41] Maimonides put it succinctly: God created only being, and all being is good (*Guide* 3.17a, citing Genesis 1:17).

---

[41] Thomas Aquinas, *Commentary on pseudo-Dionysius, De Divinis Nominibus* IV 5; see Anderson, *An Introduction to the Metaphysics of St Thomas Aquinas*, 88.

For Thomas, God was Beauty itself, just as He was Goodness and Truth itself, and the Source of the beauty, goodness, and truth in all things. The luminosity (*claritas*) that Levitan saw in the Russian landscape had God as its source, just as Levitan suspected. It is by their being, in all its variety, that created things point beyond themselves toward their Creator. As I wrote in 2001, "Creation does not – cannot – mirror divine Perfection whole, but it does refract that perfection into all the colors of nature's rainbow."[42]

---

[42] Goodman, *In Defense of Truth*, 390.

Bibliography

Adams, Robert M., "The Logical Structure of Anselm's Arguments," *The Philosophical Review* 80 (1971) 28–54.
Alston, William, *Perceiving God* (Ithaca: Cornell University Press, 1991).
Anderson, James, F. *An Introduction to the Metaphysics of St Thomas Aquinas* (Washington, DC: Regnery, 1958).
Aquinas, Thomas, *Commentary on pseudo-Dionysius, De Divinis Nominibus*, ed. and trans Michael Augros as *St Thomas Aquinas, An Exposition of the Divine Names*, full text with complete English translation of Sarrazin's Latin rendering of Pseudo-Dionysius' The Divine Names and Aquinas' Exposition in Latin and English (Merrimacck, NH: Thomas More College Press, 2021).
Armstrong, A. H., "Plotinus' Doctrine of the Infinite and Christian Thought," *Downside Review* 73 (195) 47–58.
Auerbach, Erich, *Mimesis: The Representation of Reality in Western Literature*, tr. Willard R. Trask (Princeton: Princeton University Press, 1973; 1st ed., 1946).
Bennett, Jonathan, "Spinoza's Metaphysics," in *The Cambridge Companion to Spinoza*, ed. Don Garrett (Cambridge: Cambridge University Press, 1996).
Birnbaum, Philip, *Daily Prayer Book* (New York: Hebrew Publishing Company, 1949).
Bohm, David, *Wholeness and the Implicate Order* (London: Routledge and Kegan Paul, 1980).
Calaprice, Alice, *The Quotable Einstein* (Princeton: Princeton University Press, expanded ed., 2000).
Clark, Kenneth, *The Nude: A Study in Ideal Form* (Princeton: Princeton University Press, 1956; 8th ed. 1990).
Carraud, Vincent, *Causa sive Ratio: La Raison de la Cause, de Suarez à Leibniz* (Paris: Presses Universitaires de France, 2002).
Chill, Abraham, *The Mitzvot: The Commandments and Their Rationale* (Jerusalem: Keter, 1974).

Cicero, *De Natura Deorum*, tr. Horace C. P. McGregor as *The Nature of the Gods* (London: Penguin, 1972).
  De Officiis, tr. John Higgenbotham as *Cicero on Moral Obligation* (Berkeley: University of California Press, 1967).
Cornford, F. M., *Plato's Cosmology: The Timaeus of Plato, Translated with a Running Commentary* (London: Routledge and Kegan Paul, 1937).
Craig, William Lane, "The Origin and Creation of the Universe," *British Journal for the Philosophy of Science* 43 (1992) 233–40.
Darwin, Charles, *Autobiography*, ed. Francis Darwin (New York: Dover, 1958. The work is extracted from the three-volume *Life and Letters*, compiled by Francis Darwin, London, 1887).
Dawkins, Richard, *Climbing Mount Improbable* (New York: Norton, 1999).
Descartes, René, *The Philosophical Writings*, 3 vols., tr. John Cottingham, Robert Stoothoff, and Dugald Murdoch (Cambridge: Cambridge University Press, 1985); tr. Elizabeth Haldane and G. R. T. Ross, *The Philosophical Works*, 2 vols. (Cambridge: Cambridge University Press, 1911; repr. 1967); *Oeuvres de Descartes*, ed. Charles Adam and Paul Tannery, Paris, 1897; repr. Paris: Vrin, 1969).
Dewey, John, *Art as Experience* (New York: Minton Balch, 1934).
Drozdek, Adam, "Beyond Infinity: Augustine and Cantor," *Laval Théologique et Philosophique* 51 (1995) 127–40.
Dukas, Helen, and Banesh Hoffman, *Albert Einstein: The Human Side* (Princeton: Princeton University Press, 1979).
Dürer, Albrecht. *Literary Remains*, ed. W. M. Conway (Cambridge: Cambridge University Press, 1889).
Garrett, Don, "Spinoza's 'Ontological' Argument," *The Philosophical Review* 88 (1979) 198–223.
  "Spinoza's Ethical Theory," in *The Cambridge Companion to Spinoza*, ed. Don Garrett (Cambridge: Cambridge University Press, 2nd ed. 2022).
Al-Ghazali, *Ihya' 'Ulum al-Din* (Reviving the Religious Sciences), Book 36, (Cairo, 1968); tr. Eric Ormsby, as *Love, Longing, Intimacy, and Contentment* (Cambridge: Islamic Texts Society, 2013).
  Al-Munqidh min al-Dalal (Deliverance from Error), ed. Farid Jabre (Beirut: unesco, 1959) English tr. in Wm. Montgomery Watt, tr. *The Faith and Practice of al-Ghazali* (London: Allen and Unwin, 1953).
Gödel, *Collected Works*, ed. S. Feferman, J. Dawson, W. Goldfarb, C. Parsons, and W. Sieg (New York: Oxford University Press, 2003).
Goodman, Lenn E., *Avicenna* (Ithaca: Cornell University Press, 2006).
  Creation and Evolution (London: Routledge, 2010).
  God of Abraham (New York: Oxford, 1996).
  A Guide to The Guide to the Perplexed: A Reader's Companion to Maimonides' Masterwork (Stanford: Stanford University Press, 2024).
  The Holy One of Israel (New York: Oxford University Press, 2019).
  In Defense of Truth: A Pluralistic Approach (Amherst, NY: Humanity Press, 2001).
  Judaism: A Contemporary Philosophical Investigation (London: Routledge, 2017).

"Kant's Moral Case for God," in *The Moral Argument for God's Existence*, ed. David Baggett and John Hare (Oxford University Press, forthcoming).

On Justice: An Essay in Jewish Philosophy (Oxford: Littman Library of Jewish Civilization, 2008; 1st ed., New Haven: Yale University Press, 1991).

"Respect for Nature, in *Judaism and Ecology*, ed. Hava Tirosh-Samuelson, (Cambridge, MA: Harvard University Press, 2002) 227–59.

"Time in Islam," *Asian Philosophy* 2 (1992) 3–19.

Goodman, Lenn E., and D. Gregory Caramenico, *Coming to Mind: The Soul and Its Body* (Chicago: University of Chicago Press, 2013).

Gregory, Serge. *Antosha and Levitasha: The Shared Lives and Art of Anton Chekhov and Isaac Levitan* (DeKalb: Northern Illinois University Press, 2015).

Guthrie, W. K. C., *A History of Greek Philosophy*, 6 vols. (Cambridge: Cambridge University Press, 1967).

Grünbaum, Adolf , "The Pseudo-Problem of Creation in Physical Science," *Philosophy of Science* 56 (1989) 373–94.

Guyot, Henri, *L'Infinité Divine depuis Philon le Juif jusqu'a Plotin* (Paris: Alcan, 1906).

Harris, Errol E., *Salvation from Despair: A Reappraisal of Spinoza's Philosophy* (The Hague: Nijhoff, 1973).

The Substance of Spinoza (Atlantic Highlands, NJ: Humanities Press, 1995).

Hauser, Kai, "Cantor's Absolute in Metaphysics and Mathematics," *International Philosophical Quarterly* 53 (2013) 161–88.

"Cantor's Concept of Set in the Light of Plato's Philebus," *Review of Metaphysics* 63 (2010) 783–805.

Heidegger, Martin, *Identity and Difference* (1957), tr. J. Stambaugh (New York: Harper, 1974).

Hertz, Joseph H., *The Pentateuch and Haftorahs* (London: Soncino, 2nd ed., 2001; first published, London, 1936).

Husserl, Edmund, *The Crisis of European Sciences and Transcendental Phenomenology: An Introduction to Phenomenological Philosophy*, tr. David Carr (Evanston: Northwestern University Press, 1970; the unfinished work, written in German in 1936, was published in Leiden by Nijhoff in 1954).

Itten, Johannes, *The Art of Color: The Subjective Experience and Objective Rationale of Color,* tr. Ernst van Haagen (New York: Van Nostrand Reinhold, 1973; 1st German ed., 1961).

Jacobs, Louis, "God," in *Contemporary Jewish Religious Thought*, ed. A. A. Cohen and Paul Mendes-Flohr (New York: The Free Press, 1987).

James, William, *The Varieties of Religious Experience: A Study in Human Nature* (New York: Random House, 1929; The Gifford Lectures of 1901–2, first published, 1902).

Kass, Leon R., *The Beginning of Wisdom: Reading Genesis* (Chicago: University of Chicago Press, 2006).

Kirk, G. S., Raven, J. E., and Schofield, M., *The Presocratic Philosophers: A Critical History with a Selection of Texts* (Cambridge: Cambridge University Press, 2nd ed., 1985).

Koren Tanakh – Exodus (Jerusalem: Koren, 2019).
Leigh, Fiona, "Being and Power in Plato's *Sophist*," *Apeiron* 43 (2011) 63–85.
Lovejoy, Arthur. *The Great Chain of Being* (Cambridge, MA: Harvard University Press, 1936; repr. New York: Harper and Row, 2005).
Maimonides, *Guide to the Perplexed*, tr. L. E. Goodman and Phillip I. Lieberman (Stanford: Stanford University Press, 2024).
Mar, Gary, "Gödel's Ontological Dreams," in *Space, Time and the Limits of Human Understanding*, ed. S. Wuppulluri and G. Ghirardi (Cham: Springer, 2017).
Mason, Richard, *The God of Spinoza: A Philosophical Study* (Cambridge: Cambridge University Press, 1997).
Melamed, Yitzhak, "Cohen, Spinoza and the Nature of Pantheism," *Jewish Studies Quarterly* 25 (2018) 1–10.
Miller, Jon, "Spinoza and the 'A Priori,'" *Canadian Journal of Philosophy* 34 (2004) 555–90.
Moody, Ernest, *The Logic of William of Ockham* (New York: Sheed and Ward, 1935) 252–80.
Neisser, Ulric, "Five Kinds of Self-Knowledge," *Philosophical Psychology* 1 (1988) 35–59.
Niehoff, Maren, *Philo: An Intellectual Biography* (New Haven: Yale University Press, 2018).
Owens, Joseph, *The Doctrine of Being in Aristotelian Metaphysics* (Toronto: Pontifical Institute of Mediaeval Studies, 3rd ed., 1978).
Pais, Abram, *Subtle Is the Lord: The Science and the Life of Albert Einstein* (Oxford: Oxford University Press, 1982).
Pepper, Stephen C., "Some Questions on Dewey's Esthetics," in *The Philosophy of John Dewey*, ed. Paul Schilpp (La Salle, IL: Open Court, 2nd ed. 1951; 1st ed. 1939).
Polkinghorne, John, *Belief in God in an Age of Science* (New Haven: Yale University Press, 1998).
Proclus, *A Commentary on the First Book of Euclid's Elements*, tr. Glenn R. Morrow (Princeton: Princeton University Press, 1970).
 Elements of Theology, ed. and tr. E. R. Dodds (Oxford: Oxford University Press, 1963).
Runia, David, *Philo of Alexandria and the Timaeus of Plato* (Leiden: Brill, 1986).
Ryle, Gilbert. *The Concept of Mind* (Chicago: University of Chicago Press, 1949).
Saadiah al-Fayyumi, *The Book of Theodicy* (Commentary on Job), tr. Goodman (New Haven: Yale University Press, 1988).
 Kitab al-Mukhtar fi'l-Amanat wa'l-I'tiqadat (The Book of Critically Chosen Beliefs and Convictions) ed. with Hebrew tr. Joseph Kafih (Jerusalem: Yeshiva University, 1970); tr. Samuel Rosenblatt as *The Book of Beliefs and Opinions* (New Haven: Yale University Press, 1948).
Sacks, Jonathan, *The Koren Siddur* (Jerusalem: Koren, 2009).
Scruton, Roger. *The Aesthetics of Music* (Oxford: Oxford University Press, 1997).
 Spinoza (Oxford: Oxford University Press, 1986).
Seligman, Paul, *Being and Not-Being: An Introduction to Plato's Sophist* (The Hague: Nijhoff, 1974).

Spinoza, Baruch. *Opera Omnia*, ed. C. Gebhardt (Heidelberg: Winters, 1972; 1st ed., 1926).
Steane, Andrew. *Science and Humanity: A Humane Philosophy of Science and Religion* (Oxford: Oxford University Press, 2018).
Sweeney, Leo, *Divine Infinity in Greek and Medieval Thought* (New York: Peter Lang, 1992).
  "Infinity in Plotinus," *Gregorianum* 38 (1957) 515–35.
Tapp, C., *Kardinalität und Kardinäle* (Wiesbaden: Steiner, 2005).
Teilhard de Chardin, Pierre, *The Phenomenon of Man* (London: Collins, 1966; 1st French ed., 1955).
Tlumak, Jeffrey, *Classical Modern Philosophy* (New York: Routledge, 2007).
Troy, Nancy, J. "Telling Tales: The Kröller-Müller Collection and the Narrative of Modern Art," in *Van Gogh to Mondrian: Modern Art from the Kröller-Müller Museum*, ed. David A. Brenneman (Atlanta: High Museum of Art, 2004).
Van der Veen, Joanna, and Leon Horsten, "Cantorian Infinity and Philosophical Concepts of God," *European Journal for Philosophy of Religion* (2013) 117–38.
Wang, H., *Reflections on Kurt Gödel* (Cambridge, MA: MIT Press, 1987).
Wertheimer, Max, *Productive Thinking*, enlarged ed., ed. Michael Wertheimer (Chicago: University of Chicago Press, 1982; original ed., 1945).
Williams, A. N., "Mystical Theology Redux: The Pattern of Aquinas' *Summa Theologiae*," *Modern Theology* 13 (1997) 53–74.
Wilson, Margaret, "Spinoza's Theory of Knowledge," in *The Cambridge Companion to Spinoza*, ed. Don Garrett (Cambridge: Cambridge University Press, 1996).
Winston, David, *Logos and Mystical Theology in Philo of Alexandria* (Cincinnati: Hebrew Union College, Press, 1985).
  Philo of Alexandria [Selections]: The Contemplative Life, The Giants and Selections (Mahwah, NJ: Paulist Press, 1981).
Wolfson, Harry, *Philo: Foundations of Religious Philosophy in Judaism, Christianity, and Islam*, 2 vols. (Cambridge, MA: Harvard University Press, rev., 1962; 1st ed., 1947).
  Spinoza: Unfolding the Latent Processes of His Reasoning, 2 vols. (Cambridge, MA: Harvard University Press, 1934).
Zabel, Gary, "Excursus: A Short History of Infinity before Spinoza" from *All Things in Common: Spinoza and the Collegiant Letters*.

Index

a priori, 4, 38–44, 49, 121, 133
Aaron, 18
Abraham, 1, 17–21, 47, 52–53, 60, 62–63, 145, 173
Absalom, 3
Abu Nuwas, 157
action at a distance, 125, 133
Adam and Eve, 14–15, 140, 144, 176
adaptation, 31, 131, 135, 157, 176
adequate idea, 38, 47–48, 85–86
Aeschylus, 162
aesthetic value, 30, 58, 118–20, 134, 149–57, 169
African masks, 156
agency, 83–87
akeda, 145
Akiva, cosmic unity 116; delegated powers, 83–84
Albers, Josef, 163
Alcibiades, 3
Alkabetz, Shlomo, 173
Alston, William, 28
Anaximander, 70–71, 82
Anselm, 4, 14–15, 22, 25, 29, 50
anthropocentrism, 7, 100, 107, 110–12, 131, 140
apeiron and *peras*, 69–70, 75, 78, 82
appetite, imagination, convention, 8, 35, 39, 58, 144
appreciation, 74, 91, 108, 111–12, 116–20, 155, 160, 165–67, 174–75
Aquinas, 52–53, 90, 118, 126, 179–80
arbitership, 144–45

Archimedes, 109
Aristotle, Active Intellect, 27 adaptations, 131; cosmos, 16, 62, 88–91, 117; cross-categoricals, 178; determinacy, 71; divinity, 65, 76; doable good, 173; *dynamis*, 80; eternity, 5, 113–15; first philosophy, 61–62; friendship, 129; history, 134; Homer, 156; infinity, 5–6, 70–72, 80–81; matter, 71; mimesis, 151; nature does nothing in vain, 140; Parmenides, 16, 105; reason, 39; social animal, 14–15; substance, 42; taxonomy, 14–15; time, 84, 112; truth from any source, 160; unities, 16, 88–91, 117
Armstrong, A. H., 71–73, 76
art, 8, 26, 129, 150–67
Ashʻarites, 140
aspiration, 2, 4, 16, 23, 35–36, 56–58, 86, 127, 146–48, 178
atheism, 25, 50, 99, 127, 130, 144
attributes, 2, 5–6, 22, 27, 38, 42, 46–48, 52–54, 58, 72, 75, 81–82, 87, 90–96, 125, 146
Auerbach, Erich, 167
Augustine, 22, 50, 66, 68
Australian mateship, 172
autonomy, 10–11, 137, 170
Averroes, 14
Avicenna, 4, 13–14, 22, 32–34
ʻavodah, 60
awe, 3, 60–62, 98, 132
axioms, 29–30, 37, 40–41, 48–51, 69, 77

Index

Bahya ben Asher, 2
bal tashhit, 10–11
Barnes, Albert C., 150, 155, 166
Barr, Stephen, 6–7, 100–7, 118, 127
beauty, 1, 3–4, 8, 21–24, 33–35, 53, 56–58, 62, 68, 71, 77, 86–88, 108–9, 112, 116–23, 133–35, 141, 150, 154, 158–60, 164, 178–80
Beckmann, Max, 161
Behaviorism, 150
being, and value, 4–5, 9–10, 14–18, 21–24, 33–37, 42, 48–50, 58, 70, 73, 114–17, 136–38, 140–42, 146–49, 166–69, 174; *qua* being, 61
Ben Azzai, mitzvah begets mitzvah, 178
Bentham, Jeremy, 149
Bergson, Henri, 82
Berkeley, George, 122
Bezalel, 26
Big Bang, 101–2
birds, 10, 107, 135, 137, 141, 175
Blake, William, 105, 113–14
blessedness, 21, 39, 52–56, 73, 76, 116
blessing God, 60–61, 97, 141
Bohm, David, 95–96
Bonheur, Rosa, 152
Bosanquet, Bernard, 153
Brouwer's axiom, 51
Buber, Martin, 150
burning bush, 4, 15, 19–21, 35–37, 49, 52, 57, 75, 146
by Thy light, 27

Cantor, Georg, 5, 65–69
Carousel, 129
Carter, Brandon, 6, 100
Carver, George Washington, 178
Causa Sui, 37–38, 42–45
causation, 1, 7, 16, 23, 33–49, 62, 71, 79–86, 89, 95–99, 109–10, 118–19, 122–27, 131–33, 136–38, 140–43, 179
chance, 7, 9–10, 71, 99, 109–10, 124
character, 1, 2, 129, 140, 170–71, 176
charity, 2, 11, 129, 169–71; see also *hesed*
Chekhov, Anton, 8, 158–60
chemistry, 7, 101–7, 124
Chill, Abraham, 10–11
choice, 57–59, 83, 114, 128–29, 134, 145, 148–51, 170, 176; see also *agency*
Chrysippus, 108, 111
Church, Frederick, 160–61

Cicero, 6, 107–15, 117, 171
claritas, 180
Clark, Kenneth, 154
coherence, 7, 29, 42, 86–87, 91, 109, 120, 134, 153–57
Cole, Thomas, 158
collaboration, 15, 26, 56, 141, 178–79
commitment, 7, 13–14, 18–20, 50, 65, 68, 89, 99, 115–19, 128–30, 134, 175–77
common notions, 39, 44, 78
community, 15, 128, 171, 177
complexity, 30, 105, 126–27, 136–37, 164, 168, 176
conatus, 9, 42, 58, 86–87, 90, 117, 137, 146, 168, 175
consciousness, 10, 31, 55, 58, 123, 137, 142, 153, 157, 168, 175, 178
consilience, 7, 91, 119–21, 133
constellations, 109
contemplation, 7, 46, 52–53, 59–60, 156, 164
continuum, 5, 68, 71, 81–82, 86, 104–5
contract, 157, 169–71
convention, 8, 79, 144
Copernicus, Nicolaus, 134
Cordelia, 128
Cornford, F. M., 78, 162–63
corrigibility, 148–49
cosmological argument, 12, 22–25, 32–33, 37, 43, 67, 91
cosmos, 5–6, 16, 23, 27, 62, 70–71, 80–82, 87–89, 97–104, 108–23, 139, 141
Costa, Emmanuele, 87
covenant, 17, 19, 53, 60, 65, 106, 147
creation, 5–7, 11, 14, 18–23, 25–27, 31–33, 52–53, 57–58, 65–68, 75, 88–92, 97, 99, 105–18, 123, 136–42, 146, 160, 173, 179–80; and conservation, 20, 97–99, 147; and expression, 6, 20–21, 75, 110–12, 127, 139; and grace, 70; *ex nihilo*, 12, 33–34, 67, 70, 116; how?, 113–14
creativity, 6–8, 45, 58, 60–62, 75–76, 79–80, 87, 96, 107–8, 114–19, 138–40, 151, 157, 166, 175–76, 178–79
culture, 10, 30, 60, 93, 111, 147–48, 169, 172–73
curiosity, 4, 18, 60, 132
Cyclopes, 156

Darwin, Charles, 106, 110, 115–16, 119, 130–31, 133

Darwin, Francis, 131
David, dances before God, 62–63; devotion, 59–60
Dawkins, Richard, 126–28, 130
debt, 17
Decalogue, 27–29
Democritus, 96, 122
Dennett, Daniel, 99, 126, 128
de Sade, 134
Descartes, René, the a priori, 40–41 doubt, 37, 43; a geometrical world, 6, 89, 133; God, 15, 30–31, 37, 46, 50; knowledge, 39, 43, 56; substance, 6, 38, 42; the Church, 130; world's preservation, 99
deserts, 2, 9–11, 33, 54, 58, 67, 70, 132, 142, 145–49, 168–70, 174–75
design, 1, 6–7, 23, 25–28, 58, 87, 97–99, 106–12, 117, 122, 126, 146
destruction, 10–11, 99
dhawq, 28
dignity, 3, 10
dimensions, 78–79, 104, 158
Dirac, Paul, 118–19, 122
disenchantment, 123, 132
diversity, natural and cultural, 6, 16, 88–91, 94, 120, 125, 167
Divided Line, 23, 35–36
divine command theory, 8, 139, 145
Dix, Otto, 161
Dostoevsky, Fyodor, 9
doubt, 25, 31, 37–38, 40, 43, 52, 94, 99, 109, 130, 154
Dürer, Albrecht, 156, 160–61
dynamis, 80

education, and discovery, 165, 178
egoism, 15, 170–71
Ein Sof, 92–93
Einstein, Albert, 66, 83, 103–4, 119, 122, 126, 133
El Adon, 98
Eldad and Medad, 74
election, 48
electrical induction, 133
electromagnetism, 102, 105, 122, 133
elements, 17, 101–7, 113–17, 124, 136, 142
emanation, 73, 92
embodiment, 35
emergence, 55, 103, 118, 124–25, 132, 135, 142–43

empathy, 149, 159
Empedocles, light by light, 27
empiricism, 13–14, 122–25, 149
energy, 6, 58, 101–4, 117, 125, 135–36; entropy, 135
Epicurean, cosmology 7, 90–91, 109, 113, 118–20, 126; dilemma, 99, 111–14; gods, 114, 123; justice, 170; dissolution, 114
esti, 15
ethos, 167, 169–73, 177; see also character
Euclid, 77–80
Eustachio a Sancto Paulo, 40
evil, 42, 72, 114, 142, 146, 167
evolution, 9–10, 55, 125–27, 130–37, 142, 176; evolutionary psychology, 31, 119
ex consensu gentium, 30
exegesis, 27, 29, 45, 49, 162
existence as a perfection, 43, 49
existential propositions, 12–13
Existentialist forlornness, 123, 145
explanation, 14, 68, 85, 90–91, 110–11, 122–26, 132–36
expression, 6–9, 16, 110, 127–29, 137–42, 146–47, 151, 157–66, 174–78
'*ezer ke-negdo*, 15

facts, 123, 134, 144, 169, 175
fallacy of composition, 108, 110
family, 34, 147, 171, 176–77
fellowship and friendship, 100, 107, 128, 147, 176
fields of force, 125
Form of the Good, 16, 23–24, 80, 88
Fragonard, Jean Honoré, 167
fusion, 102

Galen, teleology, 55, 131
Gandhi, Mohandas, 9, 178
Gauguin, Paul, 155
Gaunilon, 4, 29
Gauss, Karl, 45
generosity, 1, 18, 37, 53, 70, 73, 114, 116, 127, 139–40, 170–74, 177–78; see also *hesed*
geometry, 6, 36, 40–41, 76–84, 89, 113, 128, 133
Ghazali, 27–28, 33, 49, 84, 113
Gilgamesh, 106
Glackens, William, 150, 155

Gnosticism, 92
God, a category error?, 129 absolute, 5, 47–48, 57–61, 64, 67, 80, 90, 93, 118, 123 and love, 1–5, 16–19, 25, 28, 35, 49, 52–64, 128–29, 145, 159, 173, 177; and virtue, 56–59, 111, 114, 177; authority, 8, 123, 144–45, 149; "back", 146; Creator, 3, 31–33, 58, 65, 89, 98, 107, 112–17, 132, 139–41; formal and final cause, 34–36; idea of, 12–13, 25, 32, 38, 42, 47, 68, 94; glory, 4, 57, 95, 98, 106, 132, 139; image, 21; necessary being, 12–24, 31–34, 37–38, 42–44, 51, 65, 115; perfection, 4–6, 13–16, 21, 25, 29–49, 56–60, 72–79, 90; unity and infinity, 1, 5–6, 33, 38, 45–48, 53–56, 65–96, 125–26; the Real/the Truth, 21, 26, 32, 36, 144; transcendence and engagement, 17, 75, 93–95
God-of-the-gaps, 124
gods, their disqualifiers, 129
Gödel, Kurt, 4, 49–51
Golden calf, 2
goodness, 1–2, 21, 24, 49, 62, 70–71, 75, 80, 88, 97, 114, 118, 123–25, 129, 134–35, 138–42, 154, 178–80; the doable good, 173
Gould, Stephen Jay, NOMA, 130–31
governance, 2, 27, 74, 90, 93, 145–46
Goya, Francisco 167
grace, 1–3, 8, 27–28, 33, 37, 58–59, 68–70, 74, 99–100, 114–17, 125–27, 138–42, 145–46, 170–73
gravity, 103–4, 122, 126, 133
Gregory, 53
groping, 125
Grosz, George, 161
Grünbaum, Adolf, 115

hadar, 3
Halevi, Judah, 27
Hamadhani, 157
Harris, Errol, 6, 38–39, 43–48, 54, 82, 86–87, 90, 95
Hasidism, 2, 92–94
health and healing, 11, 135–73, 177
Hegel, G., W. F., 72, 152–53
Heidegger, Martin, 62
Heisenberg, Werner, 104
Heraclitus, 16, 84, 109, 117
Hertz, Joseph, 3, 70
hesed, 1, 95, 145, 170–71
heurism, 41, 132–34

hierarchy, of being and value, 4, 14, 23, 35–36
Hillel, 88, 117
hineni, 17
history, 17, 19, 28, 31, 50, 83–84, 92, 124, 164 historicism, 155–56
Hockney, David, 156
Hokusai, 156
holiness, 4, 17, 35, 58, 95, 116, 125, 129, 171–72
holism, 6, 82, 85–87, 95
Homer, 156–57
Homer, Winslow, 158
Hoyle, Fred, 101
hubris, 8
human image, 176
humanitas and *pietas*, 95 humanity, 148
Hume, David, 4, 13–14, 38–39, 106, 122–23, 126, 154
Husserl, Edmund, 77
hypotheses, 24, 119–20, 126–30

I am, 4, 17–21, 27–29, 32, 58; *its prescriptivity*, 29
I sleep, but my heart waketh, 61
Ibn Ezra, Abraham, 2, 27–28
idealism and materialism, 94
imagination, 8, 43, 60, 78–79, 81–89, 99–100, 136, 159, 166; as the serpent, 144
indeterminacy, 70, 77, 134
individuality, 9, 96, 147, 167–68, 176
induction, 25, 30, 133
infinite regress, 114
Inness, George, 158
inspiration, 2, 6, 21, 29, 47, 57, 64, 71, 75, 83, 111, 157–58, 167
intellectual love of God, 54–55, 89
interdependence, 90, 148, 175
intuitions, 4–5, 15, 22–30, 41–45, 49, 62, 68–69, 119
inverse square law, 104
Isaac, 1, 17, 145
Isaac Israeli, truth, 179
Isaiah, 3, 57–58, 70, 84, 88, 94–95, 106–7, 117–18, 139, 145
Israel, covenant, 4–5, 17–20, 31, 53, 57–59, 64–65, 128, 145–46, 171 land and state, 173, 178; mission, 171; peoplehood, 64–65, 93; skepticism and acceptance, 20–22, 28, 32, 38, 52, 74
Itten, Johannes, 164

Jacob, 17; Jacob's ladder, 34–35, 70–72
Jacobs, Louis, Kabbalah, 6, 92–93
James, William, 28, 91, 153, 157
Jeremiah, 31–32, 59, 144, 172–73
Johanan, 94
Jose ben Halafta, 73
Joshua, 74
joy, 54, 93, 98
justice, 1–3, 8, 21, 37, 53, 75, 94, 98, 113, 139–40, 145–49, 162, 170–71
Juwayni, 27

Kabbalah, 6, 91–94
kalam, 32, 41, 140
Kant, Immanuel, causality, 49 coherence, 153–54; human sensibility, 165; morals, 8, 12, 145; nebulae, 121; the ontological argument, 4, 12–14, 33, 43; rational intuitions, 28; time, 50, 84
kashrut, 10
Kass, Leon, 112
katalepsis, 154
Keats, John 150, 160
Kepler, Johannes, 134
Kiefer, Anselm, 161
Kim, Jaegwon, 124, 127–28
kinship, 147
kitsch, 9, 167
knowing and loving God, 5, 22–27, 47–48, 52–61, 127–30
knowledge, 8; of the third kind, 37–49

ladder of love, 35–36
Lanfranc, 22
language, 29, 52, 85, 95, 127, 135, 138, 166, 173; prophetic language, 29
Lear, 128
Leibniz, G. W., 48, 50–51, 89, 96
Lekha dodi, 173
Leucippus, 96
Levi, Primo, 152
Levitan, Isaac, 8, 157–60, 164, 180
libertarians, 170
life, 7–11, 17–19, 31, 36, 53–62, 70, 73–75, 78, 97, 100–12, 118–27, 131–33, 136–37, 142, 147, 151, 156–59, 165–68, 174–77
light, 23, 26–27, 97, 102–5, 117, 133, 140, 155, 158–59
Locke, John, 122

logic, 4, 12–15, 29, 34, 41, 48, 104–5, 174; modal, 50
Logical Positivism, 50, 126
Logos, 75, 90
love, 1–2, 5, 16–19, 25, 28, 33–35, 44, 49, 52–61, 64, 89, 100, 128–29, 145, 148–49, 159, 162, 164, 177
loyalty, 4, 57, 65, 93–94
Lucretius, 9

magic, 47, 67, 92–93, 133, 138
magnetism, 102, 125, 133
Mahler, Gustav, 161
Maimonides, on Abraham, 132; the Active Intellect, 34; agency, 83–84; analytic exegesis, 20, 41, 45; anthropocentrism, 111, 131, 140–41; on asceticism, 95; Adam's image, 176; on attributes, 72, 87; being is good; blessedness, 39; evil a privation, 34, 42, 138, 179–80; contemplation, 59; cosmic unity, 7, 91, 117; creation/ conservation, 71, 112–15, 138–39; Gibeon, 132; God absolute, simple, unique, 5, 37, 42, 45–46, 49, 57, 65, 69–70, 89, 95; God's glory, 139, 142; God's justice, 8, 145; God's name, 4, 15, 20–22, 49; God's power, 71–72; God's transcendence, 46, 92; God's will/ wisdom, 87; human fulfillment, 52–53, 60–63, 89, 93; imagination, 43, 46, 60; Jacob's ladder, 35–36; knowing/loving/ serving, 5, 27–34, 38, 42–43, 52–63, 84, 89, 92–93; nature, 62, 66, 83–84, 91, 138–42, 146; punishment, 147; questioning, 43; reason, 39, 46, 176; ritual, 148; time, 112; virtue, 177
Makki, 27
Mandeville, Bernard de, 170
Manet, Édouard, 167
manna, 74
Maqom, 62, 73
Mason, Richard, 40–41, 65, 85, 161
mastery/stewardship, 109, 122, 169–70, 177
mathematics, 5, 13, 28–29, 31, 36, 45, 49, 65–91, 113, 119
matter/form, 34, 69–71, 75–80, 89, 94, 117, 125, 133
McGuinn, Warner, 177
McTaggart, J. M. T., 50

means infect ends, 2, 60, 171
mechanism, 90, 108–10, 125, 133–38
Megarians, 80
Melville, Herman, 167
Mendeleev, Dmitri, 105
metaphysics, 14–15, 22, 31, 34, 37, 48–50, 61–62, 67–68, 87–89, 95, 125, 131, 138–39, 150, 156
middat ha-rahamim, 75 *middat hesed*, 170
miracles, 22, 46, 74, 114
mitzvot, 11, 29, 59, 178
modalities, 12, 51
Molnar, Ferenc, 129
Mondrian, Piet, 163–64
Monet, Claude, 155
monism, 6, 15–16, 50, 65, 82, 84–86, 90–91
monotheism, 6–7, 12, 37, 62, 65, 69, 84, 91, 95, 113–15, 123, 132, 139, 173
moral principle, 58; moral realism, 8, 134, 144–45; moral truths/their truth-bearers, 67, 125, 142, 146–48, 168
mores and norms, 148
Morgenstern, Oscar, 50
Moses, his active life, 2, 60, 145–46; his gift shared, 74–75; his calling, 4, 15, 17–24; his God and law, 26–28, 31–32, 35–38, 49, 52–53, 57, 60, 75, 91, 95, 142, 145–46; song, 3, 26, 142
Mother Theresa, 134
multiverse, 7, 91, 117–18, 120–21
music, 8, 62, 77, 79, 157, 161, 163–66
mystical experience, 25, 28–30, 52–53, 68, 73–75, 92–93
myth, 25, 36, 47, 62, 92, 94, 106, 134, 161

Nahmanides, 170–71
natural law, 7, 47, 87, 90, 107, 117–18, 120–21, 137–38, 170, 174
naturalism, 12, 109–10, 125, 132
nature, 6–8, 10–11, 14, 16, 18–20, 27–28, 33–34, 36–37, 43, 46–47, 55–58, 66–71, 78–93, 95–125; monuments of nature, 142; nature-worship, 123
naval, 171
necessary being, 5, 7, 12–15, 21–24, 31–34, 37–38, 42–43, 46, 50–51, 65, 115
Neisser, Ulric, 150
neo-Darwinism, 119, 130
Neoplatonism, 5, 37, 57, 65, 80, 89, 91–92, 138, 140, 142

Newton's Laws, 121, 126, 133.
Nietzsche, Friedrich, 144
Noah/Noahidic laws, 2–3, 106, 177
noesis and *dianoia*, 23, 25
not good for a man to be alone, 14, 107
Nous, 75

obligations, 9–11, 64, 147–49
occasionalism, 141
Ockham, William, the a priori, 39–40; ontological parsimony, 67
offspring, 17, 53, 135, 147–49, 177
Oldenburg, Henry, 46, 86–87
ontological argument, 4, 12–17, 22, 25, 28–30, 32–36, 41–43, 48–51
oppression, 19–20, 65, 173
Orwell, George, 167
Owens, Joseph, 71–72

pagan gods, 5, 106; pagan piety, 1, 3, 16, 25–26, 57, 62, 115
Paine, Thomas, 3
Pais, Abram, 119
Paley, William, a watch on the heath, 106; orbital stability, 104
Parmenides, against creation, 105, 113–14; monism, 15–19, 65, 88
Pascal, Blaise, 59, 62
Peirce, C. S., abduction, 133; qualia, 154; the relational, 150
Pepper, Stephen, 152–56
perfection, 80, 87–90, 94, 108, 116–18, 125–26, 137, 142, 146, 166, 174, 180
Pericles, funeral oration, 163
persons, 2–3, 10–11, 30, 50, 56, 59–60, 67, 86, 114, 125, 127, 137, 140, 157, 165–79
Pharaoh, 4, 19
Philo, allegory, 62 cities of refuge, 172; cosmic unity, 89; creation, 113; *eupatheiai*, 54; inspiration shared, 74–75; knowing God, 4–6, 22–33, 37–38, 41, 43, 47, 49, 70–76; the Place, 73; time, 112
Philoponus, John, 113
Picasso, Pablo, 155–56, 163
Plantinga, Alvin, 129
Plato, "a likely story", 91, 113–14
anamnesis, 25; being and becoming, 16, 88; corrigibility, 148; cosmic unity, 88, 117–18; cosmic preservation, 114;

design, 107, 113; dialectic, 24, 174; the divided line, 23, 35–36; divinity, 5, 15–16, 22–25, 28, 32, 35–36, 65–68, 72–73, 76, 80; escape, 19; the Forms, 23–24, 35–37, 50, 72, 80, 118, 153–54; the indefinite dyad, 80; macrocosm, 89; mathematics, 67–69, 91–93, 113; method of division, 14, 68; *mimesis*, 26; *noesis*, 23–25; oneness, 16, 88; *philia*, 89; relative and absolute, 24, 118; stars, 109; time, 112; truth and seeming, 88; the *Menexenus*, 163; the *Meno*, 77; the *Philebus*, 25, 68, 75; the *Republic*, 23–24, 35–36, 72, 171; the *Timaeus*, 25, 72, 80, 84, 89–91, 112–14, 118
Platonic solids, 89, 113, 133
plenitude, 142
Plotinus, God known directly, 26–27 the Infinite, 1, 5–6, 46–48, 53–58, 65, 69, 72–76, 80; intellectual sharing, 75; ontic hierarchy, 142
poetry, 4, 15, 29, 35, 45, 58–61, 68, 76, 80, 94, 97, 100–1, 110, 112, 127, 129, 138, 151, 156, 162
Polkinghorne, John, 118–21
Popper, Karl, 130
pornography, 152
Posidonius, 171
Pragmatism, and art, 8, 152–56; the ideal observer, 145
prescriptivity, 29, 39, 67, 116, 169, 173–74
Principle of Sufficient Reason, 48–49
Proclus, the arc of emanation, 75 eternal creaion, 113, 115; Euclid, 78; the point, 78–80
procreation, 107, 135, 137–38
propaganda, 9, 167
prophecy, 20–21, 29, 31–32, 35, 47, 74–75, 127
providence, 17, 23, 42, 54, 97–99, 111–12, 114, 137–38
Ptolemy, 134
purpose, 138–41
Putnam, Hilary, 132
Pythagoras/Pythagoreans, 68–72, 77–82, 93, 113, 128

quantum properties, 104–5, 121–23, 134
Quine, W. V. O., 41, 122–23, 128, 179

radiation, 124
rainbow and God's covenant, 106, 180
rational mysticism, 68
Rawls, John, 169
Razi, Muhammad b. Zakariyya, 84
reason, 12–14, 24–29, 35, 38–39, 44–46, 56, 66, 81, 86, 90–92, 108–11, 121, 124, 133, 142–44, 159, 162
Rebecca, 1
reciprocity, 147
red shift, 7, 103
reductio ad ignorantiam, 110, 121
reductionism, 87, 109, 136, 161–62
religion, and science, 7, 132, 143; and adaptive utility, 31
Rembrandt, 134, 156, 164, 167
Rensch, Bernard, 100
reproof, 148
revelation, 2, 20, 25, 29–30, 47–48
reverence for life, 54
rights and dignities, 3, 10, 148, 168, 178
ritual, 58–60, 92–94, 129–30, 148, 161–62, 169, 173
Ryle, Gilbert, 129

Saadiah, boundless grace, 68–70 causal ultimacy, 124–26, 133; God as Truth, 144
Sabbaths, 98, 173; for the soil, 10
Sacks, Jonathan, 64
satyagraha, 9, 178
Schweitzer, Albert, 54
science, 56, 61, 66–69, 71, 73, 85, 88, 91, 110–11, 114, 119–27, 130–35, 138, 143, 165; scientism, 116, 132–36
Scruton, Roger, music, 164–66; Spinoza, 85
Sedgwick, Adam, 133
seeds, 107–8, 141; seed time and harvest, 97, 106
sefirot, 92–93
self-perfection, 137; see also conatus
sensation, 149
sexual reproduction, 9–10
Shaddai, 22
Shammai, 88
sharing, 171, 177; intellectual, 9, 15, 22, 26–28, 47, 53, 56, 74–75, 94, 108, 138, 151, 158

Shekhina, 30
Shelley, Percy Bysshe, 160
Shema, 64
shepherd's rod, 99
Shiviti ha-Shem le-negdi tamid, 60
Simeon, pot and lid, 88, 117
Sinai, 2, 21, 28, 31, 53, 107
slavery, 17, 28, 74, 107, 169, 173
Socrates, 25, 36, 148, 174
Sodom, its ethos, 170
solitude, 14, 60
Sophists' questions, 138
species, 14, 16, 88, 95, 99, 127, 130–37, 169, 176–77
Speusippus, 71
Spinoza, Baruch, the a priori, 38–49 active emotions, 54; analysis/ synthesis, 62; asceticism, 95; attributes, 6, 46, 95; causation, 42, 48, 95; collaboration, 15, 170; conatus, 42, 56, 99, 131, 137; doubt, 37; eternalism, 57; expression, 9, 57; fragmentary ideas, 48; God, 6, 32, 37–38, 43–46, 50, 65, 81–86, 94–95 his hopes, 56–58, 94; imagination, 43; inboard forces, 90; infinity, 81–86; intelligence in nature, 46; intuition, 49, 54–55; Judaism, 93; knowing/loving God, 5, 47, 52–56; knowledge, 43–45, 55; macrocosm, 86–91; monism, 86, 91; *natura naturans*, 87; ontological argument, 4, 15, 48–49; reason, 39, 44, 54; science, 56; space/time, 81–86; teleology, 110–11, 131; truth, 179; worm in the bloodstream, 87
stars, 3, 97–99, 101–2, 109, 111, 116, 121, 124, 140–43
Steane, Andrew, 122–30
stewardship, 169, 177
Stoic, allegory, 62 anthropocentrism, 110, 140; caring, 114; cosmic unity, 88; conflagrations, 110; design, 6–7, 23, 107–11, 131; divinity and the god idea, 6, 25, 30; *eupatheiai*, 54; immanence, 23, 46; *katalepsis*, 154; logos, 90; nature and culture, 111; pantheism, 109–10, 123; providence, 17, 99; time, 50, 83; vitalism, 89
Strato, 123–24
sub specie aeternitatis, 85
sublimity, 4, 35, 112, 126

Sufism, 27–28, 33, 91–92
Sweeney, Leo, 71

Teilhard de Chardin, Pierre, 176
teleology, 23, 131, 141–42
teshuvah, 61
Tetragrammaton, 4, 19, 22, 32–34, 95
Theaetetus, 19, 77, 113, 133
theistic subjectivism, 8, 139, 145
theoria, 52
theory choice, 134
Thomists, 52
Thucydides, 163
Tlumak, Jeffrey, 85–86
tohu va-vohu, 67, 100, 107, 117
Tolstoy, Leo, 9
tongs, 114, 117
Torah, 93–95, 105–6, 112, 116–17, 135–44, 148, 170–77
Trinity, 5, 93
Tschirnhaus, E. W. von, 46, 89
twilight of the sixth day, 114, 117
Tyndale, William, 15
tzaddik, tzedakah, 1–2, 11

ukiyo-e prints, 156
ultimates, 52, 62, 125
uniqueness of events, 99, 175
unity in infinity, 1, 5–6, 65, 69, 80–81, 85–88, 92–94

values, 59, 62–64, 99–100, 116–17, 123–25, 128, 130–40, 144–45, 149–54, 157–58, 165, 179
Van Gogh, Vincent, 155–56, 164
van Inwagen, Peter, 127
via negativa, 75
viciousness, 147, 149, 172
virtue, 56–59, 111, 114, 127, 162, 171–72, 177
vividness, 154–56

Washington, Booker T., 178
water clock, 84
Watteau, Jean Antoine, 167
Wertheimer, Max, 45
Whewell, William, consilience, 133
Whitehead, Alfred North, 76
Williams, A. N., 52–53

Winston, David, 22–26, 30, 73–75
Wolfson, Harry, 89
worlds on trial, 99–100 infinite worlds, 7, 90–91, 117–21; possible worlds, 51; see also multiverse
worship, 23, 58–63
Wyeth, Andrew, 156

Yah, 22

Zabarella, the a priori, 40
Zechariah, God's covenant, 59
Zen, 15
Zeno of Elea, 83
Zeno of Citium, 108

For EU product safety concerns, contact us at Calle de José Abascal, 56–1°, 28003 Madrid, Spain or eugpsr@cambridge.org.

www.ingramcontent.com/pod-product-compliance
Ingram Content Group UK Ltd.
Pitfield, Milton Keynes, MK11 3LW, UK
UKHW041905270226
468510UK00013B/232